THE ASSOCIATION FOR SCOTTISH LITERARY STUDIES

NUMBER TWENTY-FIVE

'SCOTLAND'S RUINE': LOCKHART OF CARNWATH'S MEMOIRS OF THE UNION

THE ASSOCIATION FOR SCOTTISH LITERARY STUDIES

The Association for Scottish Literary Studies aims to promote the study, teaching and writing of Scottish literature, and to further the study of the languages of Scotland.

To these ends, the ASLS publishes works of Scottish literature (of which this volume is an example), literary criticism in *Scottish Literary Journal*, scholarly studies of language in *Scottish Language*, and in-depth reviews of Scottish books in *SLJ Supplements*. It also publishes *New Writing Scotland*, an annual anthology of new poetry, drama and short fiction, in Scots, English and Gaelic, by Scottish writers. ASLS has also prepared a range of teaching materials covering Scottish language and literature for use in schools.

All the above publications, except for the teaching materials, are available as a single 'package', in return for an annual subscription. Enquiries should be sent to: ASLS, c/o Department of English, University of Aberdeen, Aberdeen AB9 2UB, telephone number 01224 272634.

A list of Annual Volumes published by ASLS can be found at the end of this book.

THE ASSOCIATION FOR SCOTTISH LITERARY STUDIES

GENERAL EDITOR—C.J.M. MACLACHLAN

'SCOTLAND'S RUINE'

LOCKHART OF CARNWATH'S MEMOIRS OF THE UNION

Edited by

Daniel Szechi

with a Foreword by

Paul Scott

ABERDEEN

1995

15.12.95

First published in Great Britain, 1995
by The Association for Scottish Literary Studies
c/o Department of English
University of Aberdeen
Aberdeen AB9 2UB

ISBN 0 948877 28 6

A catalogue record for this book is available from the British
Library.

The Association for Scottish Literary Studies acknowledges
subsidy from the Scottish Arts Council towards the publication
of this volume.

Typeset by Roger Booth Associates, Hassocks, West Sussex
Printed by Cromwell Press, Melksham, Wiltshire

Contents

Acknowledgements

I must first acknowledge my debt to Dr Mary Kuntz of Auburn's fledgeling Classics program for her help in translating and identifying the various Latin quotations in the text. Dr Christopher MacLachlan, the ever-courteous General Editor for the Association for Scottish Literary Studies, was especially helpful in identifying poems whose provenance had escaped me and in catching my errors before they reached the press. Clyve Jones of the Institute of Historical Research Library and David Hayton of the History of Parliament Trust both also merit my special thanks for resolving mysteries I could not crack with the resources available to me in Auburn. I would, finally, be a monster of ingratitude if I did not acknowledge the help, support and, above all, intellectual stimulation provided by my colleagues in the History Department (in particular Dr Donna Bohanan) in sustaining me to a conclusion.

D.S.

Abbreviated References

APS	*The Acts of the Parliaments of Scotland*, 11 vols (1832)
Baillie	*Correspondence of George Baillie of Jerviswood 1702–1708*, ed. G. Elliot, Bannatyne Club (Edinburgh, 1842)
CP	G. E. Cokayne, *The Complete Peerage of England, Scotland, Ireland, Great Britain and the United Kingdom Extant, Extinct or Dormant*, ed. V. Gibbs, 13 vols (1912)
Crossrigg Diary	*A Diary of the Proceedings in the Parliament and Privy Council of Scotland. May 21, 1700—March 7, 1707. By Sir David Hume of Crossrigg, one of the Senators of the College of Justice*, ed. J. Hope, Bannatyne Club (Edinburgh, 1828)
DNB	*Dictionary of National Biography* eds L. Stephen and S. Lee, 63 vols (1890)
GL	George Lockhart of Carnwath (the author)
HMC	Historical Manuscripts Commission
Lockhart Letters	*Letters of George Lockhart of Carnwath 1698–1732*, ed. D. Szechi, *Scottish History Society*, 5th series, vol. 2 (Edinburgh, 1989)
PS	*The Parliaments of Scotland. Burgh and Shire Commissioners*, ed. M. D. Young, 2 vols (Edinburgh, 1992)
Seafield Letters	*Letters Relating to Scotland in the Reign of Queen Anne by James Ogilvy, First Earl of Seafield, and Others*, ed. P. Hume Brown, *Scottish History Society*, New Series vol. xi (Edinburgh, 1915)
Stair Annals	*Annals and Correspondence of the Viscount and the First and Second Earls of Stair*, ed. J. M. Graham, 2 vols (Edinburgh, 1875)

Foreword

Scope of the Present Publication

George Lockhart of Carnwath's *Memoirs Concerning the Affairs of Scotland from Queen Anne's Accession to the Throne to the Commencement of the Union of the Two Kingdoms of Scotland and England in May 1707* has appeared before in only two editions. The first, in 1714, was pirated from a copy of the manuscript without Lockhart's knowledge or permission and indeed to his great embarrassment and danger. The second, just over a century later in 1817, was printed from Lockhart's own manuscript which he had left to his descendants for the purpose. This publication, in two large and handsome volumes, known as *The Lockhart Papers*, contains much additional material. Together this is more than twice the length of the original *Memoirs* and includes: *Commentarys of George Lockhart of Carnwath, Esq., Containing An Account of Publick Affairs from the Union of the Two Kingdoms in May 1707 to the Death of Queen Anne in August 1714* and *A Register of Letters Twixt the King and George Lockhart of Carnwath, Containing also a Short Account of Public Affairs from 1706 to 1728* exchanged between Lockhart as principal Jacobite agent in Scotland and the exiled James 'VIII' in Rome along with a short account of affairs from 1716 to 1728. There are also miscellaneous letters, speeches and pamphlets by Lockhart and, by another hand altogether (since Lockhart died in 1732), *Journals* and *Memoirs* relating to the Jacobite rising of 1745.

This present edition is confined to the original *Memoirs*, the book pirated in 1714, but now reprinted from the 1817 text, with some connected papers. The 1714 edition included Lockhart's preface along with an introduction, 'Shewing the Reason for

Publishing these Memoirs at this Juncture', as it said on the title page. The book itself, the preface and the introduction were all anonymous, as was common at the time. In fact, the introduction was by Sir David Dalrymple,[1] who was responsible for the 1714 publication, and it was clearly intended as an antidote to the dangerous contents of the *Memoirs* themselves. People mentioned in the book were indicated only by the first and last letters of their names, but their identity is usually obvious from their titles and offices. In any case, a key to the names was issued separately by another publisher in the same year and this is often found bound together in copies of the 1714 text. The 1817 edition (which gives the names in full) reprints the original preface and Dalrymple's introduction along with yet another preface by Lockhart in which he replies to Dalrymple. Some copies also contain a facsimile of a letter from Lockhart to his son with instructions for the safe keeping and eventual publication of the manuscripts.[2] (Both prefaces, Dalrymple's introduction and the letter of instructions are now reprinted.) The *Memoirs* were followed by an important appendix about bribery which appeared in both the 1714 and 1817 editions and some letters which were in the 1817 edition only.

The subsequent accounts and letters in the 1817 edition are of considerable interest and value, but they deal with a separate subject, the Jacobite endeavours to recover the throne for the Stuarts. The *Memoirs* are complete in themselves as an account by an active participant of the events between 1702 and 1707 which led to the Parliamentary Union. As such the *Memoirs* have long been recognised by historians as one of the principal sources for the period. Lockhart is fiercely partisan and he makes no secret of his feelings, particularly in his judgements of people. On the other hand, as I shall argue below, his account of events is consistent with all the other evidence and he has never been proved wrong on any point of substance. It is also a very lively historical narrative, full of tension, suspense and drama, and ultimately tragic in its conclusion. Lockhart's sentences are sometimes Latinate and involved, but he is also a master of the pungent phrase. His *Memoirs* are the best thing of this kind in our literature since John Knox's *History of the Reformation*.

Reasons for the Comparative Neglect of the Memoirs

Why then has there been no new edition since 1817? This is indeed very puzzling and it is very satisfactory that this serious omission is now being made good. The historian Hume Brown speculated in his Ford Lectures in Oxford in 1914 about the reasons for the general ignorance among Scots of the events leading to the Union, 'one of the most fateful periods in their national history'. The first reason, he thought, was a sense of shame, 'an unconscious instinct' which made us try to forget it. The Union was a subject which the Scots 'must regard with mingled feelings, among which pride is not predominant... A people does not gladly turn its eyes to a period when its representative men, whether from their own natural failings or as a result of temporary circumstances, compromise the national character in the eyes of the world.' Hume Brown may well be right that the subject was simply too painful, but he goes on to suggest an additional reason. This is that the general ignorance of the circumstances of the Union might be due to the absence of a contemporary account which could 'permanently stamp its characters and its events on the mind of posterity'.[3]

Although Hume Brown denied it, I believe that Lockhart's *Memoirs* are precisely such an account. The trouble from the point of view of those, like Hume Brown, who wanted to try to justify the Union (and that was the predominant attitude in the nineteenth century) was that Lockhart gave the game away in an unflinching exposure of a very sordid transaction. If you wanted to conceal the facts and maintain that the Union was an act of enlightened statesmanship, then you certainly did not want to encourage people to read Lockhart. His book has been suppressed by tacit censorship. For this reason, it has never received the recognition which it deserves as a work of literature as well as an important historical source.

Sir Walter Scott was aware of the *Memoirs*. He wrote to Robert Cadell in May 1829: 'I wish you could get me the Lockhart papers (use of them) two volumes quarto. I have not brought them from the country and they are indispensable to copy of tales'.[4] The reference is to his *Tales of a Grandfather*, which Scott was writing at the time. Thanks largely to Lockhart, Scott's account of the Union in that book is, as far as I am aware, the most honest and revealing of any written in the nineteenth century. He draws heavily on Lockhart and quotes, for example, the evidence of bribery which Lockhart had uncovered. Byron, too, knew about the *Memoirs*. In 1822 he was looking for an oppressed country to liberate, for he considered others before he decided on Greece. He wrote from Pisa on 16 May 1822 to John Murray in London: 'Could you send me the Lockhard papers a publication upon Scotch affairs of sometime since'.[5] We do not know if the two volumes ever reached him. If they had, they might have turned his crusading zeal towards Scotland, to which he felt a strong attachment. The *Memoirs* had the capacity, I think, to convince him, in Tom Scott's words, that the Union 'was a historical iniquity with no right but might behind it, and to be overthrown by all good men and true'.[6]

George Lockhart's Life[7]

George Lockhart was a member of the family of the Lockharts of Lee who have held the same land in Scotland for over 700 years. His father, Sir George Lockhart of Carnwath (1630–1689), was the second son of the twelfth laird of Lee, who became an advocate in 1656. Two years later, during the Cromwellian occupation of Scotland, he was appointed the Protector's Advocate and he represented Lanarkshire in the Cromwellian Parliament from 1658 to 1659. He was the first member of the family to acquire the Barony of Carnwath. His marriage to a daughter of the English Baron Wharton allied him to her brother Thomas, a man who after the Glorious Revolution became prominent in English politics as a member of the Whig Junta. Wharton was Lord-Lieutenant of Ireland from 1708 to 1710 and was the target of one of Swift's Irish tracts. Sir George Lockhart won a reputation at the Scottish bar as the most skilful and eloquent pleader of his time. He defended many Covenanting prisoners during the period of their persecution and Argyll at his trial for treason in 1681. In spite of this he was appointed Lord President of the Court of Session in 1685. Four years later he was murdered in the High Street of Edinburgh by the unbalanced John Chiesley of Dalry, who was disgruntled because Lockhart had found in favour of his wife in a lawsuit between them.

The author of the *Memoirs*, George Lockhart, 2nd Laird of Carnwath (1681–1732), then succeeded to his estate and to an ample fortune when he was only eight years old. His first guardian was an uncle, Sir John Lockhart (or Lord Castlehill, to give him his title as a law lord). He did his best to have the young laird brought up in the Presbyterian and Whig tradition of the family. The Argyll children were among his playmates. His tutors were replaced by Episcopalians when Sir John died in 1694. Even so, it is something of a mystery why George Lockhart devoted his life to the Jacobite cause. As the editor of his letters, Daniel Szechi, says: 'Our stereotypical Jacobite is a declining landowner, burdened with inherited debts left over from the civil wars of the mid-seventeenth century, jealous of his social position, suspicious of the local (prospering) bourgeoisie, hostile to innovation of any kind'.[8] Lockhart could hardly have been more different. He was very young, wealthy and energetic, interested in agricultural improvements and in exploiting the coal on his land, and connected through his mother's family to one of the most powerful men in English, and after 1707 British, politics. In 1697 Lockhart married Euphemia Montgomery, a daughter of the 9th Earl of Eglinton, who was a constant supporter of the government. Lockhart's Jacobitism, which was closely related to his Scottish patriotism, was evidently a matter of personal choice and conviction, not of family tradition or habit.

For most of his life Lockhart, in one way or another, was actively and passionately involved in politics. His career falls into several distinct phases. From 1703 to 1707 he was a member of the Scottish Parliament. He was a close associate of the Duke of Hamilton and of Andrew Fletcher of Saltoun and with them vigorously opposed the incorporating union which the Parliament was eventually brought to accept by a mixture of bribery, appeals to self-interest and military intimidation. Lockhart, no doubt because of the Wharton connection, was the only opponent of the Union chosen by London as one of the Scottish Commissioners to negotiate the treaty. (Because of a *volte face* by Hamilton, described in the *Memoirs*, both teams of negotiators were chosen by the Queen on the advice of the English ministers.) The whole of this agonising debate, spread over five years, is the subject of the *Memoirs*.

In the second phase, from 1708 to 1714, Lockhart represented Midlothian in the new British Parliament in London. He was again very active in defending Scottish interests and in trying to mitigate some of the consequences of the Union in such matters as a malt tax which treated Scotland unfairly and violated the treaty. He was a prime mover in the attempt which followed to dissolve the Union. As a member of a Parliamentary Commission appointed in 1711 to examine public accounts he was able to uncover evidence of secret payments to members of the Scottish Parliament in 1706 during the debate on the treaty. He added a report about this in an appendix to the *Memoirs* as a 'further discovery' which had come to light since they were written. The writing must therefore have been completed some time between the events of 1708, with which the *Memoirs* conclude, and 1711.

While Lockhart was attending Parliament in London, it was his practice to send frequent letters about his political activities to his friend, and principal contact in Scotland, Henry Maule of Kellie, subsequently 5th titular Earl of Panmure. On 29 June 1714, Lockhart wrote to Maule about the way in which a copy of the manuscript of the *Memoirs* had come into the hands of one of his political opponents, Sir David Dalrymple of Hailes:

> An accident has hapned which gives me more vexation than I can well express. Mr Houston[9] and I have lodged and lived togather since wee came here. About 2 months ago I

lent him the memoirs I showed you, only to peruse, but
without ever asking my concent or acquainting me of it (tho
I had charged him with secresie and coud have confided in
him) he gave them to one who had been a writer lad in
Edinburgh and is half a kind of schoolmaster here to copy,
and this spark has taken a copy of it which I understand is
just now in Sir David Dalrymple's hands. You can easily
foresee the inconveniencies that will attend this discovery at
this time. There are several matters of fact which ought
to've been keept secret, and the characters given of some
people must creat me many enimyes. I know not in the
world what to do. I know Mr Houston did it out of
simplicity and he's like to hang himself for it, but it won't
help what's past. I am yours, adeiu.

[P.S.] As matters stand and are like to go I think it scarce
worth my pains to accept being a Commissioner of
Accounts. And indeed I have it under consideration to come
home and leave all publick concerns for the future.[10]

Other letters which followed showed Lockhart in a very
natural panic over this disaster. Clearly he had not intended
publication while the people he discussed so frankly were still
alive and while the political issues involved might still cause his
arrest on charges of treason. The instructions to his son, dated 3
February 1730, proposed that the manuscripts (including also the
later ones) should be kept secret and sealed until 1750 'by which
time I reckon the inconveniencies attending the publication may
probably be removed'.[11] This was presumably his intention with
the *Memoirs* themselves, although he had taken the risk of
showing the manuscript in confidence to some friends.

When Lockhart heard that a copy was in the hands of
Dalrymple, he was so alarmed that he wrote again to Maule later
on the same day: 'I never was so uneasie and concerned at any
accident [that] befell me, and must look on it as a very great
misfortune'. He hoped that Dalrymple would see that his best
course was to suppress the manuscript, but he saw 'innumerable
inconveniencies attending the discovery at this time, for the

characters will expose me to the malice and revenge of many people'. His first instinct was to deny that he was the author and to admit only that he had contributed some material to a work 'jiggled and compiled by several hands'.[12] Of course, the *Memoirs* contained the text of documents written by other people and perhaps also some narrative passages contributed by others, but no one could seriously doubt that the major part was by Lockhart himself. It was written from his known point of view and contained much which nobody else could know with the same intimacy. Only Lockhart had inside knowledge of both the Union negotiations and the tactics of the Opposition in the Scottish Parliament. The character sketches, the part of the book likely to provoke the most dangerous reaction, had an unmistakably personal flavour in the pungent phrases which enliven the whole book.

As Lockhart had already said in the postscript to his first letter of 29 June to Maule, the discovery of the manuscript meant the effective end of his parliamentary career in London. He had given too much offence to too many people in high places. By 20 July he told Maule that he was leaving London by the end of the week, 'being heartily wearie of it'.[13] Just as he was about to leave, he happened to meet James Dundas, son of Lord Arniston, who was closely associated with Dalrymple. Dundas warned him that it was proposed to prosecute him and that the reflections in the *Memoirs* against the Scottish peers could lead to a cumulative fine of £30,000. In fact, no such action was taken. Not for the only time, Lockhart might have been saved by the influence of Wharton and such other powerful friends as the Duke of Argyll.[14] Lockhart himself in his *Account of Publick Affairs* records that his childhood friendship with Argyll survived their political differences and that the Duke did him many 'good offices'.[15] For example, Lockhart was not arrested in 1708 when a scare over an abortive Jacobite landing caused the Government to round up possible sympathisers. They included opponents of the Union, and even some, like Andrew Fletcher of Saltoun, who were certainly not Jacobites.

The end of Lockhart's parliamentary career in 1714 introduced another phase. For the rest of his life he devoted himself to Jacobite conspiracy. At the time of Mar's rising in 1715 he was one of the first to be arrested. Argyll, who was now Commander-in-Chief of the army in Scotland, released him on bail. Lockhart then proceeded to raise a troop of horse and organise a general rising by the Jacobite gentry of Midlothian. This time he was arrested in earnest and held in Edinburgh Castle, under conditions which made him seriously ill. His brother, Philip, led a small Jacobite force to Preston where they were forced to surrender. Philip, who had been an officer in the British army, was immediately court-martialled and shot. This harsh treatment of his brother embittered Lockhart and no doubt strengthened his hostility to the Hanoverian and Unionist regime.

Lockhart resumed his Jacobite activities when he was released under a general indemnity in 1717. He did not at first play a leading role, but by 1720 he was in direct correspondence with James the Old Pretender who was at that time living in Rome. He was appointed one of a secret committee of trustees appointed to look after Jacobite affairs in Scotland and became in effect their secretary. This correspondence with Rome is a substantial part of the second volume of the 1817 edition of the *Lockhart Papers*.

In this position, Lockhart was sorely tried both by internal squabbles among the Jacobites in Scotland and by the public row in Rome between James and his wife, Clementina Sobieska. In a letter to a Jacobite friend on 18 January 1726 Lockhart said that he was 'pritty much wearied of what is laid on me'. Nothing, however, would induce him to give up as long as he could serve James, but he would be glad to have some liberty for himself if others could be found to do the work.[16] In fact his hand was forced in March 1727. Two of Lockhart's couriers were arrested and he was warned that his own arrest was imminent. He fled in disguise and reached Holland on 15 April. Just over a year later he was given permission to return home, thanks again to the influence of Argyll and others, on condition that he lived quietly in retirement and abandoned his links with the Jacobite cause. He was obliged to travel through London and 'bow his knee' to George II. This he did reluctantly on the introduction of Sir Robert Walpole. As he recorded in the *Register*, 'I made a bow and went off, well determined never to trust in his mercy, which did not seem to abound.'[17] Lockhart seems indeed to have lived very quietly for the remaining years of his life. Among his papers are two letters, written in 1727 and 1730 and 'intended for publication in a periodical paper called the Eccho'. They are completely innocent of politics and make somewhat blimpish complaints about the decay of standards in dress and behaviour and the increase of swearing and cursing. So obscure had he become that little is known about the circumstances of his death. He died some time in January 1732 as a result of wounds received in a duel, but we do not know the name of his opponent or the reason for their quarrel.

The Reliability of the Memoirs as a Historical Record

As we have seen, Lockhart had hoped that Dalrymple would see that his best course was to keep quiet about the *Memoirs* when a copy of the manuscript fell into his hands. This was not unreasonable. The *Memoirs* exposed the events which led to the Union in a way that was bound to be uncomfortable to those who had supported it, or at least voted for it. That included Dalrymple's own political friends and the late, distinguished head of his own family, the Earl of Stair. Anyone of this persuasion might well be supposed to favour suppression of the dangerous evidence which Lockhart had produced. On the other hand, opinion in 1714 was very different from 1707. Since the Union had come into force a whole series of measures by the new British Parliament had alienated even those who had worked to bring it about. All parties in Scotland were now in favour of its dissolution and a motion to this effect in the House of Lords in 1713 very nearly succeeded. In 1714 few people in Scotland were likely to disagree with Lockhart's objections to the Union, but many would resent his outspoken views on some of the people involved and his open adherence to the Stuarts.

This was, in fact, the position taken by Dalrymple in his introduction to the 1714 edition. He objects to Lockhart's Jacobitism as 'barbarous designs' which if they were to succeed would lead to the 'destruction of all civil and religious rights'. For Dalrymple, he whom Lockhart called the Prince or King are the 'Pretender' or 'Mock-monarch'. He defends the characters of those whom Lockhart attacked, particularly his own relation, the 'unblemish'd' Earl of Stair. He says almost nothing about the Union. He admits that 'some rights and priviledges in Scotland might have been weaken'd by it', but maintains that it secured religion and liberty by accepting the succession of the House of Hanover. He does not suggest that Lockhart's narrative of events, as distinct from his opinions of people, is in any way inaccurate.

Lockhart in his effective reply in his additional preface naturally draws attention to this: 'that they had nothing to alledge against the veracity of it is evidently apparent from the introduction published with it'. Lockhart also dismisses the insinuation implicit in Dalrymple's introduction that the opponents of the Union and the opponents of the Revolution were the same people. A great many of those in favour of the Revolution (in other words the overthrow of the Stuarts) were opposed to the Union. Even those who had supported the treaty agreed with Sir David Dalrymple himself, who now 'frequently and publickly declared' how much he regretted that he had helped to promote it.

The argument on this point between Lockhart and Dalrymple is continued in two other papers included in the 1817 edition. One, ascribed to Sir David Dalrymple, agrees that 'seven years experience of the fatall consequences of this unhappy Union hath so much opened the eyes of the nation to see it drawing a graduall ruin on us... that not one thing so much employs the thoughts and time of honest men as a dissolution of the Union.' He argues that this should be achieved without the participation of the Jacobites. Lockhart's reply, dated 18 December 1714, argues that the Jacobite support for the dissolution, which is against their tactical interest, shows that they are true Scotsmen who put the interest of their country before their own particular views.[18] In a sense, the attitude which many historians have taken towards Lockhart's *Memoirs* is a curious echo of this dispute between him and Dalrymple. Many references to him come close to implying that his evidence can be dismissed simply by saying that he is a Jacobite. 'The charge of bribery brought against the Scottish statesmen who carried the Union was first deliberately formulated by the Jacobite Lockhart—a witness, to say the least, capable of making such statements against his opponents'—so writes Hume Brown, for example, and he continues, 'Lockhart's statements do not bear a close examination'.[19]

These remarks tend to confuse judgements of people with accounts of facts. On the first, it is true that Lockhart did not mince words about people of whom he disapproved. He admitted as much himself in his first preface: 'my indignation against the betrayers of my country is so great, I never could, nor will, speak or write otherwise of them.' (But even in these cases he often admits their good points.) Facts about the sequence and nature of events are another matter and here I think that Lockhart does stand up very well to close examination. No one, as far as I am aware, has ever detected him in any serious inaccuracy or misrepresentation in this respect. I have been through the evidence as carefully and minutely as I could in the course of writing two books on the period. I have often been struck by the way in which Lockhart's account is supported by documents of which he could not have been aware and which have come to light very many years later.

The most obvious example of this is over the issue of bribery. This is the point on which many Unionist historians, as in the example of Hume Brown which I have just quoted, have attempted to cast doubt on Lockhart's reliability as a witness. In fact, Lockhart's own account in the appendix to the *Memoirs*, is convincing enough, based as it is on original documents reluctantly surrendered to a parliamentary commission. Long afterwards other documents, of which Lockhart could not have had knowledge, have come to light to confirm his account beyond any possibility of doubt. The first is a letter from the Earls of Seafield and Glasgow on 20 July 1707 to the Duke of Queensberry for the information of the Earl of Godolphin as Lord Treasurer of Great Britain. It says that it would be impossible to account for the distribution of the £20,000 'unless it were to bring discredit upon the manadgement of that Parliament'. Like so many secret and incriminating documents, it ends with the desperate hope that 'your Grace may be pleased to burn this letter when you have read it to my Lord Treasurer'. Godolphin evidently insisted on keeping it as a receipt because it remained in his family papers until it was sold to the British Museum in 1892.[20] There is further confirmation, if more were needed, in a letter of 22 November 1711 from the Earl of Glasgow, the man responsible for the disbursement of the money in Scotland. As he says, if it had been known at the time, 'the Union had certainly broken'.[21]

Time and again, when Lockhart's version of events is compared with the private correspondence of men on the Government side, it is impossible not to be struck by his reliability as a witness and by his knowledge and understanding of the motives and attitudes of his political opponents. His account of the nature and objectives of the Marquess of Tweeddale's period of office as High Commissioner, for example, is amply supported by his secret instructions and his correspondence with the Queen and Godolphin in London.[22] Lockhart's allegation that the Scottish Commissioners in the Union negotiations made only a token gesture in favour of federalism is confirmed by two witnesses on the Government side, Sir John Clerk of Penicuik and the Earl of Mar.[23] There is similar confirmation from a host of witnesses, Mar, Seafield, Clerk, Defoe and many others, about the hostility of the people of Scotland to the treaty and the reaction of the crowds on the streets of Edinburgh.[24]

Comparison of the 1714 and 1817 Editions

We have seen from Lockhart's letters the circumstances of the 1714 edition. His letter of directions to his son and Anthony Aufrere's prefatory note, 'To the Reader', in the 1817 edition explain how that came to be published after an interval of more than 100 years. Lockhart's wish was that the manuscripts should be kept secret and sealed until 1750, by which time he thought that 'the inconveniencies attending the publishing may probably be removed'. The rising of 1745 and his grandson's part in it made that impossible. In 1802 the papers came into the hands of Anthony Aufrere through his marriage to Lockhart's great granddaughter, as he recorded in a genealogical table printed in the book. For reasons which he explains in his note, he was able to begin preparation for the press only in 1814.

The conditions in which the two editions were produced were therefore very different. The first was a hurried and surreptitious act of literary piracy with no opportunity for proof corrections by the author and evidently very little by anyone else. The second was a leisurely work of family piety using the author's own manuscript, which he had carefully prepared for the purpose in his admirably clear and bold handwriting. Aufrere says that he was 'diligent' in this task. All the evidence confirms that this was a fair claim. The editor of Lockhart's letters, Daniel Szechi, has said that his research has many times confirmed the authenticity of Aufrere's edition and 'his reputation for painstaking scholarship'.[25] In several readings of the *Memoirs* I have detected only two misprints. (One is the omission of the letter 'l' from 'religion' on page 46. The other is on page 104 where the 1817 text, referring to the English House of Commons, has 'were not like those of good subjects to the Queen'. The 1714 text at this point has on page 123 'were like'. The latter is correct because it refers to a speech in which Fletcher contrasted the conduct of the Commons on a particular matter with the interference of the Lords in Scottish affairs.) The two volumes of 1817 are handsome quartos (11 x $8^{1}/_{2}$ inches), finely printed on high quality paper. There is every sign that great care was lavished on them. Strangely enough, in apparent contradiction to this care, three dates for which blank spaces were left in the 1714 edition (pages 42, 212 and 299) are left blank in 1817 also (pages 6, 157 and 202). This might be taken as an indication of Aufrere's reluctance to add anything that was not in the manuscript.

In his letter of directions George Lockhart 'expressly required' that any publication should be exact 'without adding or impairing, conform to the originall manuscripts.' These manuscripts have been lost and without them it is impossible to know how scrupulously Aufrere complied. A comparison of the 1714 and 1817 texts suggests that most of the differences between them, apart from the changes in printing practice, were corrections of obvious misprints and gaps. In most cases, Aufrere was almost certainly following the original manuscript, not introducing amendments of his own. Some small changes, which were evidently intended to remove ambiguity or give more precision, may have been introduced either by Aufrere or by Lockhart. The insertion of the 'not' on page 104, which I mentioned above, was presumably the work of Aufrere. It might seem logically necessary to some one not familiar with the historical events under discussion. I have detected no other case where an error might have been introduced in 1817. Some spellings have been modernised (such as 'pathetic' for 'pathetical' or 'straiten'd' for 'streighten'd'), but there are not many instances of this. A curious exception to the evident respect with which the original text has been treated is the substitution of 'prorogue' for 'adjourn' in reference to Parliament. This occurs no fewer than twelve times. For all we know, of course, even this change may have been introduced by Lockhart himself.

The 1714 edition is very different in general appearance from the two volumes of 1817. It is a small volume of about 8 by 4 inches and of 420 pages. The printing looks careless with gaps and incorrect alignments as well as many obvious typographical errors. Most of the names of people are indicated only by their first and last letters, although some, especially towards the end of the book, are given in full. It follows the printing conventions of the time in the lavish use of capitals and italics, the long 's' and in punctuation. Numbers appear in figures, not in words as they do in the 1817 edition. The book itself, the preface (by Lockhart) and the introduction (by Dalrymple) are all anonymous.

In his 'Additional Preface' in the 1817 edition Lockhart says of the earlier one that it 'appeared under all the disadvantages imaginable; for the copy from which that printed edition was taken, was noways prepared and designed for the press, and many errors appeared in it; several words, nay sentences being, some omitted, and some inserted instead of others, by which in many places the sense of the whole was confounded'. This is fair comment, as the analysis which follows confirms. At the same time, it may give an exaggerated impression. In spite of the gaps and errors in the earlier edition, and the differences in printing style, the two editions are substantially the same in most of their text. I give below two tables of variations, one of those of a word or two and the other of longer passages. Different considerations apply to each.

The short variations fall into three categories:
1. Words replaced by another similar in appearance, but different in meaning.
2. Differences in the spelling of the same word.
3. Minor changes to correct grammar or remove ambiguity.

It is with the first of these categories that, as Lockhart complained, the sense is often confounded. Sometimes the meaning is reversed as in the following examples: support/ suspect (40/60), excuse/accuse (76/79), repeated/repealed (283/ 200), returned/retired (360/235). More often, the 1714 reading makes no sense at all, as in warning/turning (3/40), test/jest (92/ 87), proper credit/paper credit (144/117), receive/respective (209/ 154), crown laws/crown and the laws (230/167) and behalf/belief (345/255). In all such cases (with the two very small exceptions on pages 46 and 104, which I mentioned above) the 1817 text is clearly the better reading. The 1714 variations look very much like misreadings of the manuscript, often of only a letter or two, of the kind which a proof reader should have picked up from the sense. It is a reasonable assumption that they were mistakes by the copyist or type-setter in 1714, and that the 1817 edition restores the wording that Lockhart intended. Apart from the instances which I have already mentioned, there are very few variations in spelling, apart from some Scottish proper names. Examples are 'Seld' for 'Selkirk' (248/178), 'Lanerk' for 'Lanark' (363/236) and even 'Carnworth' for 'Carnwath' (280/198). The 1714 spellings are unlikely to have been used by a literate Scot even at that time. Lockhart tells us that the copyist of the manuscript 'had been a writer lad in Edinburgh', and these spellings were probably therefore introduced by a type-setter to whom Scottish names were unfamiliar. It again suggests that there was very little, if any, proof reading of the 1714 text.

The third category includes minor adjustments to correct grammar, usually in the agreement of subject and verb (as on pages 143/116 and 296/207) or of personal pronouns (pages 96/89, 120/102, 243/175). Some are obviously intended to remove ambiguity (349/228 or 193/145) or to give more precision (101/91, 226/165, 359/234). A few seem to be intended to give a phrase more elegance (142/115–16, 268/191). It is impossible, of course, to say whether the 1817 readings appeared in the original manuscript, were amended later by Lockhart or were introduced by Aufrere.

The longer passages omitted from one edition or the other present a few problems. Most of the omissions from the 1714 text look like the result of the eye of the copyist or type-setter accidentally jumping over a line or two. That on page 336, for example, suggests a jump from one use of the word 'protestation' to the next. It introduces an error, which should have been obvious to a proof reader, because it goes on to refer to two protestations when only one had been mentioned in the truncated version. The omissions on pages 36, 51, 71, 217, 263, 354, 380 and 384 also look like omissions of this kind. Those on pages 175, 254 and 379 look like deliberate amendments to achieve more accuracy. Both the language and the knowledge of the circumstances suggest that they are more likely to show the hand of Lockhart than of Aufrere. As we have seen, Lockhart complained that the manuscript copied in 1714 had not been prepared for the press. This implies, I think, that he intended to check and, if necessary, amend it.

On the other hand, there are three passages in the 1714 edition which are omitted from that of 1817, those on pages 24–5, 272 and 339–40. We have no means of knowing why the first of these, in the account of Seafield's character, was considerably amended for the later edition. It is presumably one of Lockhart's amendments; perhaps he discovered that he had been wrong about Ogilvy of Boyn. There is nothing surprising in the addition of a favourable remark about Seafield's abilities. Throughout the book Lockhart combines criticism of his political opponents with recognition of their good points. Again, there is no obvious explanation of the omission in 1817 of the references on page 272 of the earlier text to the English East and West India Companies. Possibly Lockhart decided that he wanted to make the reference more general and not limit it to the companies alone. The passage on pages 339–40 in the 1714 edition is a digression in which some rather strained coincidences of dates are used as an excuse for Jacobite name calling. If it was part of Lockhart's original manuscript, he or Aufrere made the sensible decision that the book was better without it. It contains two more examples of the 1714 type-setter's difficulty with Scottish proper names, 'Stavis' for Stair and 'Gourie' for Gowrie.

There are two substantial passages in the edition of 1817 which do not appear in that of 1714. The anecdote about Seafield on pages 222–3 of the former is one of the best known remarks in the book and indeed in the whole of Scottish history. It was presumably either an accidental omission in 1714 or a later addition by Lockhart. The concluding lines of the *Memoirs* in the 1817 edition, from 'for the Almighty God' to the end, were almost certainly a late addition. They probably record the feelings of Lockhart as he placed the manuscripts in the box that was to be sealed and entrusted to his son.

In bringing out a new edition of Lockhart's *Memoirs*, we have to decide, in the absence of the manuscript, between following the text of 1714 or 1817. The earlier one has the advantage of the flavour of the period in which it was written with the long 's' and the lavish use of capitals and italics. It does, however, have severe disadvantages. The skeleton form of the names of people give whole pages the appearance of heavy censorship. There are evident signs of the lack of care and proof reading in the many omissions and errors. The author himself complained about its inadequacies. On the other hand, the 1817 text is from the author's own manuscript as finally revised by him for eventual publication. It was obviously printed with scrupulous care and, from all the evidence, with fidelity to the manuscript. It appeared in accordance with the printing conventions of the early nineteenth century in its punctuation and use of capital letters, but the wording was probably very close to the intentions of the author. I have no doubt that we cannot hope to do better than follow it for this new edition which restores an important book to the canon of Scottish history and literature.

In drawing up the tables of variant readings I was greatly assisted by my good friend, Bert Davies, who died before the book appeared in print.

Paul H. Scott

Brief Variations Between the 1714 and 1817 Editions

1714	1817
3 Warning the Convention	40 turning the Convention
19-20 adjourn; adjourn'd	50 prorogue; prorogued
32 memoirs	56 memories
33 Seared the cavaliers	57 scared
34 went Pleasingly on	57 went pleasantly on
38 so entirely	59 so avow'dly
39 conveniendum	60 meeting
40 Support his integrity	60 suspect
53 many of the Country party	67 all the Country party
59 Adjourned	70 prorogued
62 adjourn'd	71 prorogued
68 made a great interest	74 had a great interest
72 Adjourned	77 prorogued
74 Design and Conclusions	78 design and consequences
76 upon these	79 upon those

76 excuse	79 accuse
76 'twixt whem	79 'twixt whom
77 and likewise	79 and that too
80 adjourn'd	81 prorogued
80 these persons	81 those Persons
81 Mr Furguson	81 Mr Ferguson
87 to avouch to them	84 to assure them
92 drive the Test	87 drive the jest
94 irritate the Cavaliers	87 irritate and cement the Cavaliers
96 his, and his family	89 he and his family
101 his Parents were	91 his predecessors were
108 rebauce	95 revenge
108 hardest headed	95 significant
110 in whom	97 on whom
111 these bad measures	97 the bad measures
112 and proposed to attack	97 and attack
112 But tho' others	97 But the others
113 And 'twould have been	98 It would indeed have been
117 approve of it	101 get it approven
120 He moved the Vote	102 I move the vote
120 adjourned	103 prorogued
128 adjourned	105 prorogue
135 And I never could hear	135 Nor ever could I hear
142 and yet so much deluded	115–16 and yet were so deluded
143 Zeal and Fervour of the members goes off	116 Zeal and fervour of the members goes off
144, 145 a proper credit [twice]	117 a paper credit
145 it was so found, that	117 it was so contrived, that
145 more momentous	117 more material
165 by plurality	130 by a plurality
166 adjourned	130 prorogued
170 they did not expect should have	132 they did not expect would have
178 adjourned	137 prorogued
193 their disadvantage	145 their own disadvantage
209 receive Laws	154 respective laws
226 *Edinburgh's* Privileges	165 Edinburgh's right to their privileges or other occassions
230 the Crown Laws of the Land	167 the crown and the other laws of the land
243 your Benefices	175 their benefices
248 abide the Test	178 stand the test

248 Earl of Seld — 178 Earl of Selkirk
249 promis'd — 178 premised
253 Lord Tarficton — 181 Lord Torphicen
258 pick'd — 184 picqued
258 Remarks of Favour — 184 rewards and marks of favour
259 punctually — 185 so punctually
260 a valiant War — 185 a bloody war
264 Deligates — 188 delegates
265 motion mention'd in the 255 Pag — 189 last mentioned motion
268 but no Care taken — 191 but no care was taken
272 the Prospect of — 193 disappointing her prospect of
275 [we] refers — 195 refer
278 Reswick — 197 Ryswick
280 with the Negotiates — 198 with the Negotiators
280 Carnworth — 198 Carnwath
283 Parliament repeated — 200 Parliament repealed
295 so many, and so considerable numbers — 206 so many and such considerable members
296 does chiefly depend — 207 do chiefly depend
324 convoy — 213 attend
324 esteemed the second part — 213 play'd the second part
325 prorogate — 214 prorogue
329 Inherint — 216 inherent
334 may Instruments — 219 I take instruments
338 through paced — 222 thorough paced
345 Behalf and Expectation — 225 belief and expectation
348 Audenard — 227 Ramillies
349 Obedience to him — 228 obedience to his Grace
359 hanged any Man — 234 hanged many honest men
360 so that having waited — 234 and having waited
360 returned — 235 retired
361 That they got — 235 and that thought they got
361 Stenhope — 235 Stanhope
362 Convey'd — 236 convoy'd
363 Lanerk — 236 Lanark
371 Wachop — 242 Wauchope
392 Dantzick etc — 254 Dantzick and other places

Longer Variations Between the 1714 and 1817 Editions
1714   1817

1714	1817
24-5 ...when his Interest led him to it, (which was the only Thing on Earth he was ever Firm and Stedfast to) a notable Instance of which, was his Ingratitude to Sir *James Ogilvy of Boyn* and his Family who had been at the Charge of Educating him at the Schools and Colleges at Home; and of Sending and Maintaining him Abroad, Studying the Law; and being a Lord of the Session in King *James's* Time, Patroniz'd and Protected him when he entered Lawyer.	53 ...interest (which he was only firm to) did not stand in competition. He made a good figure, and proceeded extremely well in Parliament and Session, where he dispatch'd business to the general satisfaction of the Judges.
36 ...dreaded most; and therefore that unless...	59 ...dreaded most; and therefore insisted that unless...
51 ...Signed by Mr *George Meldrum*...	66 ...Signed by their moderator Mr George Meldrum...
71 ...often in Parliament Stuck close to the Country Party,...	76 ...often in Parliament acted a part by himself, tho' in the main he stuck close to the *Country party*
175 ...and consequently those Members I spoke of, not deserted...	136 ...and consequently, if those members I spoke of had not deserted...
217 ...as a Sample that induc'd...	154 ...as a sample of the motives which induc'd...
254 ...and his Adherents, to renew...	182 ...and he craved that he and such as had adhered to him might renew...
263 ...would be continu'd and perform'd; and...	187 ...would be continu'd and perform'd as England pleased? and...
272 ...a present of it to the English East and *West India Companies*...	193 ...a present of it to the English...
272 ...flow from Scotland; and that Trade was monopolised by these two Companies: But...	193 ...flow from Scotland. But...

336 ...to raise Sedition; and the members, as they favoured the Parties and Cause adhered to the one or the other of these two Protestations

220 ...to raise sedition. But the Lord Balmerino enter'd another protestation against receiving this of Lord Marchmont's, as the same was unmannerlie and illegal; and the members, as they favoured the parties and cause, adhered to the one and the other of these two protestations.

339-40 ...their Independency and Soveraignty.

I shall leave this Melancholy Subject with adding a few Observes that some were pleased to remark.

First, That the first Article of the Union was approven the fourth Day of *November,* which was the Birth-day of our Dutch ironical Saviour King William, being the Day preparatory to *Gunpowder-Treason.*

Second, That the Peerage was renounced the eighth of *January,* which was the Date of the Warrant for the Religious Murder of *Glenco,* upon which Day likewise the Earl of *Stavis* [Stair], Signer of the said Warrant, after he had with more than ordinary Zeal appeared that Day in Parliament, was found dead on his Bed; or, as was reported, hanged himself.

Third, The Ratification of the Articles of the Union was upon the sixteenth of the Date of the Sentence of the Royal Martyr King *Charles* the First.

Fourth, The Dissolution of the Scots Parliament or Kingdom was upon the Twenty-fifth of *March,* being the first of the Year in *England,* and a handsome new

222-3 ...the independency and soveraignty of the Kingdom both which the Earl of Seafield so little valued, that when he, as Chancellor, signed the engrossed exemplification of the Act of Union, he returned it to the clerk, in face of Parliament, with this despising and contemning remark, 'Now there's ane end of ane old song." I have now brought...

Years Gift to that Kingdom.
Fifth, The Equivalent (*alias Price of Scotland*) came to Edinburgh on the Fifth of *August*, the Day the Earl of Gourie designed to perpetrate his horrid Conspiracy against King James VI.

I have now brought...

354 ...upon themselves. A few private men...

379 ...Opinion or instruction could have that weight...

380 ...Stirling of Cordon, having...

384 ...grievous to any, that..

403 ...Seriously consider.

Finis

231 ...upon themselves, it being too much for a few private men...

246 ...opinion or inclination (supposing the fact was true, though at the same time it was not probable) could have had such weight...

247 ...Stirling of Carden, and many others, having...

249 ...grievous to any true Scotsman that...

261 ...seriously consider. For the Almighty God, the wise and supreme Governour of the world, hath permitted such things to come to pass; yet I doubt much if the authors and abettors of them can produce any authority to justify their proceedings in the sight of God or man. 'Tis true that God hath in all ages and countries raised up wicked and tyrannicall princes and rulers, and also rebellious and treacherous subjects, both of the clergy and laity, as a scourge to sinfull nations; but their wickedness, tyrannies, rebellions, and treacheries were never to be esteemed the less criminal; and if so in preceding times, those of the present age, when they reflect upon the part they have acted with respect to Scotland, have no reason to expect to be justify'd in this world or that which is to come.

Finis

Notes

1. Sir David Dalrymple of Hailes, M.P. for Haddington Burghs.
2. Simon Macdonald Lockhart on p. 107 of his book, *Seven Centuries: The History of the Lockharts of Lee and Carnwath* (1976), states that as far as he knows his family copy of the *Lockhart Papers* was the only one which contained a copy of the facsimile letter. In fact there are others, including those in the British Library and the Bodleian, but it is missing from the copy in the National Library of Scotland.
3. P. Hume Brown, *The Legislative Union of England and Scotland* (Oxford, 1914) pp. 3–5.
4. *The Letters of Sir Walter Scott*, ed. Sir Herbert Grierson (12 vols, 1936), xi. 185.
5. *Byron's Letters and Journals: the Complete and Unexpurgated Text of all the Letters Available in Manuscript and the Full Printed Version of All Others*, ed. L. A. Marchand (12 vols, 1973), ix. 156.
6. Tom Scott in his introduction to *The Penguin Book of Scottish Verse* (1970), p. 50.
7. The main sources for Lockhart's life are the *Lockhart Papers*, the *Lockhart Letters* and Dr Szechi's introduction, Macdonald Lockhart's *Seven Centuries* and his entry in the *DNB*. Dr Szechi is also working on a full-scale social and intellectual biography.
8. *Lockhart Letters*, xiii.
9. John Houston of Houston Jr, M.P. for Linlithgowshire.
10. Ibid, p. 110.
11. See below, pp. xxxii–xxxiii.
12. *Lockhart Letters*, p. 111.
13. Ibid., p. 113.
14. John Campbell, 2nd Duke of Argyll.
15. *Lockhart Papers*, i. 394.
16. *Lockhart Letters*, p. 260.
17. *Lockhart Papers*, ii. 397.
18. Ibid., i. 581–88 and 612–16, espec. pp. 586, 613.
19. P. Hume Brown, *History of Scotland* , 3 vols (Cambridge, 1909), iii. 126.
20. British Library, Add. MSS 34, 180. Quoted in P. H. Scott, *1707, The Union of Scotland and England* (Edinburgh, 1979), pp. 43–4.
21. HMC, *Portland MSS*, v. 114–15.
22. *Lockhart Papers*, i. 127–8; National Library of Scotland, MS 7102.
23. *Lockhart Papers*, i. 153; *Memoirs of Sir John Clerk of Penicuik, Baronet. Extracted by Himself From his own Journals, 1676–1755,*

ed. J. M. Gray, *Scottish History Society*, 1st series, vol. 13 (Edinburgh, 1892), p. 60; *State Papers and Letters Addressed to William Carstares*, ed. J. McCormick (Edinburgh, 1774), pp. 743–4.

24. See, for example, HMC, *Mar and Kellie MSS*, pp. 293, 296, 302, 305, 307, 329 and *passim*; *Seafield Letters*, p. 99; *Memoirs of the Life of Sir John Clerk*, p. 58; *The Letters of Daniel Defoe*, ed. G. H. Healey (Oxford, 1955), pp. 132–6; D. Defoe, *The History of the Union of Great Britain* (1709, repr. 1768), pp. 33, 64, 229, 246.

25. *Lockhart Letters*, v.

Textual Preface

George Lockhart originally intended *The Memoirs of Scotland* to be little more than a personal *aide-memoire*. For his own purposes he had collected official publications and jotted down notes of proceedings in the Scottish Parliament while he was a Commissioner for Midlothian, and while languishing in enforced retirement after the Union he decided to put them in order. The process of putting them in order led him to write linking sections that placed his miscellaneous notes and documents in context, which in turn gave rise to his attempt to construct a coherent narrative.[1] Though he had published a short polemical pamphlet, *Letter to An English Lord*, in 1702, this was Lockhart's first essay in extended narrative, and despite its arresting pungency, drama and verve it bears all the hallmarks of inexperience.

The most obvious manifestation of the author's naivete is the way undigested documents recur in solid blocks throughout the text. Inserting telling official documents in polemical works such as the *Memoirs* was far from uncommon at the time Lockhart was writing, but writers like Defoe and Ridpath usually managed it with more dexterity. Consequently some sections of the text that follows are little more than reproductions of selected public-cum-official documents. They have, nevertheless, been retained unabridged in the text that follows because there can be no doubt it was the author's intention that they should feature in his narrative.

The revised version of the *Memoirs* found in the 1817 edition, on which the text below is based, was prepared by Lockhart, probably between 1717 and 1720, very likely as part of the process of writing up the *Commentarys* that constitute the rest of the first volume of the *Lockhart Papers* published by Aufrere in

1817. The *Commentarys* are a much more fluent, polished work than the *Memoirs*, and though Lockhart implies in his second introduction to the *Memoirs*[2] that he has corrected the errors and infelicities of his original text, it still has some very awkward, stodgy passages which are uncharacteristic of Lockhart's later writings. That he nonetheless intended it to be published in this revised form is, however, apparent from the title page he drafted for the revised text of the *Memoirs*, on which he proudly proclaimed his authorship, and his inclusion of Sir David Dalrymple's introduction with a second introduction by himself appended in rebuttal. As part of the 1817 edition Aufrere also published a facsimile of Lockhart's letter to his heirs concerning the whole body of his writings, which also indicates he considered the text of the *Memoirs* to be ready for publication:

> 3rd February 1730
>
> The papers contained in the trunk sealed up to which this is annexed are of importance and cannot for some time be divulged without manifold inconveniencies public and private, general and particular. On the other hand the publishing of them may some time or other be proper and useful on several accounts, for which reason it is expedient they be preserved in secret and safety [*sic*]. In order therto I do leave them behind me, committing them to you with and under the following rules and directions, viz: that you deposite them in some safe secret place, of which none shall be acquainted excepting one trusty person to take care of them in case of your decease. That you communicate their being any such thing left by me to no soul living but that person, under solemn promises of secresie. That you do not out of curiosity or any other motive break up the sealls or open the trunk, but let it remain intire as I have left it to you. That immediately after my death you enclose this within a letter directed to your son and heir renewing and repeating what is here contained, and joining with me in desiring the continuance of the aforesaid care and caution. That what is in this trunk be after this manner concealled and preserved

till the year seventeen hundred and fifty, by which time I reckon the inconveniencies attending the publishing may probably be removed. And lastly, if ever they be published I expresslie require that it be exactly, without adding or impairing, conform to the originall manuscripts.

Now as you and those descending from me have any regard for my earnest desire I do expect you will carefully and faithfully execute this trust according to the aforesaid instructions, as you would merite and expect the kindest blessing of ane affectionat father to attend you and yours.[3]

Geo. Lockhart

And Aufrere was, as far as we can ascertain without access to the original manuscript (unfortunately since lost),[4] faithful to the author's instructions in publishing his text as he found it in 1817.

The text of the 1817 edition thus reproduces the literary conventions of the late seventeenth/early eighteenth century.[5] Lockhart's spelling and punctuation are idiosyncratic and inconsistent. The text is not broken up into chapters but is instead a seamless robe, running on for 222 pages without interruption before pausing for an 11 page appendix. Paragraph breaks are used unsystematically. Sentences run on for the best part of a page at a time. Quotations are haphazardly signalled, and marginal notes are used in lieu of chapter-headings and an index. As well, Aufrere, as editor, judged it best to take a minimalist approach to explicating the text. Hence there are only five explanatory notes and a brief (two page) editorial preface. The net result has been that the text reproduced by the 1817 edition has steadily become less and less accessible to any but historians of Scotland specialising in the period 1703–1708.

In order to avoid falling into the same trap this edition includes a number of changes to the text designed to enhance its readability while preserving the author's emphasis and meaning. As far as possible Lockhart's spellings have been left intact, but commonplace contractions, usually denoted by an apostrophe by Lockhart, have been silently expanded whenever possible. The punctuation and paragraphing have been modernised wherever this helps clarify the author's meaning. Capitalisation has been made consistent throughout. The natural breaks the author fell into in his narrative (which is systematically chronological) have been converted into chapter breaks, and an indication that this is occurring signalled by the insertion of formal chapter headings in square brackets.

Since Sir David Dalrymple's preface to the 1714 edition and Lockhart's angry rebuttal of his and various other authors' attacks on the veracity of the *Memoirs* are of less general interest than the main text, they have been sited in an appendix at the end of this edition rather than preceding the text proper. As well, this edition omits the marginal notes Aufrere preserved in 1817 in favour of a modern index and table of contents.

Given the unfamiliarity of the society, politics and personalities of the era Lockhart is describing, it has been necessary to annotate this edition of the *Memoirs* far more heavily than that of 1817. And in order to keep these notes more easily accessible I have tried, as far as possible, to refer only to printed sources obtainable at major public and university libraries. Persons mentioned in the text solely as adherers to formal protests in the Scottish Parliament have been passed over without further explication. Wherever possible, all other individuals mentioned in the text have received a note pointing the reader towards the most accessible source of further information. In the case of those individuals singled out for character sketches by Lockhart the note pointing up further information has been inserted in the text where the character sketch appears; in all other cases it has been inserted the first time the person is mentioned. Citations without comment in notes on Lockhart's account of events indicate a source which supports his interpretation of what was happening. Notes prefaced by the notation 'Cf.' conversely indicate the source cited disagrees with Lockhart's depiction of what was going on. Secondary works on the period covered by the *Memoirs* have not generally been cited in the notes, the only exception being modern biographies of individuals mentioned in the text. Instead, relevant modern interpretations have been collected in the Select Bibliography that follows this textual preface. Unless otherwise stated all works cited were published in London.

Notes

1. See below, pp. 4–5.
2. See below, p. 273.
3. *Lockhart Papers*, xvii—n.b. I have silently expanded all the contractions and modernised the punctuation in this letter.
4. I have searched fruitlessly for several years for the 'trunk' of papers alluded to by Lockhart in the letter above, and have come to the sad conclusion that they were probably destroyed when the RAF firebombed Hamburg (where Aufrere's son appears to have settled after his marriage to a Hamburg merchant's daughter) in 1943. There is, however, the possibility that they were part of a legacy (Aufrere's papers) left by Aufrere's widow, *née* Matilda Lockhart, to *The Gentleman's Magazine* in the mid-nineteenth century. In which case they may be found wherever the archives of the magazine ended up after it shut down in the 1920s. Or, alternatively, they may have followed Aufrere's daughter to America. If any reader of this note should happen to have further information on the whereabouts of Lockhart's original manuscripts, I would be most grateful if they would contact me directly at Auburn University.
5. Though it makes very little difference to the editing of the text that follows, I disagree with Paul Scott's ascription of the punctuation, style and format of the 1817 edition to early nineteenth-century literary conventions, and am instead of the opinion that all of these were faithfully derived by Aufrere from GL's original manuscript.

Select Bibliography

Baxter, S., *William III and the Defence of European Liberty 1650–1702* (1966)

Campbell, R. H., *Scotland Since 1707: the Rise of an Industrial Society*, 2nd edition (1985)

Donaldson, G., *Scotland: James V—James VII* (Edinburgh, 1965)

Ferguson, W., *Scotland: 1689 to the Present* (1968)
Scotland's Relations with England: a Survey to 1707 (Edinburgh, 1977)

Gibson, J., *Playing the Scottish Card. The Franco-Jacobite Invasion of 1708* (Edinburgh, 1988)

Gregg, E., *Queen Anne* (1980)

Holmes, G., *British Politics in the Age of Anne*, revised edition (1987)
The Making of a Great Power. Late Stuart and Early Georgian Britain 1660–1722 (1993)

Holmes, G. and Szechi, D., *The Age of Oligarchy. Pre-Industrial Britain 1722–1783* (1993)

Hopkins, P., *Glencoe and the End of the Highland War* (Edinburgh, 1986)

Lenman, B., *An Economic History of Modern Scotland, 1660–1976* (1977)
The Jacobite Risings in Britain 1689–1746 (1980)

Miller, J., *James II. A Study in Kingship* (Hove, 1977)

Phillipson, N. T. and Mitchison, R., *Scotland in the Age of Improvement: Essays in Scottish History in the Eighteenth Century* (Edinburgh, 1970)

Prebble, J., *The Darien Disaster* (1968)

Riley, P. W. J., *The Union of England and Scotland* (Manchester, 1978)
King William and the Scottish Politicians (Edinburgh, 1979)

Scott, P. H., *1707: the Union of Scotland and England* (Edinburgh, 1979)

Shaw, J. S., *The Management of Scottish Society 1707–64: Power, Nobles, Lawyers, Edinburgh Agents and English Influences* (Edinburgh, 1983)

Smout, T. C., *Scottish Trade on the Eve of Union, 1660–1707* (Edinburgh, 1963)
A History of the Scottish People 1560–1860 (1969)

Szechi, D., *The Jacobites. Britain and Europe 1688–1788* (Manchester, 1994)

MEMOIRS

Concerning the Affairs of

SCOTLAND,

From

Queen Anne's

Accession to the Throne

To the

Commencement of the UNION of the two Kingdoms of

Scotland and England,

In MAY, 1707.

With an Account of the Origine and Progress of the Design'd
Invasion from France, in March, 1708

And some Reflections on the Ancient State of Scotland

By

George Lockhart, Esq. of Carnwath

The Preface

A book now without a preface, is thought as ridiculous as a man with a suit of fine cloaths and a slovenly sign-post hat and periwig; and therefore, since, according to the proverb, 'a man had as good be dead as out of the fashion', I must preface a little too. Though, indeed, after all, I might spare my self the pains, since the odds are more than two to one that these memoirs will never appear in publick. One thing I'm sure of, that a good space of time must needs interveen, since they make several passages that upon many accounts are not fit to be promulgated in the world, till the affairs thereof—I mean in this island—take another turn. And even supposing that obstacle were (and I pray God it may be soon) removed, yet having used a little freedom with several persons of rank and power, in the characters I have given of them, and in the relation of matters of fact, common prudence requires these memoirs should lie dormant till such be out of a capacity to resent the same either on my self or posterity.

To begin then: I do most solemnly declare, not because it is the jog-trot method of prefaces, but because it is real truth, that my writing of these memoirs did not proceed from any desire of being an author. For the true rise and origine was, as I'm now to tell you, having had the honour to represent one of the chief shires in Scotland during the last four sessions of Parliament, I did apply myself to become as useful as I could to my country. And, I thank God, my behaviour was such, that I did not procure the displeasure of my constituents. I considered that, when I first entered upon that employment, I was very young, and void of experience, and was desirous to retrieve that loss by a diligent application to observe what did occur for the future. And for that purpose I used, for the most part, to make my remarks on what I thought observable as they occurred either in or out of the Parliament house, and gather a collection of all the valuable prints, and procure extracts of such papers as I believed might be useful to lie by me. Having followed this method for four years, viz. from Queen Anne's first session of the Parliament in 1703 to the commencement of the Union in May 1707, I lived thereafter some time privately at my house in the country, and thought I could not divert myself to better purpose than by ranging my notes into order, believing they might, perhaps, prove some time or other useful, to keep in my remembrance several passages that I might otherways forget. And all I then designed was to be contained in a small volume. But, after I was once engaged in the work, I found several passages required the relation of others, without which they were not plain, which, bit by bit, drew me into a labyrinth, out of which I could not well extricate myself till it had swelled to a much greater bulk than I at first imagined. This being finished, I projected no more, but being afterwards a little curious to know if any other person had a design of writing an account of these times, and being certainly informed that there was none, at least that I could hear of (except Mr Redpath and some other mercenary party scribblers,[1] whose accounts, if ever published, will be found to want several remarkable passages the knowledge of which they could never attain to, and which are contained here), I thought it a million of pities that such considerable transactions should be altogether buried in oblivion, and therefore, since no other that I heard of did, I was resolved to attempt it.

In prosecution whereof, I found it necessary to give the reader a particular account of the lives and characters of several persons without which he could not well have had a clear and full idea of what passed. I know it is the hardest part of an historian. And how I have performed it I must refer to the judgment of others. These characters will let posterity know who they were made the greatest appearance, and had the chief ruling of the roast in these days, and the protestations and protestors' names will serve to keep in remembrance the grounds upon which they went, and to whom the country owes its ruin, and who they were stood to its defence.

After I had designed it so far as the commencement of the Union, the designed invasion from France soon followed,[2] and I thought it had so near a relation and dependance upon what preceeded that I inclined to give likewise an account of it. The disappointment of which drew me insensibly to take a short glance of the happy state from which the kingdom of Scotland was fallen, and, I am perswaded, if Scotchmen would often and seriously reflect upon it and the glorious and heroick actions of their progenitors, it could not fail of exciting in them a generous resolution of recovering what was so valiantly defended and maintained by their predecessors, and meanly parted with by this age. And I can never suffer myself to despond, or doubt, but that, some time or other, God will bless such resolutions and endeavours with success by restoring the nation to its ancient rights and liberties.

What next remains is to acquaint my reader that, besides the pains I was at to make the observations and collections I have spoke of, I had opportunities of knowing the rise of most transactions as much as any of my contemporaries, having (I say it without vanity) been trusted by the chief of the Cavaliers and Country parties. It cannot be imagined that I (though I doubt not the time will come when the truth will appear and be made publick) can, in all points, give a full account of the springs and causes of all the measures that were taken and followed during this time, many of them being the secret intriegues and resolutions of aspiring self-designing men. But, in the main, I fancy I have discovered as much as will give my reader a clear notion of the state of affairs, and the several views and motives that then prevailed. And I do most solemnly declare I have, to the best of my knowledge, neither added to nor impaired the truth, as a proof of which I think I may appeal to the characters and the general strain of the memoirs, wherein I have not spared my near relations, particular friends and intimate comrades when I thought them faulty.

As I am conscious to myself that no motive, save a true-hearted Scots one, incited me to compile these memoirs, so I beg and hope what imperfections they contain may be excused by all such into whose hands they fall. If I have misrepresented any person, it is a sin of ignorance, and I beg pardon for it, but I may desire my reader to give their vindications no credit, unless they be as well vouched [for] as my accusations, which I am sure are so well founded that was there (as we say in Scotland) a right-sitting sheriff, I would not doubt to see some gentlemen string.[3] This remembers me, that I foresee it may be objected I write too much against a certain party. It is true my indignation against the betrayers of my country is so great I never could, nor will, speak otherwise of them. But, when it does not induce me to deviate from the truth on so provoking a subject, I [hope I] may be granted that grain of allowance which you know is never refused losing gamesters.

All I have to add is that perhaps in the process of time some of these persons whose characters I have drawn, and of whose behaviour I have given an account, may alter their minds and manners, some grow better and some grow worse. As to those that grow better, and I wish there may be many such, I shall honour them as much as any man, and I hope they will not take it amiss that I tell the truth and condemn what they themselves seem to disapprove of. As to the other sort of men, I shall heartily regret their falling off from what they once knew to be right and what is contained in these memoirs that seems to favour them will become their greatest reproach. Thus I see no occasion of retracting what I have said of either of these sorts of men. If the account I give of them be true, and the faults I mention were actually committed, I cannot be accused with any shadow of reason.

Notes

1. George Ridpath was paid by the Scottish administration for his services: *Baillie*, p. 24: Earl of Roxburgh to Baillie of Jerviswood, 19 Dec. 1704.
2. The abortive Franco-Jacobite invasion attempt of March 1708. See below, ch. 9.
3. Hang.

[Convention to First Election, 1689–1703]

After King James [II and VII] had retired out of England, and the Prince of Orange[1] was declared king, a Convention of Estates was called in Scotland, and met at Edinburgh on the fourteenth of March 1689, which in a little time declared that King James, having in several points violated and infringed the fundamental constitution of this kingdom, had thereby forfeited his right to the crown and that the throne was become vacant, and immediately settled the crown upon the Prince and Princess[2] of Orange during their lives, and the heirs of their body, which failing, to Princess Anne[3] and the heirs of her body, as it is contained at large in the instrument of government[4] framed by them and called the Claim of Right.[5] And according thereto, William and Mary, Prince and Princess of Orange, were proclaimed king and queen of Scotland on the eleventh of April 1689.

At the commencement of this Convention there was a very considerable party in it that designed to adhere to and support King James's interest. But jealousies and animosities arising amongst them, and several other unfortunate accidents happening, they were obliged to yield to that violent torrent which rushed down upon all such as had the least regard for the royal family, and withdraw from the Convention.

The Viscount of Dundee,[6] and some others, betook themselves to arms, but most of them retired home to their country houses. But certain it is, had they been unanimous amongst themselves, they were strong enough to have opposed the fanatic party,[7] and crossed them in most of their designs with relation to both church and state. The opinion, likewise, that matters could not long stand in the present posture, induced many of the Royalists to shun being elected members of that Convention, not desiring to homologate[8] any of the Prince of Orange's actings, and thereby many more of the fanatics came to be elected than otherwise would have been.

The Revolutioners being sensible of this, and afraid to call a new Parliament lest the Royalists, seeing whither they were driving, should lay aside their scruples and stand candidates for being elected, had recourse to a shift, altogether, I shall say no worse, unprecedented in this kingdom. And that was to pass an act, on the fifth of June 1689, turning the Convention of Estates into a Parliament, in which William, Duke of Hamilton,[9] represented the king's person as Commissioner.[10]

Next year the Parliament met again (the Earl of Melville[11] Commissioner), repealed the Act of Supremacy, abolished episcopacy and established presbytery, not pretending it was agreeable to the word of God, but as suited to the inclinations of the people.[12] And to prevent the designs of the Royalists, in being elected in the room of any vacancies that should happen in Parliament, they framed a test, called the Assurance, wherein they declared before God that they believed King William and Queen Mary to be king and queen of this kingdom *de jure* as well as *de facto*,[13] and engaged to defend their title, as such, with their lives and fortunes. Which declaration they required all persons capable to elect or be elected members of Parliament, and all in any publick trust or office, civil, military or ecclesiastical, to sign, together with the oath of allegiance, under the penalty of deprivation.[14]

To these abovementioned unfortunate jealousies of the Royalists, the turning of the Convention into a Parliament and the framing and imposing this assurance, may be imputed the difficulty that has been since found in opposing the fanatick and Court[15] parties' designs and projects. For, having once settled the government as they pleased, and got a Parliament which consisted entirely of a set of men of their own stamp and kidney (being mostly old, forfeited rebells and gentlemen of no fortunes, respect or families in the kingdom), they took care to continue that very Parliament all King William's reign and even a part of

Queen Anne's too.

Thus they went on as they listed, till at last it pleased God to open the eyes of several who were at first as blind and far seduced as any. And the vigorous appearance we find made against the Court['s] measures was in behalf of the colony of Darien.[16] The Parliament met the nineteenth of July 1698 (the Earl of Marchmont[17] being Commissioner), and the Company presented an address setting forth the indignities they had received from England, and craving the Parliament would fall upon ways and means to repair the losses they had thereby sustained.[18] This raised a hot debate in the house, the Courtiers[19] defending the king. But the Country party,[20] which then began to get that title, attacking and exposing these proceedings, at last prevailed, and carried an address to the king representing the nation's concern in the prosperity of the Company, and craving he would protect them in their just rights and privileges.[21] The Parliament having once taken the Company by the hand, the scandalous and barbarous treatment which the nation afterwards received from England on that account, and the tricks and compliance of our statesmen, with all the measures England did propose for our loss and prejudice, so inflamed this nation with resentment, that in the Parliament which met May the twenty-first 1700 (the Duke of Queensberry[22] Commissioner), they banged and forced the Court to pass several good laws which tended much to the advantage of the nation.

Thus stood affairs, and the nation was in this temper, when King William died, the eighth of March 1702. Queen Anne succeeded, and was proclaimed on the [13th] day of March 1702, to the great satisfaction of all those who were well-wishers to their country, and especially to the Cavaliers,[23] who expected mighty things from her. But, on the other hand, the Presbyterians[24] looked on themselves as undone. Despair appeared in their countenances, which were more upon the melancholick and dejected air than usual, and most of their doctrines from the pulpits were exhortations to stand by, support and be ready to suffer for Christ's cause—the epithet they gave their own. They knew the queen was a strenuous asserter of the doctrine of the Church of England. They were conscious how little respect the great men of their faction had paid her during the late reign. They saw the Church party[25] was preferred to places and favour in England. They knew the Scots nation, especially the nobility and gentry, were much disgusted at them, because of their promoting the Court interest in the last reign, against that of the Country. And upon these and such like accounts, they dreaded a storm impending over their heads.

At the time of King William's decease, the government was lodged in the hands of a set of men entirely on the Revolution foot.[26] The Earl of Marchmont was Chancellor, the Earl of Melville President of the Council, the Duke of Queensberry Privy Seal, the Earls of Seafield[27] and Hyndford[28] Secretaries of State, the Earl of Selkirk[29] Register, Adam Cockburn of Ormiston Treasurer Deputy,[30] Sir John Maxwell of Pollock[31] Justice Clerk and Sir James Stuart[32] Advocate. The Lords of the Treasury were all (except the Lord Murray[33]) of the same stamp. And, generally speaking, few or none were admitted to any post, civil or military, but such as were of undoubted antimonarchical principles, and ready to sacrifice their honour, conscience and country to the Court['s] designs, which absolutely depended on the English ministry and were determined according to English measures and maxims.

The funds allotted to support the army being near expired at King William's decease, there was a necessity to have a Parliament in the summer [of 1702]. The Revolutioners were afraid to venture on a new one lest (as was observed before) the number of the Country party and Cavaliers should increase, and therefore they used their utmost efforts to perswade the queen to continue the former, though no instance could ever be given of the surviving of a Parliament after the decease of the monarch by whom it was called. And, besides, it is inconsistent with the very nature and constitution of the Scots Parliament. And therefore the Duke of Hamilton,[34] the Marquis of Tweedale,[35] Earls Marishal[36] and Rothes,[37] and a great many of the chief nobility and gentry went to London and laid before Her Majesty the unreasonableness of such a project, but all to no purpose. For Her Majesty did not hearken to their remonstrance and advice, being, whether for fear of offending and irritating the Presbyterian party (whose power was mightily magnifyed to her), or because they were more submissive and ready to trucle under the English ministry and comply with every state measure that could be proposed to them, I know not, prevailed upon to continue the former Parliament. And in order thereto, issue[d] out a proclamation appointing it to meet on the ninth of June 1702, and name James, Duke of Queensberry to be High Commissioner thereto.[38]

He was the son of William, Duke of Queensberry, who was highly in favour with both King Charles[39] and King James, and by them intrusted with the greatest offices and employments (which he well deserved, being in all respects a great man). But after the Revolution he retired and lived privately for the most part, and continued firm to King James's interest all the time he lived.[40] But the son, notwithstanding King Charles and King James's kindness to his father and family (through which he was created a duke, and scraped together a vast fortune), and the respect and favour which King James had all alongst bestowed on himself, was the first Scotsman that deserted over to the Prince of Orange, and from thence acquir'd the epithet (amongst honest men) of 'Proto-rebel', and has ever since been so faithful to the Revolution party, and averse to the king and all his adherers, that he laid hold on all occasions to oppress and depress the loyal party and interest. Having thus made his first appearance in the world by deserting his king and benefactor, we are not to expect he will prove more faithful to his country—and had he deserted her, as he did the former, it would have been happy for us—but, alass, he stuck close by her and never left her, till he had ruined her to all intents and purposes, having undertaken and promoted every proposal and scheme for enslaving Scotland, and invading her honour, liberty, and trade, and rendering her obsequious to the measures and interest of England. This proceeded, I suppose, from his being of a lazy, easy temper, and falling at first into bad hands, he was seduced by them, and being once deeply dipt in all

projects against the king and country, he never could imagine that
repentence and amendment could be accepted of (the frequent
effects of a hardened conscience), and that he was safe against an
after reckoning. He was reputed a man of good parts, but wanted
application to business; was extreamly covetous, and, at the same
time, extreamly lavish of his money. For though he got vast sums
of money by his publick employments, most of it was squandred
away. He was well-bred, and had so courteous a behaviour, that
what by this, and the occasion of doing acts of kindness, by
having the chief administration of affairs a long time in his hands,
he engaged the favour and friendship of very many of all ranks of
people, and entirely managed the Revolution party, and such as
were willing to prostitute themselves to serve the Court
measures. To outward appearance, and in his ordinary conversation, he was of a gentle and good disposition, but inwardly a
very devil, standing at nothing to advance his own interest and
designs. Though his hypocrisy and dissimulation served him very
much, yet he became so very well known, that no man, except
such as were his nearest friends and *socii criminis*,[41] gave him
any trust. And so little regard had he to his promises and vows,
that it was observed and notour, that if he was at any pains to
convince you of his friendship, and by swearing and imprecating
curses on himself and family, to assure you of his sincerity, then,
to be sure, he was doing you underhand all the mischief in his
power. To sum up all, he was altogether void of honour, loyalty,
justice, religion, and ingenuity; an ungrateful deserter of, and
rebel to, his prince, the ruin and bane of his country, and the
aversion of all loyal and true Scotsmen.[42]

But now to return to the Parliament. As soon as the house was
conveened the Duke of Hamilton desired to be heard, and in his
own name, and the name of those that adheared to him, spoke as
follows.

> We are come here in obedience to Her Majesty's command,
> and we are all heartily glad of Her Majesty's happy
> accession to the throne, not meerely on the account that it
> was her undoubted right as being lineally descended from

the ancient race of our kings, but likewise because of the many personal vertues and royal qualities Her Majesty is endowed with. Which gives us ground to hope we shall enjoy under her auspicious reign all the blessings that can attend a nation which has a loving and gracious sovereign, united with a dutiful and obedient people. And we are resolved to sacrifice our lives and fortunes in defence of Her Majesty's right against all her enemies whatever, and have all the deference and respect for Her Majesty's government and authority that is due from loyal subjects to their rightful and lawful sovereign. But at the same time that we acknowledge our submission to Her Majesty's authority, we think ourselves bound in duty, by vertue of the obedience we owe to the standing laws of the nation, and because of the regard we ought to have for the rights and liberties of our fellow subjects, to declare our opinion as to the legality of this meeting. Viz. that we do not think ourselves warranted by law to sit and act any longer as a Parliament, and that by so doing we shall incur the hazard of losing our lives and fortunes if our proceedings shall come to be questioned by subsequent Parliaments.

Then his grace read a paper, which contains the reasons of their dissenting from the proceedings of the other members, who thought themselves impowered to sit and act as a Parliament, and is as follows:

Forasmuch as by the fundamental laws and constitution of this kingdom, all Parliaments do dissolve by the death of the king or queen, except in so far innovated by the seventeenth Act, sixth sessions, of King William's Parliament last in being, at his decease to meet and act what should be needful for the defence of the true Protestant religion, as now by law established, and maintaining the succession to the crown, as settled by the claim of right, and for preserving and securing the peace and safety of the kingdom. And seeing that the said ends are fully satisfied by Her Majesty's succession to the throne, whereby the religion and peace of

the kingdom are secured, we conceive ourselves not now
warranted by the law to meet, sit or act, and therefore do
dissent from any thing that shall be done or acted.

And thereupon his grace took instruments,[43] and craved an extract
of his protestation.[44] And seventy-nine members of the first
quality and best estates in the kingdom adhered thereto, and all
withdrew out of the house and left the other part to sit and act by
themselves.[45] As the Duke of Hamilton and the other dissenting
members passed in a body from the Parliament-house to the
Cross Keys tavern, near the Cross, they were huzzaed by the
acclamations of an infinite number of people of all degrees and
ranks. These dissenting members sent up my Lord Blantyre[46]
with an address from them to the queen, showing their reasons
for this their proceedure, which Her Majesty positively refused to
receive, but allowed my Lord Blantyre to wait upon her.[47]

In the mean time the Parliament went on, and the first thing
they set about was to preserve themselves, by passing an act
declaring this session to be a lawful and free meeting of
Parliament, and discharging any person to disown, quarrel, or
impugne the dignity and authority thereof, under the penalty of
high treason.[48] Yet when the taxes they afterwards imposed came
to be uplifted, near one half the nation refused to pay the same,
and they were raised by quartering of soldiers, poynding of goods
and the like methods usual in cases of deficiency.[49] Next the
Parliament proceeded to frame an act recognizing Her Majesty's
authority, and another for the security of the Presbyterian Kirk
government. And Sir Alexander Bruce,[50] upon account of a
speech made against the same, wherein amongst other things he
affirmed that presbytery was inconsistent with monarchy, was
expelled the house.[51] The Dean and Faculty of Advocates having
passed a vote among themselves in favour of the foresaid
protestation and address of the dissenting members, declaring
they were founded upon, and in terms of, the laws of the
kingdom, were upon that account charged and pursued by my
Lord Advocate before the Parliament, where, after several long
debates upon the matter, they were severely reprimanded.[52] But it

had been much better for the government they had not taken any notice of it. For the nation was enraged to see a learned and venerable society attacked for declaring their opinion (who are certainly the best judges) in a point of law, which so nearly concerned the foundation and constitution of the Parliament and consequently the liberty and right of the subject.

Thus the Parliament proceeded peaceably and calmly within doors (they being all one man's bairns, as we say) until the Earl of Marchmont, from an headstrong overgrown zeal, against the advice of his friends, and even the commands of my Lord Commissioner, presented an act for imposing an oath abjuring the Prince of Wales,[53] in the most horrid, scurrilous terms imaginable.[54] This divided the house and raised great heats amongst the members, many of the Courtiers being desirous the dissenting members would return to the house, to assist them in opposing it.[55] And in case it had gone on, they would have come for that end.

It may be thought strange that this act did not pass currantly[56] in such a strange, made-up meeting, and when such eminently famous and zealous Revolutioners were at the helm of affairs and acted without any to comptrole them. But I presume the reasons were: first, the Commissioner had no instructions concerning it; secondly, the uncertainty how things would go in England (the queen was but newly come to the crown, and not well fixed in the throne, and they foresaw they might expect little thanks if she afterwards should favour the interest of the distressed royal family. And I have reason to believe that the queen and her English ministry were then inclined to keep the succession in Scotland open as a check and awe-band upon the Whigs and the family of Hanover[57]); and lastly, as they pretended afterwards in England, that Parliament's title to act was contraverted, and had so little authority in the nation as it was not fit to venture upon it, there being reason to believe few would have complied with it and every body almost been highly disgusted. For these and the like reasons it is possible, I say, the Commissioners and other Courtiers resolved to wave entering upon this matter.[58] And

therefore when the day came in which it was to be under the
house's consideration, my lord Commissioner cut them short and
made the following speech:

My Lords and Gentlemen,

The chearfulness and unanimity of your proceedings in this
session of Parliament, in recognizing Her Majesty's royal
authority, securing the Protestant religion and presbyterian
government, and expeding[59] the other acts that have been
made for Her Majesty's service, and the good safety of the
kingdom, will, I am perswaded, be very acceptable to Her
Majesty, and satisfying to all her good subjects, and, I do
assure you, is very obliging to me. But I must regret that
when I was expecting we should have parted in the same
happy manner, a proposal which I had some ground to think
was laid aside was offered, to my surprize as well as that of
Her Majesty's other ministers, which occasioned some
debate and difference in the house. My early engagement
and firm adherence to the established government is so well
known that none can doubt my readiness to enter into all
measures for Her Majesty's service, and [to] secure our
happy settlement according to the Claim of Right, and I am
confident you are all of the same mind. Since then we are all
perfectly the same as to our dutifull and faithfull adherence
to Her Majesty, and that the Claim of Right is our
unalterable security, I judge it fit for Her Majesty's service,
and your own interest, to prevent further contest and debate
amongst persons I know to be entirely so well affected to
Her Majesty and for whom I have all imaginable honour, to
dismiss this session of Parliament. We have had no particular
acts or ratifications that do require an act *salvo*,[60] and I do
render you hearty thanks, in Her Majesty's name, for the
loyalty you have testifyed by publick acts, and which I shall
be careful to report to Her Majesty, and shall only
recommend to you, to let the country know the gracious
assurance Her Majesty has been pleased to give us, and to
dispose them to their duty and to comply with Her Majesty's

royal intentions for their own welfare and happiness. And thus I do, in Her Majesty's name and by her authority, prorogue this Parliament till the eighteenth of August, which my lord Chancellor is to declare in the usual form.[61]

And so we take our leave of this monstrous Parliament, which from a Convention was metamorphosed and transubstantiated[62] into a Parliament, and when dead revived again. And all this to support the interest and continue the dominion of a set of men that would, notwithstanding their pretended zeal for the liberties of their country, break in upon the same by overturning and trampling upon the most nice and sacred part of our constitution, the greatest preservative and bulwark of all that is near and dear to a free people.

But to wave this digression. As soon as the Parliament was prorogued away flew the leading men of all the different parties to make their several representations to the queen and her ministers of England.[63] The queen still continued to bestow her favours on the Church party in England, and alterations were made in Scotland, though not so much in behalf of the Cavaliers as could have been wished, yet more for their than their adversaries' advantage. Which had this effect, that it encreased their hopes of seeing better days, but as much displeased the Presbyterians, as if their all had been taken from them. The Earl of Marchmont, Chancellor, the Earl of Melville, President of the Council, the Earl of Selkirk, Register, Adam Cockburn of Ormiston, Treasurer Deputy, Sir John Maxwell of Pollock, Justice Clerk, the Earl of Leven,[64] Governor of the castle of Edinburgh and the Earl of Hyndford, one of the Secretaries of State, were all laid aside. The Duke of Queensberry and the Viscount of Tarbat[65] were made Secretaries of State, and the Earl of Seafield removed from thence and made Chancellor. The Marquis of Annandale,[66] President of the Council, the Earl of Tullibardine (now Duke of Athol),[67] Lord Privy Seal, Lord Blantyre, Treasurer Deputy, Mr Roderick Mackenzie of Preston-hall,[68] Justice Clerk, Sir James Murray of Philiphaugh,[69] Lord Register and the Earl of March,[70] Governor of the castle of Edinburgh. And though it is true all these (excepting the Earl of March and Mackenzie of Preston-hall) had been deeply enough engaged at or since the Revolution against the loyal interest, yet the Duke of Queensberry, and his two dependants, the Lord Blantyre and Sir James Murray of Philiphaugh, now pretended to be quite of another mind. Athol, Seafield and Tarbat valued themselves for having, each of them, once in their life, opposed King William, and the Marquis of Annandale, every body believed, would, if kindly dealt with, go along with the prevailing party.

But some time before this change in the ministry was perfected the scrimpness of the funds imposed by the Rump Parliament,[71] and the difficulties they found in collecting them, rendered it absolutely necessary to call a Parliament to sit in the spring of 1703.[72] And therefore the Earl of Seafield (then Secretary) came down from London to influence the elections of the members of Parliament, which, upon the dissolution of the old Rump, were to be made at the following Michaelmas 1702. And here it would not be much out of the way to give a particular account of this gentleman, since he had so great a share in many of the transactions of this kingdom.

James, Earl of Seafield, was the son and heir of the Earl of Findlater,[73] at this time alive. In his younger years, his father's family being very low and his elder brother alive, he was bred a lawyer, and entered and continued an advocate with a good reputation. In the Convention [of] 1689 he was much taken notice of by reason of a speech he made against the forfeiting of King James, but he did not long continue in these measures. For, by William, Duke of Hamilton's, means he was made sollicitor to King William, and enjoyed that office several years. During which time he prosecuted his employment to good purpose and made a fair estate. In the year 1696 he was called to court to be one of King William's Secretaries of State, and indeed it must be owned he served him very faithfully, consenting to and going alongst with any thing demanded of him, though visibly against the interest of his country, and trimmed and tricked so shamefully in the affair of Darien that he thereby, from being generally well-beloved, drew upon himself the hatred of all who wished well to that glorious undertaking. He was believed to be of loyal enough principles, but so mean and selfish a soul that he wanted both resolution and honesty enough to adhere to them. Which evidently appeared from his changing sides so often, and cleaving to that party he found rising. People were willing to excuse, at least extenuate, his first faults, because of the lowness of his worldly circumstances. But after he had raised them to a considerable height, and had a fair occasion of retrieving his reputation when he joined with the Cavaliers in the Parliament [in] 1703, to leave them as basely as he did, is altogether inexcusable. He was finely accomplished, a learned lawyer, a just judge, courteous and good-natured, but withall so intirely abandoned to serve the Court measures, be what they will, that he seldom or never consulted his own inclinations but was a blank sheet of paper which the Court might fill up with what they pleased. As he thus sacrificed his honour and principles, so he likewise easily deserted his friend when his interest (which he was only firm to) did not stand in competition [sic]. He made a good figure, and proceeded extremely well in the Parliament and Session, where he dispatched business to the general satisfaction of the Judges.[74]

But to return [to] where we left off. The great and main design of the Court at the time of the elections was to get the legality of the last, controverted, session of the Rump Parliament asserted in the ensuing Parliament. And therefore the Earl of Seafield did assure all such as he knew to be of loyal principles,[75] that the queen was resolved to take their cause by the hand, would trust the government to their management and take care of both the distressed royal family and church. And with horrid asseverations and solemn vows protested he would joyn and stand firm to the interest of both. This took with most of that perswasion, but, alas, they were not so provident as the Presbyterians who (let their several affections to the Court or Country be as they will) where they had the plurality never chose any but such as were true blew. On the other hand, the Cavaliers went into, and elected, several

Presbyterians, and even, in some places, opposed the election of those who were known to be well inclined to the royal family and church, and of as good character and reputation as any in the kingdom. And being thus divided in the beginning, it was a wonder they made not a smaller figure than they did in the ensuing Parliament though they joyned together and acted one part. But the cause of this must be chiefly attributed to [the] Duke [of] Hamilton. For the difference and discord between him and the Duke of Queensberry were so great that whilst the other was at the helm of affairs he could not be induced to comply with those measures the queen proposed, though attended with much advantage to the cause he had always stood up for, and really wished well to. And finding the Cavaliers inclined to serve and trust the queen, he divided them, and opposed many of their elections with all his might. However, he soon and often repented it, and they have since seen and smarted for their error.

But this is a rock often the Cavaliers (but never the Presbyterians) have split upon. And the reason, as I take it, from whence this comes is that the former being (I say it impartially) of generous spirits, and designing good and just things, believe every man is so too, and are not at such pains as is necessary to cement a party's councils and measures together. Whereas the Presbyterians, acting from a selfish principle and conscious of their ill actions and designs, are, like the devil himself, never idle, but always projecting, and so closely linked together that all go the same way, and all either stand or fall together. The former practice is certainly more noble and less politick and ought never to be prosecuted until we are convinced of a general reformation of minds and manners. Which I am sure this age cannot in the least pretend to.

Having so far digressed, before I return to where I left off it will not be amiss to let my reader known that James, Duke of Hamilton, was the son of William, Earl of Selkirk, second son to the Marquis of Douglas, who after his marriage with Anne, daughter to James, the first Duke of Hamilton, and heiress of both the estate and honours of Hamilton, was likewise created

Duke of Hamilton. During his father's life, and even for some time after his decease, he was designed Earl of Arran,[76] but afterwards his mother made a resignation of the honours to King William,[77] in favours of her son, which were accordingly bestowed on him. After his return from his travels he remained for the most part at court, where he was a gentleman of the bedchamber and in great favour with both King Charles and King James. At the time of the late Revolution he had the command of a regiment of horse, was brigadier-general, and amongst the small number of those that continued faithful to their unfortunate sovereign, never leaving him till he went to France. And then, returning to London, he gave a proof in a meeting of the Scots nobility and gentry that he was a faithful and loyal subject.[78] But after King William was established on the throne he retired, [and] was ready to have commanded to the north of England had not my Lord Dundee's death and some other fatal accidents prevented that design, was several times imprisoned and much harrassed upon account of his loyalty.

In the year 1698 the oppression which his native country received from England, particularly in their affair of the colony of Darien, called him to attend the Parliament, in which, with great dexterity, he framed a party very considerable for numbers and power (though it was King William's own packed-up Parliament), that stood firm to the interest of the country and asserted the independency of the nation. Had not his loyalty been so unalterable, and that he never would engage in King William and his government's service, and his love to his country induced him to oppose that king and England's injustice and encroachment upon it, no doubt he had made as great a figure in the world as any other whatsoever, and that either in a civil or military capacity. For he was master of an heroick and undaunted courage, a clear, ready and penetrating conception, and knew not what it was to be surprized, having at all times and on all occasions his wits about him. And though in Parliament he did not express his thoughts in a style altogether eloquent,[79] yet he had so nervous, majestick and pathetick[80] a method of speaking, and applying what he spoke, that it was always valued and regarded. Never was a man so well qualified to be the head of a party as himself. For he could, with the greatest dexterity, apply himself to and sift through the inclinations of different parties, and so cunningly manage them, that he gained some of all to his. And if once he had entered into a new measure and formed a project (though in doing thereof he was too cautious) did then prosecute his designs with such courage that nothing could either daunt or divert his zeal and forwardness.

The Cavaliers, and those of the Country party, had a great opinion of and honour for him, and that deservedly. For it is well known he often refused great offers if he would leave them, and was by his excellent qualifications, and eminent station and character absolutely necessary both to advise and support them. He wanted not a share of that haughtiness which is in some measure inherent to his family, though he was most affable and courteous to those he knew were honest men, and in whom he confided. He was extreamly cautious and wary in engaging in any project that was dangerous. And it was thought, and perhaps not without too much ground, that his too great concern for his estate in England occasioned a great deal of lukewarmness in his opposition to the Union and unwillingness to enter into several measures that were proposed to prevent the same. But his greatest failing lay in his being somewhat too selfish and revengeful, which he carried alongst with in all his designs, and did thereby several times prejudice the cause for which he contended. And to these two failings any wrong steps he shall be found to make are solely to be attributed. But since it is certain there is no mortal without some imperfection or other, and that his were so small and inconsiderable in respect of his great endowments and qualifications, we may well enough pass them over and conclude him a great and extraordinary man. And whensoever a loyal and true Scotsman will reflect upon his actions he cannot fail to admire and love him for the service he did his king and country, and number him amongst those worthies whose memories ought ever to be reverenced in Scotland.[81]

But now it is high time to consider where we left off. After the elections were over the Earl of Seafield returned to London. And a little thereafter the above-mentioned alterations of our statesmen were actually effected. But ere I leave the old set of ministers I must remember that upon dissolving the Old Rump Parliament the Earl of Marchmont and his crew, being baulked of their darling abjuration, and still dreading the Cavaliers, framed in Council an explanation of the assurance, by changing the engagement to defend the queen against the late King James and all her enemies, and to the pretended Prince of Wales's assuming the title of King James the Eighth, and ordered it to be signed for the future in that form, in hopes thereby to have scared the Cavaliers.[82]

Notes

1. I.e. William III.
2. Mary II, daughter of James II by his first wife, Anne Hyde. See, H. Chapman, *Mary II, Queen of England* (Westport, Connecticut, 1976).
3. Princess Anne of Denmark, second daughter of James II by his first wife Anne Hyde. The future Queen Anne.
4. A pejorative simile, since the Protectorate of Oliver Cromwell (which was generally believed to have been the worst kind of military despotism by GL and his contemporaries) took its authority from a written constitution entitled *The Instrument of Government*.
5. *The Jacobite Threat. Rebellion and Conspiracy 1688–1759: England, Ireland, Scotland and France*, eds B. P. Lenman and J. S. Gibson (Edinburgh, 1990), pp. 13–15.
6. Rect., Viscount Dundee—John Graham of Claverhouse, 1st Viscount Dundee. *DNB*, xxii. 335–50.
7. A contemporary pejorative term for Scots Presbyterians.
8. Approve.
9. William Douglas, 1st Duke of Hamilton of the 2nd creation. *DNB*, xv. 370–2.
10. *APS*, ix. 98.
11. George Melville, 1st Earl of Melville. *DNB*, xxxvii. 238–40.
12. *APS*, ix. 104, 111, 133–4.

13. The distinction was crucial to many episcopalians and Anglicans because, having already sworn allegiance to James II and VII, who lived on in exile until 1701, many believed they could not in conscience acknowledge William III as the true, *de jure*, king, but that they might obey his commands and officers as *de facto* exerciser of the kingly office.

14. *APS*, ix. 223.

15. A contemporary (and semi-pejorative) term used to denote those Commissioners and peers who supported the government of the day.

16. The failed attempt to found a purely Scottish trading settlement and colony on the isthmus of Darien (in modern Panama), for an account of which see: J. Prebble, *The Darien Disaster* (1968).

17. Patrick Hume, 1st Earl of Marchmont. *DNB*, xxviii. 231–4.

18. *APS*, x. 113, appendix 19–20.

19. GL, in keeping with contemporary usage, consistently describes the supporters of the ministry of the day as the Court party or Courtiers.

20. Those opposed to the ministry of the day, or Court, either from principle or due to being out of office.

21. *APS*, x. 135.

22. James Douglas, 2nd Duke of Queensberry. See below, pp.11–12.

23. The episcopalian cum Jacobite party.

24. A catch-all term embracing all those who supported a presbyterian settlement of the Kirk and approved of the overthrow of James II and VII.

25. The name the English Tories liked to give themselves, deriving from their support for the Church of England.

26. I.e. supporters of the Revolution settlement in Kirk and state (regardless of their personal religious inclinations).

27. James Ogilvy, 1st Earl of Seafield (subsequently 4th Earl of Findlater). See below pp. 18–19.

28. John Carmichael, 1st Earl of Hyndford; *CP*, vii. 37–8.

29. Charles Douglas (*né* Hamilton), 2nd Earl of Selkirk; *CP*, xi. 616–17.

30. See below, pp. 79–80.

31. *PS*, ii. 482.

32. Of Goodtrees.

33. Sir James Murray of Dowally, subsequently Tory M.P. for Perthshire 1710–14.

34. James Douglas, 2nd Duke of Hamilton. See below, pp. 22–3.

35. John Hay, 2nd Marquess of Tweeddale. See below, p. 66.
36. William Keith, 8th Earl Marischal. See below, p. 111.
37. John Hamilton (or Leslie), 2nd Earl of Rothes. See below, p. 64.
38. *Crossrigg Diary*, pp. 80–2: 13 Mar.—21 May 1702.
39. Charles II.
40. Cf. *DNB*, xv. 372–3. GL overlooks James II and VII's dismissal of the first Duke of Queensberry in 1686 on charges of peculation, and his acceptance of the office of extraordinary Lord of Session under William III.
41. Partners in crime.
42. Cf. *DNB*, xv. 323–6.
43. Signatures.
44. *APS*, xi. 5: 9 June 1702.
45. *Seafield Letters*, xiii, gives the number of seceders as 57.
46. Walter Stewart, 6th Lord Blantyre. William Keith, jr, of Ludquhairn also accompanied Blantyre to London (*Seafield Letters*, pp. 111–15: Duke of Hamilton to Keith, 24, 27 and 30 June and 9 July 1702).
47. Anne nonetheless indicated her willingness to receive Hamilton and the other seceders: *Baillie*, pp. 6–7: Secretary William Johnston to George Baillie of Jerviswood, 11 and 25 Aug. 1702.
48. *APS*, xi. 16: 12 June 1702.
49. *Baillie*, pp. 8, 9: Johnston to Baillie, 21 Nov. and 22 Dec. 1702.
50. Sir Alexander Bruce of Broomhall, Commissioner for Sanquhar, subsequently 4th Earl of Kincardine. *PS*, i. 76.
51. *APS*, xi. 13, 15, 16.
52. *APS*, xi. 28, appendix 4–7. GL is not quite accurate in his account of Parliament's treatment of the Faculty of Advocates, in that Parliament remitted consideration of the affair to the Privy Council on 30 June, so that any reprimand in fact stemmed from that body rather than the legislature.
53. I.e. repudiating any claim to the throne by James Francis Edward Stuart (the Old Pretender), the only surviving son of James II and VII by his second wife Mary of Modena.
54. *APS*, xi. 28: 27 June 1702.
55. *Seafield Letters*, pp. 112–13: Hamilton to William Keith, jr, of Ludquhairn, [Edinburgh, 27 and 30 June 1702].
56. Swiftly.
57. The Welfs, Electors of Hanover, had been designated Queen Anne's heirs in England by the 1701 Act of Settlement.
58. *Seafield Letters*, p. 113: Hamilton to Keith [Edinburgh, 30 June 1702].

59. Expediting.
60. The ragbag act in which extensions of existing legislation and suchlike amendments to the law were passed by Parliament.
61. *APS*, xi. 28: 30 June 1702; *Crossrigg Diary*, p. 95: 30 June 1702.
62. A pejorative simile. GL and most of his readers were Protestants who at this time were brought up to believe Roman Catholicism was full of artfully constructed falsehoods, the worst being the transubstantiation of the eucharist into the flesh and blood of Christ.
63. *Seafield Letters*, xiii. Lord Treasurer Godolphin, the Duke of Marlborough (Captain-General of the army), and Speaker Robert Harley effectively formed a triumvirate that dominated English politics in the early years of the reign of Queen Anne.
64. David Leslie (*né* Melville), 5th Earl of Leven. See below, p. 60.
65. George Mackenzie, subsequently 1st Earl of Cromarty. See below, pp. 42–3.
66. William Johnston, 1st Marquess of Annandale. See below, p. 110.
67. John Murray, created Duke of Atholl 1703. See below, pp. 40–2.
68. Commissioner for Cromartyshire and subsequently Lord Prestonhall of the Court of Session. *PS*, ii. 458.
69. *DNB*, xxxix. 370–1.
70. William Douglas, 1st Earl of March, brother of the Duke of Queensberry; *CP*, viii. 456–7.
71. A deliberate equating of the Scots Convention Parliament with the English Republican regime overthrown by General Monk in 1660.
72. Speaker Robert Harley seems to have been unaware of any financial problems when he implicitly urged Lord Chancellor Godolphin to avoid new elections in Scotland: *Seafield Letters*, pp. 142–3: Harley to Godolphin [Brampton Bryan] 9 Aug. 1702.
73. James Ogilvy, 3rd Earl of Findlater; *CP*, v. 382.
74. Cf. *DNB*, xlii. 29–31.
75. I.e. the Cavaliers.
76. Known as the Earl of Arran.
77. Scottish law, very unusually in contemporary Europe, allowed inheritance of titles through the female line and Duchess Anne was the last of the original Hamilton family.
78. Hamilton pleaded, alone, for James II and VII's restoration.
79. Cf. HMC *Portland*, iv. 211, 215: William Greg to Harley, Edinburgh, 19 July and 2 Aug. 1705.
80. In the sense of compelling, empathetic in modern usage.
81. Cf. *DNB*, xv. 326–9.
82. *Seafield Letters*, p. 116: Hamilton to Keith, [7 Aug. 1702].

[The Parliamentary Session of 1703]

The Earl of Seafield returned again to Scotland about the beginning of February 1703, being then Chancellor, full freighted with assurances of the queen's design to support the Cavaliers, who all resorted to, and were extreamly carressed by, him. And then it was you would have heard him say, 'the Grahams and Ogilvys were always loyal'. But in a short time thereafter they proved the very reverse, as you will hear anon. He brought down a new commission of Council with him, wherein many of the rotten fanaticks were left out, and Cavaliers put in their places. An Act of Indemnity was granted to all that had been enemies to the government, and guilty of treason since the Revolution, and liberty allowed them to come home within a certain limited time. And a letter was produced from the queen to the Council recommending the care for the Episcopal clergy to them, and we were told every day that she designed to bestow the bishops' rents upon them.[1] And thus affairs went pleasantly on (and no wonder the Cavaliers were elevated), when the Duke of Queensberry, who was declared Commissioner to the ensuing Parliament, and the other statesmen came from London and, with all the oaths and imprecations imaginable, assured the Cavaliers of the sincerity of the queen's and their designs to serve and promote their interest, [and] required nothing from them but to assert the legality of the last Parliament, recognize Her Majesty's title and authority and grant subsidies for the support of the army. And in requital, promised they should be taken into, and have a large share in the management of the government, a toleration be granted in Parliament to the Episcopal clergy,[2] and nothing be required of them, or even pass in Parliament, that did in the least ratify what had passed since the year 1689. This the Duke of

Queensberry declared he was instructed and commanded by the queen to promise unto them. And for his part, with a thousand oaths and protestations, assured them he would be faithful to them. But how he kept his word and vows the following account will illustrate.

At the time when the Parliament met, there were [several] different parties or clubs. First, the Court party. And these were subdivided into such as were Revolutioners, and of anti-monarchical principles, and such as were any thing that would procure or secure them in their employments and pensions. And these were directed by the court in all their measures. Secondly, the Country party, which consisted of some (though but few) Cavaliers, and of Presbyterians, of which the Duke of Hamilton and the Marquis of Tweedale were leaders. Thirdly, the Cavaliers, who, from the house they met in, were called Mitchel's Club, of whom the Earl of Home[3] was the chief man.[4] All these had their several distinct meetings, consultations and projects, and made up that Parliament which met on the third of May 1703.

The queen's letter, and the Commissioner's and Chancellor's speeches to the Parliament, tended chiefly to assure the house of her gracious inclinations towards her ancient kingdom, recommending [sic] unity and craving supplies.[5] The first matter of moment under the house's consideration was an act presented by the Duke of Hamilton recognizing Her Majesty's title and authority and declaring it to be high treason to disown, quarrel, or impugn her title to this crown. And my Lord Argyle[6] presented a clause declaring it high treason to impugn or quarrel her exercise of the government since her actual entry thereto, which he craved might be added to his grace's act. This, the Duke of Hamilton and all his party opposing vigorously, since it ruined their project of asserting the illegality of the former Rump Parliament, the Court again pressed the addition of the clause as a most material point, since they knew it saved them from what it dreaded most, and therefore insisted that unless something could be particularized that was amiss in the administration of Her Majesty's affairs, Her Majesty had all the reason in the world to expect this from her first Parliament. To which [the] Duke [of] Hamilton and his adherers made no positive reply, shifting to enter upon the main of their drift at that time, not knowing what support they would find in the house, and willing to keep it up as a reserve wherewithall to keep the Court in awe. So at last, by the concurrence of the Cavaliers (or more properly, Mitchel's Club), the clause was added to the act by a considerable majority, and then the act itself was approved.[7]

Many at that time, and the Duke of Hamilton ever since, blamed the Cavaliers for complying with the Court in this point. But in my opinion they may easily be justifyed, considering that this was the particular piece of service the queen demanded of them, in recompence of the great things she promised to do for them. And with what confidence could they have expected to be admitted into her favour and entrusted with the administration of affairs if they had opposed her in it? If she and her servants broke their engagements afterwards to them that was not their fault. But if they had flown so avowedly in her face, it would have justifyed her future conduct, [or] at least been a rare handle to have infused a jealousy in the queen that they were no further inclined to serve her than suited with, and tended to, their own particular designs. It is true indeed, if the Cavaliers had joyned with the other party this clause had been rejected. In which case it is more than probable that the Parliament would have been blown up, for the Court would not have dared to stand it out any longer. But what did this avail either the royal interest, or that of the country? A Parliament was needful for procuring some acts in favour of both, which the Cavaliers aimed at. Perhaps it might have ruined the Duke of Queensberry and his set of ministers, but what signifyed that to the Cavaliers, since (as we saw afterwards) the government would be lodged in other hands that were as much, if not more, their enemies? So that the question comes to this narrow compass: whether the Cavaliers had most reason to trust the queen and those she impowered to treat with them, or a set of men made up of all sorts of parties, some few Cavaliers, but mostly Presbyterians, Revolutioners and disgusted Courtiers who had opposed the Cavaliers being elected Members of Parliament? I must acknowledge, if they had suspected what was to follow, and acted as they did, there might have been some ground to censure them, but as matters stood then they had all the reason in the world to do as they did.

From these and such considerations the Cavaliers in a full meeting (after the abovementioned affair was over) unanimously resolved to serve the queen, and, to shew their inclinations, agreed that the Earl of Home should next day move in Parliament a supply to Her Majesty, which they were all to second.[8] And upon these accounts the Duke of Queensberry did again renew his engagements to stand firm to them and inform the queen what signal service they had done her. But this good correspondence did not last long, for in two or three days time it begun to lessen, and his grace's deportment induced many to suspect his integrity.

The great hazard being now over, such of the Court as were upon a high-flown Revolution foot begun to think how they could best secure their own, and disappoint the Cavaliers', game.[9] It is hard to determine whether or not the Duke of Queensberry did from the beginning design to act so foul a part. For my own share, I do believe he was once seriously embarked with the Cavaliers, and I was informed by a person of undoubted authority that the reason why he changed was as follows. That day in which the Earl of Home designed to move for a supply,[10] his grace called a council, and acquainted them of it. With which, all agreeing, they adjourned with a design to prosecute it. A few minutes thereafter the Duke of Argyle, the Marquis of Annandale and the Earl of Marchmont came to wait upon his grace, and, withdrawing privately with him, one of them told him the other two and himself had that morning met with a considerable number of Parliament-men, when it was resolved to move for an act ratifying the Revolution and another the presbyterian government,[11] and press to have them preferred to the Act of Supply, which they were certain to carry, but first thought it fit to acquaint his grace with their design and ask his concurrence. This his grace the Commissioner begged them to forbear, because now he had an opportunity of obtaining a supply to Her Majesty, and if slipped at this time (as did happen) never again. And promised, if this were over, to go into whatever they proposed. But still the others refused to comply, being rather willing that there should be no supply granted at all than that it should proceed from the Cavaliers. And thus they left the Commissioner in a peck of troubles. Immediately he acquainted Sir James Murray of Philiphaugh with what had passed (who was, by very far, the most sufficient and best man he trusted and advised with) and was answered by him, he well deserved it. For, notwithstanding his own experience, and his [Philiphaugh's] remonstrance to the contrary, he would have dealings with such a pack, and that this day's work would create such difficulties that he should not extricate himself out of them were he to live an hundred years, which truly came to pass. The Commissioner, you may be sure, was much confounded. He durst not venture to push the Act of Supply knowing the Duke of Hamilton and his party would joyn the Duke of Argyle and his, and so it would be rejected. So all that came of it was, the Earl of Home made the motion and it was ordered to lie upon the table.[12] On the other hand, he foresaw what Sir James Murray of Philiphaugh intimated to him, that if he joyned and supported the Duke of Argyle in his designs, the Cavaliers would leave him, and so his interest be much diminished and he be obliged to trucle and depend upon the Duke of Argyle, the Marquis of Annandale and such others.

Whilst he was thus musing and perplexed, the Duke of Argyle (who had more interest with him than any other person) soon returned, and, being privately alone with him, did so effectually represent the improbability of his succeeding by these methods he was then upon, since it was certain the Duke of Hamilton had, notwithstanding what had happened of late, more interest with the Cavaliers than any other, and that as soon as they gained their point a correspondence would soon again be commenced betwixt them, and he become the chief ruler of the roast. These, I say, and such representations, joyned to the terrour he was in of the Duke of Argyle and the Marquis of Annandale's leaving him, so

powerfully wrought upon him that he resolved to desert the
Cavaliers. This matter of fact I have from so good hands I dare
ascertain the truth of it.

Having made so much mention of the Duke of Argyle, it will
not be improper to give a more particular account of him.
Archibald, Earl, afterward Duke, of Argyle, in outward
appearance was a good-natured, civil, modest gentleman. But his
actions were quite otherwise, being capable of the worst things to
promote his interest, and altogether addicted to a lewd, profligate
life.[13] He was not cut out for business, only applying himself to it
in so far as it tended to secure his court interest and politicks,
from whence he got great sums of money to lavish away upon his
pleasures. But when he set himself to it, no man was more
capable, or could more quickly and with greater solidity and
judgement dispatch it than himself. So that, for want of
application, a great man was lost. He was always an enemy to the
loyal interest, and came over with the Prince of Orange to
England though King James had been kind to him, and given him
hopes of being restored to his estate, which stood at that time
under a sentence of forfeiture. But what other could be expected
from a man that (to curry favour with King James) had renounced
his religion and turned papist? Notwithstanding which, and his
constant vicious life and conversation, he was the darling of the
Presbyterians, being descended from, and the representative of, a
family that suffered for a cause (as they termed it) and of great
power in the country, and himself so involved in treason and
rebellion that they were confident he would never venture to
leave them. And thus they supported one another and he made a
great figure.[14]

But to return. When the Duke of Queensberry was brought
over to enter into measures opposite to those of the Cavaliers, he
resolved, the better to carry on his designs, to dissemble as much
as possible with them. But this did avail him very little. For no
sooner did they perceive some of his friends and dependents,
such as William Alves[15] and others (who were known to be
constant frequenters of the Episcopal meeting houses) appear

against an act of toleration presented by the Earl of Strathmore,[16] and in behalf of the abovementioned act presented by the Duke of Argyle, ratifying the late Revolution and all that followed thereupon, and the other act presented by the Earl of Marchmont, for securing the presbyterian government[17]; I say, no sooner did the Duke of Queensberry's friends behave after this manner, but immediately all that ever suspected the integrity of one who had been so much concerned against King James and his family, as his grace was, did conclude they were betrayed, and declared this their opinion in a meeting of the Cavaliers. Upon which it was resolved to send some of their number, viz. the Earls of Home and Strathmore, George Lockhart of Carnwath and James Ogilvy of Boyn,[18] to represent unto him how much they were surprized to find his friends behave after such a manner, and that they hoped his grace would remember his vows and promises and how they served the queen. The matter of fact would not deny for him, so he excused it as necessary to please such of the ministry as were so inclined, lest otherways the queen's affairs should suffer prejudice. And then he renewed his former promises, and swore heartily to them. To which they replyed they believed this would not satisfy those who had sent them there, and that his grace nor the queen could not blame them to look to themselves, since it was plain he was embarked with a party, and entered into measures quite contrary to the capitulation made and agreed to between him and them.[19] And so they withdrew, and, having made a report to their constituents, it was unanimously resolved not to enter into any concert with the Court, or any other party, but to stand by themselves, firm to one another, and jointly go into such measures as, when proposed by any party, should be by the plurality of themselves esteemed for the interest of their country. And this they all engaged to upon honour, and it cannot be said but they faithfully performed the same during that whole session. And to the best of my memory all this happened within three or four days after the Cavaliers had so signally preserved the Court, and particularly the Duke of Queensberry, from the danger they so much apprehended.[20]

I must do justice to all, and take notice that from this time the Earls of Balcarras[21] and Dunmore[22] left the Cavaliers and continued ever since firm to the Court, and went along with all their measures. Wretches of the greatest ingratitude! They owed all they had, and much they had squandered away, to King Charles and King James. Until now they claimed more merit than others, especially the first, who had been some time, since the Revolution, in France (where he had, nevertheless, acted but a bad part), and not many years ago obtained liberty to come home. He had some pretence for what he did, having a numerous family and little to subsist them on but what the Court bestowed, though that should never have weighed with him, who lay under such obligations to King James. But the other is inexcusable, having above five hundred pounds a year of his own, and yet sold his honour for a present which the queen had yearly given his lady since the late Revolution. But the truth of the matter lies here: they had no further ambition than how to get as much money as to make themselves drunk once or twice a day, so no party was much a gainer or loser by having or wanting such a couple.[23]

But it is now high time to enquire what the Parliament has been a-doing. The first material affair they went upon after the queen's title was recognized was the Earl of Marchmont's act for security of the presbyterian government, in these terms:

Ratifying, approving and perpetually confirming all laws, &c., made for establishing and preserving the true reformed Protestant religion, and the true church of Christ, as at present owned and settled within this kingdom, in its presbyterian government and discipline, as being agreeable to the word of God [this was more than they pretended at the time of the Revolution, as I mentioned before] and the only Church of Christ within this kingdom.[24]

There were many in Parliament argued against this act, and none with more mettle than Sir David Cunningham of Milncraig,[25] urging that it was uncharitable to affirm that none was of the church of Christ except presbyterians. To which the Marquis of Lothian's[26] zeal made this reply: that the clause was right, since he was sure the presbyterian government was the best part of the Christian religion—which set all the house in a merry temper. The act, however, passed. But it was evident the Presbyterian party was not so considerable as imagined and that if the queen had been as episcopal in Scotland as in England she might easily have overturned presbytery. For at this time the house consisted of about two hundred and forty members, thirty whereof voted against that part of the act ratifying presbytery, and eighty-two were *non-liquets*[27] (which last were all episcopals but chose to be silent because there was no formed design against presbytery at that time, or to please the Court). So that there was not, properly speaking, a plurality of above sixteen voices or thereby for the act. Amongst which several, such as [the] Duke [of] Hamilton, the Earl of Eglinton,[28] and many others, were no ways presbyterians.[29] Now had the queen designed to introduce episcopacy, it is obvious it would have been no hard task to have done it.

When this was over, the Act for a Toleration to the Episcopal Clergy was read.[30] But those who were the greatest promoters of it agreed not to insist upon it, lest thereby many well-meaning persons that opposed the Court and stood for the interest of the country might have taken offence. And therefore they delayed it till a more proper occasion. But I must take notice that a representation from the Commission of the Kirk, signed by their Moderator, Mr George Meldrum, against toleration, was likewise read, wherein was this extraordinary and unchristian expression:

> They were perswaded [that] to enact a toleration for those of that way (considering the present case and circumstances of the church and nation), would be to establish iniquity by a law, and bring on the promoters thereof, and their families, the dreadful guilt and pernicious effects that may thereupon ensue.[31]

Next, the Parliament proceeded to consider the Duke of Argyle's act approving, ratifying and confirming perpetually an act of Parliament declaring it high treason to disown, quarrel, or impugn the dignity or authority of the said Parliament, and further statuting and declaring that it should be high treason in any of the subjects in this kingdom to quarrel, or endeavour by writing, malicious and advised speaking, or open act or deed, to alter, or innovate, the Claim of Right, or any article thereof. The last clause of this act was particularly impugned, and it was alledged that the import of such a general peremptory clause would be of dangerous consequence, since these words, 'endeavour by writing, etc', might entrap innocent people in their common conversation (which was a grievance not long ago)[32] and that it bound up the wisdom of the nation from making such alterations and reformations as they should judge necessary for the state of the kingdom in succeeding ages. And James More of Stonywood[33] desired to know, if this act passed in these terms, in case the shire of Aberdeen, which he represented, and every body knew was generally of the episcopal perswasion, should address the sovereign or the Parliament (which in the Claim of Right is asserted to be the privilege of the subject) for a rectification of the present settlement of the presbyterian church government, whether or not such an address did not import treason? To whom Sir William Hamilton of Whitelaw[34] replyed, that this act did not preclude addressing for a toleration, but he was of opinion, if it were once made a law, that person was guilty of treason who owned he thought the presbyterian a wrong establishment, and that episcopacy ought to be restored. This occasioned a long and hot debate, wherein the dangers that would arise both to the government and subject were fully laid open. But being put to the vote the act was approved, there being sixty members against it and many *non-liquets* (upon the same account as in the former act ratifying presbytery), and all the Country party, that were presbyterians, the ministry and their dependents going into it, except the Duke of Athol, the Justice Clerk and some of the Chancellor's and Viscount of Tarbat's friends, which four began at this time to break with the Court and join in a particular correspondence with the Cavaliers.[35]

Whilst the rolls were calling upon this question, there fell the greatest rain that was ever seen come from the heavens, which made such a noise upon the roof of the Parliament-house (which was covered with lead) that no voice could be heard and the clerks were obliged to stop. Whereupon, as soon as it ceased, Sir David Cunningham of Milncraig took the occasion to tell the house, 'It was apparent that the heavens declared against their procedure'. And those who were inclined to take notice of such things drew several conclusions and presages from it, suitable, for the most part, to their own inclinations. Though this be but a trifle, I inclined not to pass it altogether by.

Then the Parliament proceeded to frame and finish such acts as tended to secure their liberties and freedom from the oppression they sustained through the influence of English ministers over Scots counsels or affairs, in which a long time was spent, many bold speeches and excellent overtures being made, the Court strenuously opposing them all. But the Cavaliers and Country party, as strenuously insisting, at last prevailed, and carried in Parliament these two valuable acts.[36] First, an Act Anent War and Peace, declaring, among other things, that after Her Majesty's death, and failing heirs of her body, no person at the same time king or queen of Scotland and England shall have the sole power of making war with any prince, state or potentate whatsoever, without consent of Parliament.[37] Which was absolutely necessary considering how much the nation had lost by being brought into all England's wars. And secondly, that excellent and wisely contrived Act of Security which has since made such a noise in Britain, and, from the admirable clauses it contains, justly merits the title it bears.[38] An act which in all probability would have made this nation happy had all those who were concerned and assisted to frame and advance it, continued to act by the maxims and motives whereupon this act was founded, and not basely changed both principles and parties. But being very long, and to be found in the printed Acts of Parliament, I shun inserting it here. All efforts were in vain to obtain the royal assent to this act, though the other (in hopes thereby to have obtained a subsidy for the army) was passed into a law.[39]

It is needless, and would be endless to repeat, suppose I could, the discourses that were made *pro* and *con*, whilst the Parliament was upon overtures to secure their liberties and redeem the nation from the oppression it groaned under. It is sufficient to say that the Court opposed every thing that could be proposed for that end, and, in return, were so baffled in all their schemes and designs that on the fifth of September, when a motion was made for granting a first reading to the Act for a Supply, the Parliament flew in the face of it, some demanding the royal assent to the Act of Security, others asking, if the Parliament met for nothing else than to drain the nation of money to support those that were betraying and enslaving it? And after many hours' warm debates on all sides a vote was stated: whether to proceed to overtures for liberty or a subsidy? And the house being crowded with a vast number of people, nothing, for near two hours, could be heard but voices of members, and others (it being late and candles lighted), requiring 'liberty' and 'no subsidy'.[40]

The throne,[41] being confounded with this vigorous appearance in behalf of the Country, was at a stand and knew not what hand to turn to.[42] And the Earl of Roxburgh[43] declared if there was no other way of obtaining so natural and undeniable a privilege of the house as a vote, they would demand it with their swords in their hands.

Whether the Commissioner had got information that the house would that day stand stiffly to what they proposed to be done for the country, I know not. But certain it is that the foot-guards were ordered to be in readiness. And several days before this a guard was set every night upon the Nether-bow port and Lieutenant-General Ramsay[44] was heard to say in his cups that ways would be found to make the Parliament calm enough.

However, the Commissioner perceiving he would be torn in pieces if he withstood the formidable opposition he saw against him, ordered the Chancellor to acquaint the house that it was yielded the act for a subsidy should continue to lie upon the table, and that the house should next day proceed upon overtures for liberty, which put a period to that day's debate. But when the next day came instead of performing his promise the first thing he did in the house was to call for such acts as he was impowered to pass into laws, and, having given them the royal assent, immediately made the following speech:

My Lords and Gentlemen,

We have now passed several good acts for liberty and trade, which, I hope, will be acceptable to all Her Majesty's good subjects. I wish you had also given the supplies necessary for the maintaining Her Majesty's forces and preserving the peace and safety of the kingdom. But since, I hope, this may yet be done in due time, and besides, some questions and difficulties are fallen in which in all probability you can have no time to determine, and, withall it is fit Her Majesty should have some time to consider on such things as are laid before her, and that we may know her mind therein more perfectly, a short recess seems at present to be necessary, and that this Parliament be prorogued for some time. And therefore I have ordered my Lord Chancellor to prorogue this Parliament to the twelfth of October next.[45]

Which he accordingly did.

But before we leave this Parliament to consider what were the consequences of it, we must remember that the Earl of Marchmont having one day presented an act for settling the succession on the house of Hanover, it was treated with such contempt that some proposed it might be burnt, and others that he might be sent to the castle, and it was at last thrown out of the house by a plurality of fifty-seven voices.[46] Such then was the temper of the nation that, if duly improved, might have done great things. Neither must I omit the opposition made to the act allowing the importation of wines, which was carried by the assistance the Court got from the trading boroughs and brought in a great deal of money to the customs.[47]

And thus I have gone through this session of Parliament, which did more for redressing the grievances and restoring the liberties of this nation than all the Parliaments since the 1660 year of God. And it cannot be thought strange that Scotsmen's blood did boil to see the English (our inveterate enemies) have such influence over all our affairs, that the royal assent should be granted or refused to the laws the Parliament made, as they thought proper, and, in short, every thing concerning Scots affairs determined by them, with regard only to the interest of England. And to see bribing and bullying of members, unseasonable adjournments and innumerable other ungentlemanny [sic] methods made use of to seduce and debauch people from the fidelity they owed to that which ought to be dearest to them—I mean the interest, welfare and liberty of their country and fellow-subjects, by whom they were entrusted in that office.[48] These considerations, I say, enraged and emboldened a great number of members to such a degree that many strange and unprecedented speeches were made, enveighing against and exposing the government, especially by that worthy and never-enough-to-be-praised patriot, Andrew Fletcher of Salton.[49]

After the Parliament was prorogued the queen was pleased to confer several titles of honour on such as had served her. The Marquis of Douglas (though a child)[50] and the Marquis of Athol were made Dukes. The Viscount of Stair,[51] Viscount of Roseberry,[52] Viscount of Tarbat, Lord Boyle,[53] James Stuart of Bute[54] and Charles Hope of Hopeton[55] were created Earls of Stair, Roseberry, Cromarty, Glasgow, Bute and Hopeton, and John Craufurd of Kilbirnie[56] and Sir James Primrose of Carrington,[57] Viscounts of Garnock and Primrose.

Having made mention of the Duke of Athol, the Earl of Cromarty and Mr Fletcher of Salton, it would not much out of the way to give a particular character of them before I go any further. John, first Marquis, then Duke, of Athol, made no great figure in the first part of his life. And the first mention I find of him was his conveening as many of his friends, followers and vassals as he could to oppose my Lord Dundee. But that being a work contrary to their grain, few joined with, or would be assistant to, him, so his grace soon quitted the field. In the year 1699 he was made one of King William's Secretaries of State, and thereafter his Commissioner to Parliament, and was all that time a most zealous Presbyterian, and so great an admirer of his master, King William, that he mimicked him in many of his gestures. But being disobliged that Sir Hugh Dalrymple[58] was made President of the Session, and not Sir William Hamilton of Whit[e]law whom he had recommended, and finding his colleague the Earl of Seafield had much more interest both with King William and his favourite, the Earl of Portland,[59] than himself, and that he would not long be in that post without he depended on the Earl of Seafield, he resigned his office and would serve no longer. And, returning to Scotland, he joyned the Country party and continued a leading man therein till after Queen Anne's accession to the throne, that he was created Lord Privy Seal. In the Parliament [of] 1703 he trimmed betwixt Court and Cavaliers, and it is probable would have continued so, had not the Duke of Queensberry trumped up the plot upon him, which did so exasperate him against the Court that he joyned entirely with the Cavaliers. And from being a friend to the Revolution and an admirer of King William he became all of a sudden a violent Jacobite, and took all methods to gain the favour and confidence of the Cavaliers, which in some measure he obtained, particularly in the shires of Fife, Angus, Perth, and other northern parts, and thereupon affected extreamly to be the head of that party and outrival the Duke of Hamilton. Yet notwithstanding this his profession in state matters he still courted, and preserved his interest with, the presbyterian ministers, professing always to be firm to their Kirk government, hearing them in the churches, and patronizing them much more than those of the episcopal perswasion. Which induced many to doubt the sincerity of his professions in other points and believe he was honest and loyal because he had no occasion of being otherwise. But, for my own part, I had an opportunity to know that he was very frank and chearful to enter into any, though the most desperate, measures in the years 1706 and 1707, to obstruct the Hanoverian succession, and especially the Union, because, perhaps, he had but a small estate and could not expect to make so great an appearance after the Union as if the kingdom of Scotland remained. But be the reasons what they will, certain it is he would have gone to the field rather than it should have passed, had others been as forward as himself.[60]

He was of great significancy to any party, especially the Cavaliers, because he had a mighty power, and when upon a loyal bottom could raise 6000 of the best men in the kingdom, well armed and ready to sacrifice all they had in the king's service. He was endowed with good natural parts, though by reason of his proud, imperious, haughty, passionate temper, he was no ways capable to be the leading man of a party, which he aimed at. After he betook himself to the Cavaliers he much affected popularity, but it was still attended with such an unpleasant air his kindest addresses were never taking. He was selfish to a great degree, and his vanity and ambition extended so far that he could not suffer an equal, and did therefore thwart the Duke of Hamilton's measures. He was reputed very brave, but hot and headstrong, and, though no scholar nor orator, yet expressed his mind very handsomely on publick occasions.[61]

The satyrist, in his lampoon, speaking of George, Viscount of Tarbat, since Earl of Cromarty, uses these words:

> Some do compare him to an eel
> Should mortal man be made of steel?

And certainly this character suited him exactly, for never was there a more fickle, unsteady man in the world. He had sworn all the contradictory oaths, complyed with all the opposite governments that had been on foot since the year 1648, and was an humble servant to them all till he got what he aimed at, though often he did not know what that was. He was full of projects, and never rejected one, provided it was new. Since the Revolution (though he had a large share in carrying it on) he pretended to favour the royal family and Episcopal clergy: yet he never did one action in favour of any of them, excepting that when he was Secretary to Queen Anne he procured an Act of Indemnity, and a letter from her recommending the Episcopal clergy to the Privy Council's protection. But whether this proceeded from a desire and design of serving them, or some political views, is easy to determine when we consider that no sooner did Queen Anne desert the Tory party and maxims but his lordship turned as great a Whig as the best of them, joined with Tweedale's party to advance the Hanoverian succession in the Parliament [of] 1704, and was, at last, a zealous stickler and writer in favour of the Union. He was certainly a good-natured gentleman, master of an extraordinary gift of pleasing and diverting conversation, and well accomplished in all kinds of learning. But, withall, so extreamly maggoty and unsettled that he was never much to be relyed upon or valued. Yet he had a great interest in the Parliament with many of the northern members. Though his brother, Mr Roderick Mackenzie of Prestonhall, was altogether so chymerical as his lordship, yet in their politicks they seldom differed. But he still pretended a greater zeal for the service of the royal family than his lordship did, though both proved alike faithful at the latter end.[62]

Andrew Fletcher of Salton in the first part of his life did improve himself to a great degree by reading and travelling. He was always a great admirer of both ancient and modern republicks, and therefore the more displeased at some steps which he thought wrong in King Charles the Second's reign, whereby he drew upon himself the enmity of the ministers of that government, to avoid the evil consequences of which he went abroad. During which time, his enemies' malice still continuing, he was upon slight, frivolous pretences summoned to appear before the Privy Council, and, their designs to ruin him being too apparent, he was so enraged that he concurred—and came over with the Duke of Monmouth when he invaded England, upon which he was forfeited. Thereafter he came over with the Prince of Orange, but that prince was not many months in England till he saw his designs and left him, and ever thereafter hated and appeared as much against him as any in the kingdom. Being elected a Parliament man in the year 1703, he shewed a sincere and honest inclination towards the honour and interest of his country. The thoughts of England's domineering over Scotland was what his generous soul could not away with. The indignities and oppression Scotland lay under galled him to the heart, so that in his learned and elaborate discourses he exposed them with undaunted courage and pathetick eloquence. He was blessed with a soul that hated and despised whatever was mean and unbecoming a gentleman, and was so stedfast to what he thought right that no hazard nor advantage, no, not the universal empire nor the gold of America, could tempt him to yield or desert it. And, I may affirm, that in all his life he never once pursued a measure with the prospect of any by-end to himself, nor furder than he judged it for the common benefit and advantage of his country. He was master of the English, Latin, Greek, French and Italian languages, and well versed in history, the civil law and all kinds of learning. And as he was universally accomplished he employed his talents for the good of mankind. He was a strict and nice observer of all the points of honour,[63] and his word [was] sacred. As brave as his sword, and had some experience in the art of war, having in his younger years been some time a volunteer in both the land and sea service. In his travels he had studied and come to understand the respective interests of the several princes and states of Europe. In his private conversation affable to his friends, but could not endure to converse with those he thought enemies to their country, and free of all manner of vice. He had a penetrating, clear and lively apprehension, but [was] so extreamly wedded to his own opinions that there were few (and those too must be his beloved friends, and of whom he had a good opinion) he could endure to reason against him, and did for the most part so closely and unalterably adhere to what he advanced (which was frequently very singular) that he would break with his party before he would alter the least jot of his scheme and maxims. And therefore it was impossible for any set of men that did not give up themselves to be absolutely directed by him to please him, so as to carry him along in all points. And thence it came to pass that he often in Parliament acted a part by himself, though in the main he stuck close to the Country party and was their Cicero. He was, no doubt, an enemy to all monarchical government—at least thought they wanted to be much reformed. But I do very well believe his aversion to the English and the Union was so great [that] in revenge to them he would have sided with the royal family.[64] But as that was a subject not fit to be entered upon with him, this is only a conjecture from some innuendos I have heard him make. But so far is certain: he liked, commended and conversed with high-flying Tories more than any other set of men, acknowledging them to be the best Country men, and of most honour, integrity and ingenuity. To sum up all, he was a learned, gallant, honest and every other way well accomplished gentleman. And if ever a man proposes to serve and merit well of his country, let him place his courage, zeal and constancy as a pattern before him, and think himself sufficiently applauded and rewarded by obtaining the character of being like Andrew Fletcher of Salton.[65]

Notes

1. The episcopalian clergy were those who had refused to conform to the new presbyterian settlement of the Kirk after 1689, instead seceding to establish a rival church that was strongest north of the Tay. The 'Bishops' rents' were the revenues from formerly episcopal lands.
2. The Episcopalian clergy were theoretically subject to heavy penalties for conducting services outside the Kirk, though in practice they were only occasionally harassed.
3. Charles Home, 6th Earl of Home. See below, pp. 133–4.
4. Cf. *Stair Annals*, i. 204.
5. *APS*, xi. 36–7: 6 May 1703.
6. Archibald Campbell, 1st Duke of Argyll. See below, p. 32.
7. *APS*, xi. 37, 41.
8. *APS*, xi. 41.
9. HMC *Laing MSS*, ii. 7: Argyll to Queen Anne, Edinburgh, 26 Apr. 1703.
10. 19 May.
11. Of the Kirk.
12. I.e. the proposal was not acted upon; *APS*, xi. 45: 26 May 1703.
13. A reference to Argyll's fondness for his mistress over his wife and his death, allegedly, from stab wounds incurred during a brawl in a brothel, for which see: *The Argyle Papers*, ed. J. Maidment (Edinburgh, 1834), xiv-xv, pp. 66, 68–9, 83. GL knew the Duke and his family personally, having been sent to Inveraray as a boy by his presbyterian relatives in order to erase the influence of his episcopalian tutor (*Lockhart Papers*, i. 394, 571).
14. Cf. *DNB*, viii. 338–9.

15. Commissioner for Sanquhar. *PS*, i. 15.
16. John Lyon, 2nd Earl of Strathmore and Kinghorne; *CP*, xii. (1) 396–7.
17. *APS*, xi. 46.
18. Commissioner for Banffshire; *PS*, ii. 547.
19. *Stair Annals*, i. 205.
20. GL's memory played him false here: it is apparent from *APS* that the events he outlines took place over 2–3 weeks from 19 May onwards.
21. Colin Lindsay, 3rd Earl of Balcarres.
22. Charles Murray, 1st Earl of Dunmore.
23. *DNB*, xxxiii. 286–7, suggests GL's anger with Balcarres got the better of him here; see xxxix. 350 for Dunmore.
24. *APS*, xi. 46.
25. Commissioner for Lauder. *PS*, i. 168.
26. William Kerr, 2nd Marquess of Lothian; *DNB*, xxxi. 66–7.
27. Abstained.
28. Alexander Montgomery, 9th Earl of Eglinton, GL's father-in-law; *DNB*, xxxviii. 300–1.
29. *Stair Annals*, i. 206. Hamilton was trying to preserve his reputation with both presbyterians and episcopalians.
30. *APS*, xi. 47.
31. *APS*, xi. 46. It was generally believed at this time that schism in the Kirk was an affront to God which tainted the whole community.
32. Possibly a reference to the grounds on which the Whig martyr Stephen Colledge was found guilty of treason in 1681, for which see, *A Complete Collection of State Trials*, ed. T. B. Howell, 33 vols (1816–26), viii. 714–16.
33. Rect., Moir, Commissioner for Aberdeenshire. *PS*, ii. 500.
34. Commissioner for Queensferry. Hamilton was a Lord of Session, which gave the legal opinion he expressed below considerable weight. See below, p. 79.
35. *APS*, xi. 47: 3 and 7 June 1703; *Stair Annals*, i. 206; HMC, *Laing*, ii. 28–9, 30–3: Atholl to Godolphin, Holyrood, 17 and 23 July 1703; ii. 29–30: Tarbat to Queen Anne, 18 July 1703.
36. *Stair Annals*, i. 205.
37. *APS*, xi. 75, 107: 17 Aug. and 16 Sept. 1703.
38. *APS*, xi. 63, 74: 22 June and 13 Aug. 1703.
39. *APS*, xi. 101–2.
40. In fact the debate was on 15 Sept.: *APS*, xi. 104; HMC *Portland*, iv. 66–7: Henry Guy to Robert Harley, London, 23 Sept. 1703.
41. The Court party.

42. Even a political veteran like the Earl of Stair failed to foresee this *impasse* (*Stair Annals*, i. 208), despite the fact that the Court had been having trouble controlling Parliament since May: HMC *Laing*, ii. 18: Seafield to Godolphin, 29 May 1703.

43. John Ker, 5th Earl (subsequently 1st Duke) of Roxburghe. See below, p. 64.

44. George Ramsay, Commander-in-Chief of the Scottish army.

45. See *APS*, xi. 112 for a slightly different version of this speech.

46. *Crossrigg Diary*, pp. 131–2: 6 Sept. 1703. According to Hume it was GL who advocated the burning of the proposed bill.

47. *APS*, xi. 102: 13 Sept. 1703; HMC *Laing*, ii. 37: Seafield to Godolphin [14 <*recte* 15?> Sept. 1703].

48. HMC *Laing*, ii. 32, 33: Atholl to Godolphin, 23 July 1703; ii. 35: Seafield to Godolphin, 28 July 1703.

49. Commissioner for Haddington Constabulary. See below, pp. 43–5.

50. Archibald Douglas, 3rd Marquess and 1st Duke of Douglas, was nine years old when he was promoted in the peerage; *DNB*, xv. 286–7.

51. John Dalrymple, 1st Earl of Stair. See below, pp. 130–2.

52. Archibald Primrose, 1st Viscount Primrose; *DNB*, xlvi. 379.

53. David Boyle, 1st Lord Boyle. See below, p. 61.

54. *CP*, ii. 440–1.

55. *CP*, vi. 572–3.

56. *CP*, v. 622.

57. *CP*, x. 682.

58. *PS*, i. 174–5.

59. Hans Willem Bentinck, 1st Earl of Portland of the 2nd creation. *DNB*, iv. 285–92.

60. See below, ch. 9.

61. Cf. *DNB*, xxxix. 383–5. Atholl was so alarmed (or outraged) at GL's characterisation of him that he made the opening moves in challenging GL to a duel, though nothing seems to have come of it (*Lockhart Letters*, p. 115: Atholl to GL, London, 13 Oct. 1714).

62. Cf. *DNB*, xxxv. 145–8.

63. See, for example, the account of his abortive duel with the Earl of Roxburghe in 1705: HMC *Portland*, iv. 209: William Greg to Harley, Edinburgh, 17 July.

64. The exiled (Catholic) Stuarts.

65. GL's sketch of Fletcher's character finds strong support in: P. Scott, *Andrew Fletcher and the Treaty of Union* (Edinburgh, 1992).

[The Scots Plot]

Let us now return back again, and acquaint you that after the Parliament was prorogued mutual engagements of fidelity and sincerity to stand firm to one another were renewed betwixt the Cavaliers on the one part, and the Duke of Athol and the Earls of Seafield and Cromarty on the other. And accordingly when these lords, with the Earl of Eglinton, went to London they were entirely trusted by the Cavaliers. The Courtiers again, they made as great haste, and all parties strove who should outdo one another in paying their respect and shewing their submission to the good will and pleasure of the Duke of Marlborough and Lord Godolphin. The queen indeed, for fashion['s] sake, was sometimes addressed to, but such application was made to these two lords that it was obvious to all the world how much the Scots affairs depended on them.

I myself, out of curiosity, went once to their levies,[1] where I saw the Commissioner, Chancellor, Secretary and other great men of Scotland hang on near an hour, and, when admitted, treated with no more civility than one gentleman pays another's valet-de-chambre. And for which the Scots have none to blame but themselves. For had they valued themselves as they ought to have done, and not so meanly and sneakingly prostituted their honour and country to the will and pleasure of the English ministry, they would never have presumed to usurp such dominion over Scotland as openly and avowedly to consult upon and determine in Scots affairs.

After the Scots nobility had waited and attended the English ministers some six or eight weeks, without knowing what was to be done, a flying report was spread about as if a plot had been discovered wherein a certain number of the chiefs and heads of the Cavaliers had engaged to rise in arms against Queen Anne in favour of the pretended Prince of Wales (as they termed the king). And this story was propagated to blacken those people's endeavours to liberate their country from the slavery and dominion which England usurped over it.

But because this plot was the foundation of a mighty superstructure, made a great noise, and was the handle the Courtiers laid hold on to ruin the Cavaliers and Country parties [sic], I must go back a little and trace it from its original, that the design and consequences of it may be the better understood, and the whole looked upon with that detestation and horrour by future ages which all good men had of it at the time. For certainly never was there a more villainous design, and which, in all probability, would have had its dismal effect had not the wise providence of God discovered and brought to light the hellish contrivance.

You must know then, that after the Duke of Queensberry had, as above narrated, broke his vows to the Cavaliers, and seen them, when joined to the Country, so strong and zealous a party that there was no hope of being able to stand it out against so violent and united a torrent, he bethought himself how to undermine their reputations and so diminish their interest with the court,[2] and find a pretence to vent his wrath and execute his malice against those that thwarted his arbitrary designs. And knowing, to his certain experience, that the poet was very much in the right when he asserted that:

Plots, true or false, are necessary things
To set up Commonwealths, and ruin kings[3]

he, with the special advice and consent of his dear friends the Duke of Argyle, the Earls of Stair and Leven and Mr Carstairs (a rebellious presbyterian preacher and one of Her Majesty's chaplains),[4] resolved one way or other to frame such a plot, as, when lodged upon those they designed it against, should, in all humane probability, be their utter ruin and destruction.

They pitched upon one Simon Frazer of Beaufort[5] as the tool to carry on this wicked design and be evidence to accuse such persons as they directed. This gentleman some three or four years

before had been guilty of a scandalous rape upon the person of
the Lady Dowager Lovat,[6] sister to the Duke of Athol, for which
crime the Lords of Justiciary had condemned him to die. And
letters of fire and sword were raised and a detachment of King
William's troops sent against him and his adherents, who were
pretty numerous, betwixt whom several skirmishes happened.
But finding the Duke of Argyle, who was his great patron (for no
other reason that I know of, but because he had been guilty of a
vile, lewd and detestable crime, and that too upon the person of
one of the family of Athol, which two houses bore each other a
constant grudge), I say, Frazer finding Argyle was no longer able
to protect him against the force of law and justice, quitted the
kingdom and retired to France. But King James having got an
account of the crimes he was found guilty of, for which he had
left his native country, would not, during his life, allow him to
come to the court of St Germains.[7] This person being made
choice of, as well qualifyed for such a design, was sent for from
France to England, and afterwards brought from thence to
Scotland. But before he left France, by the advice of his friends at
home, he turned Papist, and finding a way to be introduced to the
French king[8] by the Pope's Nuncio,[9] he represented himself as a
person of great interest in Scotland and oppressed for his zeal to
the royal family, and that, with encouragement and a small
assistance, he could contribute to make a great diversion to the
English arms and much promote the royal interest. And for that
end proposed that His Most Christian Majesty[10] would furnish
him with two or three hundred men and a good sum of money to
take along with him to Scotland, where he would perform
wonders. But the French king, unwilling to hazard his men and
money without a further security and more probability than his
assertions, gave him a fair answer, desiring him to go first to
Scotland and bring him [back] some credentials from those
persons over whom he pretended so much power. Which he
agreed to, and got, for that purpose, a little money and, by the
French interest, such credit at St Germains as to obtain a
commission from King James[11] to be a Major-General, with a

power to raise and command forces in his behalf, which was the main thing he aimed at. But at the same time Captain John Murray, brother to Mr Murray of Abercarnie,[12] and Captain James Murray, brother to Sir James Murray of Stanhope, were likewise, under the protection of Queen Anne's Act of Indemnity, sent over to Scotland to be a check upon him and bring intelligence how they found the tempers of the people and their inclinations towards King James.

Thus provided, Frazer arrived in England and on the borders of Scotland was met by the Duke of Argyle and by him conducted to Edinburgh, where he was kept private. And, being fully instructed what he was to do, the Duke of Queensberry gave him a pass to secure him from being apprehended in obedience to the letters of fire and sword emitted against him. And now he goes into the Highlands, introduces himself into the company of all that he knew were well-affected to King James and his interest, there produces his Major-General's commission as a testificate of the trust reposed in him, and proposes their rising in arms and signifying the same under their hands, that the king might know assuredly who they were and what numbers he had to trust to, and regulate his affairs accordingly. Some were so far seduced as to assure him they were ready to serve the king, though I believe there was none did it in the terms he demanded, but generally there were few that did not regret the king's reposing any trust in so bad a character and, fearing he would betray them, refused to treat or come to particulars with him. After he had trafficked here and there through the Highlands with small success, when the Parliament was prorogued he went to London to consider of what further use he might be to his constituents, resolving (though the *primum mobile*[13] and his patron, the Duke of Argyle, was now dead) to continue in their service. And they, finding he had made but a small progress and could not yet fix any thing at the doors of those persons against whom they levelled, resolved to send him again to France to demand letters and further encouragement to the Dukes of Hamilton and Athol, the Earls of Seafield and Cromarty, and the Cavaliers. And for that end the Duke of

Queensberry procured him and two others with him a pass from the Earl of Nottingham,[14] Secretary [of State] of England, under borrowed names.

If he went upon a good design, as the Duke of Queensberry afterwards alleged, why needed he have made their persons and business such a secret to the queen's Secretary, as [if] he must know neither? But before Frazer reached Paris and had executed his black design, it came to light in a great measure. For the famous Mr Ferguson[15] soon discovered and consequently defeated the project when it was as yet but in embryo. For Frazer, whilst he was in London, having addressed himself to him and one Mr William Keith (son to Sir William Keith of _____,[16] and a great depender on the Duke of Athol), he acquainted them with his pretended design and project for King James and mightily pressed Keith that he would use his endeavours to perswade the Duke of Athol to forgive him and allow him access to his grace, since he was heartily sorry for the crime he had committed and was promoting so good a design. But Keith (though he played the fool and dipt deep enough with him in all other points) told him that was what he could not presume to propose, and what he knew the Duke of Athol would never grant.

But Ferguson, an old experienced plotter, understanding his character, suspected his integrity. And it coming to his knowledge that he[17] was often privately with the Scots Courtiers, was by them supported, and had obtained a pass, as above related, he soon concluded that there was some base design in hand and thereupon gave the Duke of Athol notice of it. And he again, having enquired at the Earl of Nottingham's, and finding Ferguson's informations to hold good and his suspicions to be well grounded, acquaints Queen Anne of the whole proceedure, accusing the Duke of Queensberry in particular, and his other friends and partizans, of corresponding with and protecting a person outlawed in the kingdom of Scotland, guilty of the most horrid crimes and a trafficker with France. Whereupon the Duke of Queensberry, to vindicate himself, declared that Frazer, when he came to Scotland, wrote to him that he could make great discoveries for the queen's service, that upon that account he had sent for him, given him a protection in Scotland and again procured him a pass in England, with a design he should go to France and make a clearer discovery, which he did not doubt he would have performed had not the matter come too soon to light. And as a convincing proof thereof he produces a letter from the Queen Mother, directed to L_____ M_____, which initials he interpreted [as] the Lord Murray, formerly the title of the Duke of Athol before his father died. But his grace[18] made use of such solid arguments and convincing proofs to shew the fallacy of that letter, that Queen Anne herself could not deny but that she thought it not genuine.

Now let any impartial judge consider if it is probable that Frazer, with whom no honest man in Scotland would converse, who was under sentence of death and not such a fool as to imagine that he had interest to do any thing of moment for King James's service could have had the impudence to address the French king in the terms he did, and come over to Scotland, unless he had been put upon it and protected by such as could support him at home. If he only proposed to cheat the French king of a little money, why came he to Scotland with it, since he knew he could not fail, in time, to be discovered, and then could neither hope to be protected there or dare return to France? These, I say, and many other shrewd presumptions, make it clear what was the design of this pretended plot, and, if successful, how dismal the consequences of it would have proven, viz. the destruction of those who opposed the designs of the Scots Courtiers and English ministry against Scotland. How happy it was in being rendered abortive before the designed conception had come to full maturity, and how odious the thoughts of such a hellish conspiracy, and abettors thereof, ought to be in the eyes of all good men!

I must likewise acquaint you that David Baily wrote a letter, about the same time that the pretended plot was discovered in London, to the Duke of Hamilton, then at Edinburgh, intimating that the Duke of Queensberry and [the] Marquis of Annandale had been at great pains to engage him to go to London with them and be a concurring evidence of such things as he should afterwards be informed of against the Dukes of Hamilton and Athol, the Earl of Home and several others. Which he positively refused to do, and thought it his duty to make a discovery thereof that these noble persons might be on their guard, lest the Duke of Queensberry should still endeavour, and at last find out, proper persons to be his accomplices.

This information, upon the back of the pretended plot, made a great noise. The Duke of Hamilton tabled it before the Scots Privy Council and desired their lordships should take it and its consequences under consideration. Upon which Baily was imprisoned and examined. But having no proof besides his own assertions, he was ordered to stand upon the pillory and was banished out of the kingdom. The first part of which sentence was executed, but other taken off when the Marquis of Tweedale came to the government.

It is hard to make a judgment of this story. If it was true it is a further proof of the Court's designs. But, for my part, though I am convinced the Duke of Queensberry was capable of it and did as ill with Frazer, I do believe it was all a lye, being only a counter-plot framed by Mr Baily of Jerviswood[19] to exasperate the nation against the Duke of Queensberry, [David] Baily being his near relation and Tweedale's party appearing most earnest for his being acquitted in Council, and at last, when they came to have power, taking off the sentence of banishment. Let me add too, this Baily was so scandalous a fellow he would scarcely have been allowed as an habile[20] witness in any judicatory in Europe where his character was known. But I leave the reader, as he pleases, to give credit or not to his report, there being sufficient evidence without it to convince the world what a horrid design the Duke of Queensberry was upon.

While all this was a-doing, the Duke of Queensberry, to preserve the interest he had obtained with the Tories and Church party[21] in England, had brought up to London those two renegadoes the Earl of Balcarras and [John] Paterson,

Archbishop of Glasgow, to assure them of his inclinations to serve and protect the Tories and Church party in Scotland. The Archbishop was a man of extraordinary parts and great learning, but extreamly proud and haughty to all the inferiour clergy of his diocese and very much destitute of those virtues that should adorn the life and conversation of one so highly exalted in the church. He had a great management of the government of both church and state before the Revolution. After the abolishing of episcopacy he lived privately, indulging that avaricious, worldly temper which had sullied his other qualifications in all the capacities and stations of his life. And which likewise moved him to embark on this design, which, when he left Scotland, and even after he came to London, he kept as a mighty secret, pretending to the Cavaliers he undertook that long journey in the middle of winter, so dangerous to his grey hairs (his own expressions), only to supplicate Queen Anne to bestow the vacant bishops' rents on the poor, starving episcopal clergy. Yet when this matter was under the consideration of Queen Anne and her servants, his charitable zeal did allow him to accept of four hundred pounds sterling per annum out of them, though there remained but twelve hundred pounds after his four hundred was deducted (to be divided among his numerous needy brethren) that was not appropriated to other uses. And his lordship was worth twenty thousand pounds of his own.[22]

I have already accounted for the Earl of Balcarras, so let me proceed to tell you that this noble lord and reverend prelate served the design they came for most religiously. And the latter had the impudence to assure Queen Anne that the Duke of Queensberry was the best friend the episcopal clergy had in Scotland, and would have procured them a toleration (which, it seems, they knew she desired) had he not found they were so disaffected to her interest that to shew them favour would be to encourage and enable her enemies. Adding, with tears in his eyes, 'she might depend upon the truth of this information since it came from him who could be no great gainer, but, on the contrary, was a great loser by their being kept under.' This last part I had in half an hour after it was performed, from one who had it from Prince George,[23] who declared he and Queen Anne were confounded at the account.

During all this the plot made a great noise. And accounts of the affair being soon wafted over to France, Frazer was immediately clapt up in the Bastile.[24] But since a plot (though of the Duke of Queensberry's and his accomplices' own composure) was pretended to be discovered, the assertion must be made good. And therefore the Duke of Queensberry throws himself upon the English Whig lords,[25] craving their assistance to bring him off by finding there had been a plot and laying it upon those that were his, and consequently their, enemies. They, according to the laudable practice of that party ever ready to support every person and every measure that tended to advance the 'good old cause',[26] taking him and his cause into their own omnipotent protection, tabled it in the English Parliament, and imprisoned and examined several persons. And sundry papers framed for the purpose were laid before the house and the consideration thereof referred to a committee of seven lords, who did and found what they pleased, though never so gross and absurd, and at last the House of Lords came to the following resolution:

> Resolved. That there had been a dangerous conspiracy in Scotland, toward the invading that kingdom with a French power, in order to subvert Her Majesty's government, and the bringing in the pretended Prince of Wales. That it was their opinion nothing had given so much encouragement to these designs as the succession of the crown of Scotland not being declared in favour of the Princess Sophia and her heirs.[27] That the queen should be addressed to use such methods as she thought convenient for having the succession of the crown of that kingdom settled after that manner. And that being once done, then they would do all in their power to promote an entire union of the two kingdoms.[28]

But, notwithstanding the Lords were so clear, there was not one unbyassed person that did not see it was all trick and villainy.

And the Lords themselves, conscious thereof, would gladly have had some further proofs to justify their proceedings in the matter and for that purpose did prosecute Mr David Lindsay (who had been in France, but came home to Scotland and, before he went to England, was declared by the Privy Council to be comprehended within the terms of Queen Anne's Act of Indemnity), and, finding he had been in France, by virtue of an English act of Parliament in King William's time, condemned him to die, though he did plead he was a native of Scotland and pardoned by Her Majesty as sovereign of that kingdom. Yet nevertheless, so far did they drive the jest, and so much did Queen Anne allow herself to be imposed upon, that he was carried to Tyburn[29] and the rope put about his neck, the sheriff telling him he could expect no mercy unless he would acknowledge his crime and discover (which was the one thing needful) who were concerned in the Scots conspiracy—thus tempting him to save himself by charging others with what he knew they were innocent of. But he—to his immortal honour be it said—answered, he was willing to die rather than save his life on such terms. Whereupon the sheriff ordered the cart to drive on, but finding he was resolved to stand it out, in behaving as became a good Christian, and worthy gentleman, produced Queen Anne's reprieve, suspending the execution. And Lindsay, having thus by his heroick behaviour disappointed the designs of those who hoped by this severe method to force a confession (true or false, all was one) out of him to justify their proceedings, was remitted close prisoner to Newgate,[30] where he remained in a miserable, starving condition for three or four years, and was then banished out of Britain and died in Holland for want of necessary food and raiment.

Several Scots Councils were called, and met this winter in Queen Anne's presence in London, where [there] were several hot debates, and many proposals were made as [to] proper methods to be followed at this critical juncture, with relation to the management of Scots affairs. The most remarkable of which was that which came from the Earl of Stair, who (considering that this proceedure of the House of Lords would so exasperate the Scots nation, and the discovery of the designed plot so irritate and cement the Cavaliers [*sic*] and Country parties, that it was to no purpose for the Duke of Queensberry and his partizans to imagine to succeed there) proposed that an English army should be sent to Scotland, to be maintained by England, and remain there till Her Majesty's decease, and that during her life another session of Parliament should not meet. The first would keep Scotland in awe and the second prevent her being able to redress herself and assert her just rights in a legal manner. But this was so dangerous an expedient the English ministers did not think it proper, lest it had raised such a combustion in that kingdom as would not easily be extinguished.

Having made mention of this extraordinary proposal, it will be very proper to give a particular account of its author. John, Earl of Stair, was the origine and principal instrument of all the misfortunes that befel either the king or the kingdom of Scotland. It was he advised King James to emit a proclamation remitting the penal laws[31] by virtue of his own absolute power and authority, and made him take several other steps, with a design— as he since bragged—to procure the nation's hatred and prove his ruin. It was he that, underhand, carried on the Revolution in Scotland, thus acting the same part as the Earl of Sunderland[32] in England. It was he that, to secure his court interest in King William's time, contrived, and was the author of, the barbarous murder of Glencoe, and had a main hand in the plot just now mentioned to cut off the chief of the Cavalier and Country parties. And in this to whom can he be so well compared as to Catiline?[33] It was he that first suffered, I should rather say, taught and encouraged, England arbitrarily and avowedly to rule over Scots affairs, invade her freedom and ruin her trade. It was he that was at the bottom of the Union, and to him, in a great measure, it owes its success. And so he may be stiled the Judas of his country. As he was thus the bane of Scotland in general, so he and his family were the great oppressors of all the particular persons that did not depend upon him and go along with his designs. And that so openly and barefacedly that a Cavalier or anti-Courtier was not to expect common justice in the Session, where his brother[34] was President. Whereby he and his family were, at the same time, the most dreaded and detested of any in the kingdom, ruling over whom, and after what manner, they pleased. This family had rose but lately from nothing. And it was so much the stranger that they pretended, and others suffered them, to usurp such a dominion as extended not over the Cavaliers alone, but even such of the Revolution party as were of any interest beside theirs felt the heavy effects of it. From this short abstract of the Earl's life, it is easy to gather that he was false and cruel, covetous and imperious, altogether destitute of the sacred ties of honour, loyalty, justice and gratitude. And lastly, a man of very great parts, else he could never have perpetrated so much wickedness. He had, indeed, a piercing judgment, a lively imagination, a quick apprehension, a faithful memory, a solid reflection and a particular talent of dissimulation and cunning in their greatest extents, so that he was seldom or never to be taken at unawares. He was extreamly facetious and diverting company in common conversation, and, setting aside his politicks (to which all did yield), good-natured. To these qualifications was likewise added that of eloquence; being so great a master of it that he expressed himself on all occasions and subjects with so much life and rhetorick, and that likewise so pointedly and copiously, that there was none in the Parliament capable to take up the cudgels with him.[35] Had a judgment of his inside been taken from the outside he might well enough have passed for that of which he was the least. These endowments, much improved by long experience and application in business, may justly entitle him to be ranked among the greatest, though, at the same time, among the worst men, in this age. And what has been said of him may serve for a character of his two brothers, Sir Hugh and Sir David Dalrymple,[36] yea, the whole name, only with this difference: that though they were all equally willing, yet not equally capable of doing so much evil as his lordship.[37]

Having thus given a full account of the Earl of Stair, before I return to where I left off I think it convenient to say somewhat of those persons who were chiefly concerned and assisting to him in his projects, and shall at this occasion confine myself to the Earls of Loudoun,[38] Leven and Glasgow.

Hugh, Earl of Loudoun, was of all the persons concerned in the government without doubt amongst the best. He had nothing in his nature that was cruel and revengeful, was affable, courteous and just betwixt man and man, and though he pursued his own maxims and designs, yet it was in a moderate gentlemanny way. Being descended of a family enemies to monarchy, and educated after that way and his fortune in bad circumstances, he easily dropt into Court measures, was soon taken notice of, and first made an extraordinary Lord of the Session, in which post he behaved to all men's satisfaction, studying to understand the laws and constitution of the kingdom, and determine accordingly. He was endowed with good natural parts and had much improven them in his younger years by reading. And though he did not much affect to show them in publick, yet there were few exceeded him in contriving and carrying on a design, having a clear judgment and ready apprehension.[39]

David, Earl of Leven, in the beginning of his life was so vain and conceity that he became the jest of all sober men. But as he grew older he overcame that folly in part, and from the proudest became the civilest man alive. He was a man of good parts and sound judgment, but master of no kind of learning. And though he had once the command of a regiment, and was at last created Lieutenant-General and Commander-in-Chief of the forces in this kingdom, yet his courage was much called in question upon sundry accounts not necessary to be mentioned here.[40] He was born and bred an enemy to the royal family, and therefore chearfully embraced, and significantly promoted, every thing against its interest. However, he was no ways severe, but rather very civil to all the Cavaliers, especially such as were prisoners in the castle of Edinburgh when he was governour. From whence he gained more of their favour than any man in the government.[41]

David, Earl of Glasgow, had nothing to recommend him save that his surname was the same with the Dutchess of Queensberry,[42] being upon no account to be reckoned a man of more than ordinary sense. He was esteemed proud, arrogant, greedy, extreamly false and a great speaker at random; was so ridiculously vain that he affected a great deal of respect and reverence as his due. Nothing pleased him so much as to dedicate a book to his lordship. And he was sure to take it and its author into his protection provided much and frequent mention was made in the preface of his illustrious and ancient family, though he and all the world knew his predecessors were not long ago boatmen, and since married to the heiress of Kelburn, a petty little family in the shire of Ayr, the representatives of which until his father's time were never designed the laird, but always the goodman of Kelburn. However, having, by being concerned in farming the publick revenues, scraped together a good estate, he wanted not ambition to be a man of quality, and concerned in the government. Both which the Dutchess's favour and his own impudence procured him. Thus we see to what height ambition and impudence, without any merit, will bring a man in this world. There was no man had such a sway with the Duke of Queensberry as he, and I look upon him as the chief of those evil counsellors that perswaded and engaged him to follow, at least persevere in, such pernicious ways.[43]

I have now been so long out of the way [that] I must refresh my reader's memory with telling him I left off after I had given him an account of the methods and proposals that were under consideration in England concerning the management of Scots affairs, which induced the Duke of Athol to write to his friends in Scotland to send up two or three of their number to support him against the torrent he was unable singly to oppose. Upon this account the Duke of Hamilton wrote to, and conveened at Edinburgh, a considerable number of the Cavalier and Country parties. But before they came to a general, there were several previous, meetings betwixt the Duke of Hamilton on the one side and the Marquis of Tweedale, the Earls of Roxburgh, Rothes,

Balmerino[44] and Haddington,[45] Lord Belhaven,[46] Baily of Jerviswood, Home of Blackadder[47] and Haldane of Glenaegles[48] [*sic*], on the other (who, though they were opposite to the Court, were never esteemed staunch friends to the royal interest). And although there were several of the Cavaliers at that time in town, such as the Earls of Home and Strathmore, the Viscount of Stormont,[49] Cochran of Kilmaronock,[50] Lockhart of Carnwath and several other gentlemen, yet his grace never imparted the least of his mind to any of them, but in conjunction with the other set advises and resolves to pitch upon the Earls of Rothes and Roxburgh and Baily of Jerviswood, and accordingly at the general meeting proposed these three to be sent to London to negotiate and manage their affairs in conjunction with Athol.

The Cavaliers could not well oppose these persons in their meeting, after they had been publickly named, but they did not stick to tell [the] Duke [of] Hamilton they were afraid they would mind their private, more than [their] publick concerns, which came too truly to pass. They were instructed to inform Queen Anne that they were sent by a very considerable number of Parliament men to acquaint Her Majesty that, being informed that there had a great deal of pains been taken to perswade Her Majesty that a considerable party in this kingdom had been conspiring against her (designing thereby to incense Her Majesty against her good subjects), and that to make this the more feasible a plot was pretended to be discovered. And being likewise informed of several designs on foot, and advices given (particularly narrating the above-mentioned proposal made by the Earl of Stair) which were inconsistent with the laws, honour and welfare of the kingdom, they thought it their duty to represent to Her Majesty the necessity of allowing the Parliament to meet as soon as possible, where this plot might be enquired into and such as were found guilty be punished, and such measures taken as would for the future prevent all designs against Her Majesty and her government, discourage all endeavours to create groundless jealousies betwixt Her Majesty and her good subjects, and secure the kingdom from the effects of those pernicious projects that were on foot, with design at one stroke to debase the honour and enslave the freedom of this her ancient and independent kingdom. And though these gentlemen had afterwards the impudence to deny that they received any instructions at all, yet I am positive I heard them read unto, and approved of by, the meeting, and afterwards I saw them delivered unto them, and they promised to fulfill them. And had they faithfully performed it, they had done good service to their country, and gained a great deal of honour to themselves.

It is true indeed they did attend the queen and deliver their commission, but they were not long in London before they were prevailed upon to depend as sneakingly on the English ministry as those against whom they had often exclaimed on that very head, and did engage to serve and promote their designs against the interest of their country, whose rights and privileges they had, till now, pretended to maintain preferable to any other thing, and distinguished themselves by their zeal therein. It is hard to say whether they had this project of raising themselves and turning tail to their friends before they left Scotland, or if they were prevailed upon after they came to London. For my part, I am of the last opinion because I am certain my Lord Yester[51] (who was conscious to all their private views, and their oracle) was against the measure of sending up any to London. Next, the measure came from the Duke of Athol, who had no other design but that a formidable appearance might be made in opposition to the swarm of Courtiers that appeared this winter at court. And lastly, the chief, if not the only, reason that induced the Duke of Hamilton to pitch upon these three was to unite them and that party to stand fixed by him, against the Duke of Queensberry, his inveterate enemy. So they were not the authors of the measure, and were but by chance entrusted with the management of it. But no satisfying reason can be alledged why the Duke of Hamilton did altogether neglect advising with, or so much as communicating his design therein to the Cavaliers, and not add some of their number to the other three, in whom he and they might have entirely confided.

As affairs stood at this time in Scotland, the Lord Godolphin was fully convinced that the Duke of Queensberry would not be able to carry through Queen Anne's, or rather England's, designs there. And he lay under a necessity to endeavour to have the succession of the House of Hanover established in that kingdom, because his enemies in England asserted he was an enemy to it and that it might have been done, had he not secretly opposed it. And now being resolved to clear himself of that imputation, he advises how to effectuate it to the best purpose and resolves to draw up with the Earls of Rothes and Roxburgh and Baily of Jerviswood, proposing, by thus dividing the Cavaliers and Country parties, to carry his designs through.

The Earl of Rothes had not, that I know of, one good property to recommend him, being false to a great degree, a contemner of honour and engagements, extreamly ambitious, ridiculous, vain and conceited (though of very ordinary parts and accomplishments), extravagantly proud and scandalously mercenary. No man was more forward in the Country party, nor did any profess greater regard to the royal family than his lordship, and that with repeated oaths and asseverations, but, alass, he had neither enough of sense nor honesty to resist the first temptations.[52]

John, Earl, afterwards Duke, of Roxburgh, made his first appearance in the world to the general satisfaction of all men. He was a man of good sense, improven by so much reading and learning that, perhaps, he was the best accomplished young man of quality in Europe, and had so charming a way of expressing his thoughts that he pleased even those against whom he spoke. And it was a thousand pities a man so capable to do good should have proven the very bane and cut-throat of his country, by being extreamly false and disingenuous, and so indifferent of the ties of honour, friendship, vows and justice, that he sacrificed them all, and the interest of his country, to his designs, viz. revenge and ambition.[53]

George Baily of Jerviswood was morose, proud and severe, but of a profound, solid judgment, and by far the most significant man of all his party, to whom he was a kind of dictator. In King William's time he had gained a great reputation by standing so stiffly by the interest of his country, but being of a rebellious race he never had the least thought of serving the royal family. And though he joined with [the] Cavalier and Country parties in opposition to the Duke of Queensberry and the Court measures, yet he always favoured the Hanoverian succession. And therefore, as soon as the Court of England inclined to that measure, he left his maxims and measures, and, being once dipped, never fell off, but served them to the latter end.[54]

The Lord Godolphin knowing, no doubt, that these gentlemen were fit for his business, employs Johnstoun (who was Secretary to King William, and so vile and execrable a wretch that he deserves not so much room here as to have a large character, though indeed he was a shrewd, cunning fellow)[55] to manage it with them. And being very intimate with them and their friends, he soon brought it to a conclusion. They engaging for themselves, the Marquis of Tweedale and other friends at home, that if the queen would impower them to pass a few inconsiderable limitations upon her successors into laws and give them the management of the government and disposal of all offices and employments, they would prevail with the Parliament of Scotland to settle the succession of that crown after the same manner as in England. Which the English ministers acquiesced to, knowing well they could easily repeal the limitations in a subsequent Parliament if once the main point, viz. the succession, were granted.

All this, however, was to be kept a mighty secret. So when these gentlemen returned to Scotland (a meeting of those that commissioned them being called), they reported the effects of their journey, and, in short, made it to have no effects at all. But by this time there were some little surmises of their going over to the Court, and though the Duke of Hamilton and the Cavaliers knew well enough the nature of the bargain that was agreed to, and what was designed by them, yet they resolved to appear ignorant and behave towards them as if they had not the least apprehension of their designing any thing that was bad, but in the meantime leave nothing undone to advance their own concerns. And therefore it was recommended to every one to be as diligent as possible in setting matters in a true light, that honest well-meaning people might not be deceived by specious pretences, and to understand other people's sentiments, that a judgment might be made how matters would go in the Parliament, in whom they might confide, and whom they should distrust.

The Marquis of Tweedale never obtained any other character than that he was a well-meaning, but simple, man. And I have the charity to believe he was forced against his will, by his friends and those he trusted (who made a meer tool of him), to enter into many of the bad measures he pursued. So I may safely say he was the least ill-meaning man of his party, either through inclination or capacity.[56]

About the time it was owned Queen Anne had appointed him Commissioner to the next Parliament, the Duke of Queensberry was laid aside from being one of the Secretaries of State, and his conjunct, the Earl of Cromarty, remained sole Secretary all the ensuing Parliament. The Earl of Leven was reinstalled governour of the castle of Edinburgh in the Earl of March's place. The above-mentioned Mr Johnstoun succeeded Sir James Murray of Philiphaugh as Lord Register and the Earl of Glasgow (Treasurer-Deputy) was turned out. But no body was named to fill up that vacancy, nor any others that were in employments deposed at this time, designing to gain over some to their measures by promises and expectations of preferments, and bubble others that were overlooked with the hopes of being continued, provided they went cordially along with this new set of Courtiers. All this time, and even during the whole session of Parliament, the Earls of Rothes and Roxburgh (with their wonted oaths and imprecations, though few gave them any credit) still pretended to the Duke of Hamilton and the Cavaliers to be as honest as ever, [and] that they would never go into any measure that was against the interest of the royal family or country, and that their only design of coming into the government was to dispossess the Duke of Queensberry and his accomplices and attack them for their horrid designed plot. But the other[s], having resolved to enter into no measures with them, replyed that it was time enough to think of these things when the Parliament was met, and still carried fair with them above-board.

But in the meantime, by the negotiations of the Earl of Home and Cochran of Kilmaronock on the one side, and the Earl of March and Sir James Murray of Philiphaugh on the other, it was agreed that the examination of the plot should not be pushed any length, provided the Duke of Queensberry's friends in Parliament (for he came not down to Scotland himself) would join with the Cavaliers to oppose the succession and other measures of the Court.[57] And, to tell the truth, it was no great difficulty to obtain this from them, for most of them, when left to themselves, were very well inclined and had been dragged against their wills to do many things they naturally abhorred by their friendship to, and dependence on, his grace. But I must say the Dukes of Hamilton and Athol gained a great deal of honour by consenting to this agreement since they had a fair occasion of being sufficiently revenged upon the Duke of Queensberry and his partisans, and it was generous in them to prefer the publick good to their own private resentments. It would indeed have been good for them, and us too, if they had oftener done the same.

The Earl of Seafield, Chancellor, soon left his friends and worshipped the rising sun, and the Earl of Cromarty behaved after the same manner, and made a long, ridiculous speech in favour of the succession, though his friends, which were numerous, stood firm to the Cavaliers. The Marquis of Montrose[58] (but without being followed by any of his friends except Graham of Gorthie,[59] which he resented extremely), the Marquis of Tweedale, the Earls of Rothes, Roxburgh, Haddington and Selkirk, and the Lord Belhaven; Dundass of Arnistoun,[60] Cockburn younger of Ormistoun,[61] Sir John Home of Blackadder, Sir William Ker of Greenheed,[62] Bennet younger of Grubbet,[63] Baily of Lamingtoun,[64] Baily of Jerviswood, Sinclair younger of Stevenson,[65] Haldane of Glenaegles, Sir William Anstruther of Anstruther,[66] Douglass of Strenie,[67] Halyburton of Pitcurr[68] and Bruce younger of Kinross,[69] barons; Patrick Bruce,[70] Alexander Edgar,[71] Sir John Anstruther,[72] Sir John Erskine of Alva,[73] James

Spittle of Leuchat[74] and Sir James Halket of Pitfirran,[75] burrows, all formerly of the Cavalier or Country parties, did now desert them, and in the succeeding Parliament promote[d] the measures of England with all their might. And they were very confident they would be able to carry all before them successfully. Particularly Johnstoun the Register (though he saw he was odious to the nation) took so much upon him that he had the imprudence, or rather impudence, to say several times publickly before the Parliament met that the Parliament must and should swallow down the succession. But he soon found it was not such a mean, servile Parliament as he had to do with in 1695, to suffer him to bully and dictate to them.[76] For notwithstanding of this great defection of so many, and so considerable numbers, and their great diligence and assurance of success, what by the assistance of the Duke of Queensberry's friends (who were now left to themselves) and the courage and conduct of the Cavaliers, the designs of the Court were all frustrated and the honour of the nation asserted.

Notes

1. Rect., *levées*: their early morning reception of visitors. Statesmen receiving supplicants as they first got up in the morning was a practise whose development is usually ascribed to Louis XIV, and accordingly carried connotations of servility on the part of the visitors; hence GL's use of the term is probably contemptuous.
2. I.e. the queen and her English ministers.
3. John Dryden, 'Absalom and Achitophel', lines 83–4 (J.Kinsley (ed.), *The Poems of John Dryden*, 4 vols., Oxford, 1958).
4. William Carstares, Principal of the University of Edinburgh and subsequently Moderator of the General Assembly of the Kirk; *DNB*, ix. 187–90.
5. Subsequently 12th Lord Lovat; *DNB*, xx. 216–22.
6. Lady Amelia Murray, widow of the 10th Lord Lovat.
7. GL is obfuscating here, since Fraser was certainly allowed to visit St Germain from 1701 onwards: *Original Papers; Containing the Secret History of Great Britain from the Restoration to the Accession of the House of Hannover*, ed. J. J. Macpherson, 2 vols (1775), i. 650: Fraser to the Earl of Middleton, Paris, 15 Jan. 1704 ns.
8. Louis XIV.

9. Cardinal Gualtiero. I am indebted to Dr Anne York of Youngstown State University, Ohio, for her help in identifying Gualterio.
10. The customary formal title of the kings of France.
11. James 'VIII', the Old Pretender (son of James II and VII).
12. William Murray.
13. First mover.
14. Daniel Finch, 2nd Earl of Nottingham; H. Horwitz, *Revolution Politicks. The Career of Daniel Finch, Second Earl of Nottingham, 1647–1730* (Cambridge, 1968).
15. Robert Ferguson 'The Plotter', by this time a dedicated Jacobite; *DNB*, xviii. 350–3.
16. Possibly Ludquhairn.
17. Simon Fraser.
18. Atholl.
19. George Baillie of Jerviswood, Commissioner for Lanarkshire. See below, pp. 64–5.
20. Able (fit).
21. The 'Church party' usually denoted the Tories at this time, so GL may be trying to distinguish between the politicians and their clerical supporters.
22. Cf. *DNB*, xliv. 18–20.
23. Prince George of Denmark, Queen Anne's consort.
24. He was in fact more comfortably sequestered, in the Château d'Angoulême, until 1715.
25. A reference to the English Whig 'Junto' lords (the Earls of Sunderland and Orford and Lords Somers, Wharton and Halifax), who were, in effect, the leaders of the Whig party. N.b. Lord Wharton was GL's uncle, and he or those about him may have been the source of much of GL's information on the Scotch plot.
26. 'The Good Old Cause of God and his people', was a slogan that was much bruited about in Britain by supporters of the various Republican factions vying for control of the state 1659–60. It was subsequently used by the Whigs' opponents to tar them with Republicanism (as in this instance), and taken up by more extreme Whigs as a symbol of their radicalism.
27. Sophia was Electress of Hanover by her marriage to Ernst August, Elector of Hanover, and, as grand-daughter of James I, Queen Anne's nearest Protestant relative; hence her status as the queen's designated heir. In fact she was considerably older than Anne and predeceased her by a few months, leaving her son, the future George I, as heir at the time of Anne's death.

28. GL is paraphrasing here the much longer statement made by the House of Lords on 22 March 1704, for which see: *Journals of the House of Lords* (henceforth *LJ*), xvii. 505–6. For details of the Lords' examination of the Scotch plot see, *LJ*, xvii. 394–502: 3 Feb.—20 Mar. 1704.
29. The traditional site for executions in London.
30. Eighteenth-century London's most notorious prison.
31. Laws laying heavy fines, imprisonment and even death on those convicted of practising catholicism.
32. Robert Spencer, 3rd Earl of Sunderland, a notoriously ambitious and temporising statesman who managed to serve both James II and VII and William III; J. P. Kenyon, *Robert Spencer, Earl of Sunderland 1641–1702* (1958).
33. The notoriously self-interested Roman politician whose rebellion in 63 B.C., which aimed at cancelling all debts, was savagely suppressed by the then Consul, Cicero.
34. Sir Hugh Dalrymple of North Berwick; *DNB*, xiii. 406–7.
35. Cf. HMC *Portland*, iv. 224: Greg to Harley, Edinburgh, 16 Aug. 1705.
36. Of Hailes, Commissioner for Culross; *PS*, i. 174.
37. Cf. *DNB*, xiii. 415–20.
38. Hugh Campbell, 3rd Earl of Loudoun.
39. Cf. *DNB*, viii. 359–60.
40. This may be an oblique reference to a reluctance to duel.
41. Cf. *DNB*, xxxvii. 237–8.
42. Mary Boyle, daughter of Lord Clifford and grandaughter of the Earl of Burlington and Cork.
43. Cf. *CP*, v. 661–2.
44. Rect., John Elphinstone, 4th Lord Balmerino. See below, p. 111.
45. Thomas Haddington, 6th Earl of Haddington. See below, p. 84.
46. John Hamilton, 3rd Lord Belhaven. See below, p. 84.
47. Probably Sir John Home of Blackadder, Commissioner for Berwickshire; *PS*, i. 349.
48. John Haldane of Gleneagles, Commissioner for Perthshire; *PS*, i. 306.
49. David Murray, 5th Viscount Stormont; *CP*, xii (1). 294–5.
50. William Cochrane of Kilmaronock, Commissioner for Dunbartonshire; *PS*, i. 127.
51. Charles Hay, heir-apparent to the Marquess of Tweeddale; *CP*, xii (2). 79.
52. Cf. *DNB*, xxxiii. 103–4.
53. Cf. *DNB*, xxxi. 50–1.

54. *PS*, i. 30.
55. James Johnston; *DNB*, xxx. 64–5.
56. *DNB*, xxv. 270.
57. HMC *Portland*, iv. 99–100: Earl of Leven to Harley, Edinburgh, 11 July 1703.
58. James Graham, 4th Marquess of Montrose. See below, pp. 92–3.
59. Mungo Graham of Gorthie, Commissioner for Perthshire; *PS*, i. 292–3.
60. Sir Robert Dundas of Arniston, Lord of Session and Commissioner for Edinburghshire; *PS*, i. 215.
61. John Cockburn, Commissioner for Haddingtonshire; *PS*, i. 133.
62. Sir William Ker of Greenhead, Commissioner for Roxburghshire; *PS*, i. 392.
63. Captain William Bennet of Grubbet, Commissioner for Roxburghshire; *PS*, i. 49.
64. William Baillie of Lamington, Commissioner for Lanarkshire; *PS*, i. 32.
65. John Sinclair of Stevenson, Commissioner for Lanarkshire. *PS*, ii. 644.
66. Sir William Anstruther of that ilk, Commissioner for Fife; *PS*, i. 20.
67. Robert Douglas of Strathendry, Commissioner for Fife; *PS*, i. 199.
68. James Haliburton of Pitcur, Commissioner for Forfarshire; *PS*, i. 308.
69. Sir John Bruce of Kinross, Commissioner for Kinross-shire; *PS*, i. 79.
70. Patrick Bruce of Bunzion, Commissioner for Cupar; *PS*, i. 76.
71. Commissioner for Haddington; *PS*, i. 221.
72. Sir John Anstruther of that ilk, Commissioner for Anstruther Easter; *PS*, i. 20.
73. Sir John Erskine of Alva, Bandeath, and Cambuskenneth, Commissioner for Burntisland; *PS*, i. 228–9.
74. Rect., James Spittal of Leuchat, Commissioner for Inverkeithing. *PS*, ii. 655.
75. Commissioner for Dunfermline; *PS*, i. 311.
76. P. W. J. Riley, *King William and the Scottish Politicians* (Edinburgh, 1979), pp. 81–102.

[The Parliamentary Session of 1704]

But now I proceed to the Parliament itself, which met the sixth of July 1704, the Marquis of Tweedale being Commissioner thereto.

The queen's letter, Commissioner's and Chancellor's speeches, were of the ordinary strain, exhorting to unity, promising good laws and encouragement to trade, and demanding supplies for the support of the army. But the settlement of the succession of the crown on the house of Hanover was the main scope, and chiefly insisted on and recommended as necessary to establish peace and secure the Protestant religion.[1] And I observe that generally both these are in danger at the approaching of a Parliament, the best things being often thus made a bad use of, viz. to squeeze and drain the country of money, to gratify the ambition and supply the avarice of its greatest, viz. domestick, enemies.

The first two days being spent in constituting the house and discussing of controverted elections, on the third *sederunt*[2] (being the thirteenth of July) the Duke of Hamilton presented the following resolve: 'that this Parliament will not proceed to the nomination of a successor to the crown until we have had a previous treaty with England in relation to our commerce and other concerns with that nation.' This resolve was compiled and presented, after serious consideration, in order to put a bar upon the succession's being established before the Courtiers had time to work upon and seduce the members. The Court was much surprized and perplexed, not expecting the Cavaliers would have begun so early on that subject.[3] And they hoped to have had time to gull over some of the members with passing a few inconsiderable limitations. After the resolve was read, and some bickering discourses followed thereon, it was agreed that the resolve should lie upon the table till next *sederunt* (being the seventeenth of July), and the consideration thereof be reassumed in the first place.[4] Which the Duke of Hamilton having on the said day accordingly moved, after some debates (wherein many members, particularly Mr Fletcher of Salton, did elegantly and pathetically set forth the hardships and miseries to which we have been exposed since the union of the two crowns of Scotland and England in one and the same sovereign,[5] and the impossibility of amending and bettering our condition if we did not take care to prevent any design that tended to continue the same without other terms and better security than we have hitherto had) the Earl of Rothes presented another resolve in these terms:

> Resolved. That the Parliament will proceed in the first place to the considerations of such conditions of government as may be judged proper for rectifying of our constitution, and to vindicate and secure the sovereignty and independency of the nation; and then the Parliament will take into consideration the other resolve offered for a treaty previous to the nomination of a successor to the crown.

The Court being very positive they would be strong enough to give this last the preference, and thereafter get it approven, and reject the other resolve, moved that a vote might be stated, which of the two resolves should come first under the house's consideration? Whereupon brisk speeches and sharp repartees were made by both parties, and great heats arose, which continued a long time, till somewhat allayed by that worthy and learned judge, Sir James Falconer of Phesdo,[6] who spake to this purpose: that he was very glad to see such an emulation in the house upon account of nation's interest and security. That he thought both the resolves under their consideration so good and necessary that it was [a] pity they should justle with one another, and therefore moved that both should be conjoined in the following manner: resolved, that this house will not proceed to the nomination of a successor until we have had a previous treaty with England for regulating our commerce and other affairs with that nation. And further resolved, that this Parliament will proceed to make such limitations and conditions of government for the rectification of our constitution as may secure the religion, independency and liberty of this nation before they proceed to the nomination of a successor to the crown. 'And this motion', added he, 'will, I hope, be satisfying and agreeable to both sides', since there was nothing repugnant in the one to the other, and that both had their desires granted.

The whole [of the] Cavaliers seconded the motion, but the Courtiers as unanimously opposed it. For, since their darling succession was impeded by the first resolve, they were more averse to the second than any others, their only design of proposing the limitations being to promote the succession. And, therefore, if the first resolve must pass, they would willingly have dropped the other, though it was their own child. And next, this resolve, if approven, propaled, at the very beginning of the Parliament, their incapacity to manage the nation and make good their engagements to the English ministry. But the Cavaliers insisting upon it as what comprehended every man's wish, viz. religion, liberty and trade, and observing that it took with the house, called for and pressed a vote upon it. Which, being often shifted and postponed by the Court (the Chancellor not giving orders, as he ought, to the clerks to call over the rolls upon any question offered by a member and seconded by others) a certain member, in answer to a discourse made by the Earl of Roxburgh, told the house he remembred very well what a noble lord (meaning his lordship) in the last session of Parliament in such a parallel case when a vote was refused to a considerable number of members demanding it, was pleased to express himself thus:

'that if the nation was to be so treated he knew no way to be taken but to demand the vote with sword in hand.' And [continues the member] I cannot see but the encroachment upon the liberties of the house is as great now as then. And if such measures were allowable and necessary then, they are certainly so still. To avoid which, and the pushing matters to the last extremity, I move the vote may be stated, 'approve the resolve or not', and if I am seconded in the motion, I will not sit down till the vote be begun.[7]

And the Cavaliers having unanimously seconded the motion, and required the vote, the Court dared not any longer obstruct it, contenting themselves by proposing a previous state of a vote, viz. whether the two resolves should be voted jointly or seperately, the former of which was carried by a great majority. And thereafter the two resolves, as conjoined together, being voted were approven by a vast plurality of voices.[8]

The temper and inclinations of the people were very remarkable on this occasion. For, after the Parliament was that day prorogued, the members that had appeared more eminently in behalf of the resolve were caressed and huzzaed as they passed in the streets, by vast numbers. And the Duke of Hamilton was after that manner convoyed from the Parliament-house to the Abbey, and nothing was to be seen or heard that night but jollity, mirth and an universal satisfaction and approbation of what was done, and that by people of all ranks and degrees. This, you may be sure, did much exalt the Cavaliers, to see themselves, from being a poor, despised, oppressed party, become so powerful as to carry such a material point in Parliament and gain the love and good wishes of the nation for so doing. This, I say, did much encourage them, and induce them to renew their assurances of continuing faithful in defence of the monarchy and [the] country.

But to return to the Parliament. The Courtiers now perceiving they could do nothing unless they divided the Cavaliers and the Duke of Queensberry's friends, resolved to throw a bone amongst them that should set them together by the ears. The eighth of August being appointed for nominating commissioners to treat with England (of which more hereafter), several motions were made on that head, and the house was proceeding upon it. But the Lord Belhaven, in a long discourse, left the matter in hand and gave a full account of the plot. And having by this means spent so much of the day that it was impossible for the house to reassume and finish the former debate, Mr Fletcher of Salton (to give the Court a Rowland for their Oliver)[9] spoke to this purpose: that he was sorry the debate had been interrupted, but since the plot and proceedings of the English House of Lords had been mentioned, he was of opinion the house could not pass it by without taking it into consideration. And he having thereafter exposed the encroachments of the House of Lords on the freedom of this nation by presuming to judge of what they termed 'a Scotch conspiracy', as the greatest step that ever was made towards asserting England's dominion over the Scots crown, he hoped the house would show its resentment of it. And for that end presented the following resolve:

> Resolved. That the House of Lords address to the queen in relation to the nomination of their successor to our crown, and their examination of the plot, in so far as it concerned Scotland and Scotsmen, was an undue intermeddling with our concerns and an encroachment upon the honour, sovereignty and independency of this nation. And that the proceedings of the House of Commons were not like those of good subjects to the queen and good neighbours to us.

Though the Earl of Roxburgh, the Lord Belhaven and Baily of Jerviswood, and many more of the Courtiers, were amongst those that were bespattered by this plot, and would willingly all of them have prosecuted the authors of it to the utmost extremity, yet durst they by no means consent to this resolve, because it loaded, and was levelled against their superior powers, the peers of England. And therefore they opposed it with all their might.[10] But the matter was so hotly handled, and the injustice, incroachment and usurpation of the House of Lords so clearly proven, and the necessity of resenting the same (lest in a few years the English should pretend their dominion and power over us was prescribed) so effectually represented, that when it was put to the vote, the first branch, with relation to the Lords, was approven by a great majority.[11] But the other branch, concerning the Commons, was rejected, many being of opinion it would have been an undue intermeddling in English concerns for the Scots Parliament to declare its opinion whether the English were in the right or the wrong to the queen, as Queen of England, and below the Scots Parliament to return them thanks for not invading the rights and liberties of Scotland. This clause was not much valued by the

Cavaliers, since the only design of inserting it was to cajole the House of Commons—at that time on very bad terms with the House of Lords.[12] But the kind reception the other branch met with very much humbled the Courtiers, for they knew not what apology to make to their masters, the English Lords. And now perceiving they had and would be still baffled in all their other designs, they would have blessed their stars could they have been so happy as to obtain some subsidies and prorogue the Parliament upon it. But no sooner was that motion made, than the Act of Security was set in opposition to it, and afterwards (in imitation of an English custom called *tacking*[13]) presented as a clause to the Cess Act.[14] And the Court perceiving that the first would not pass without the second, proposed, and the other party agreed, that the Act of Security first, and then the act for a subsidy, should have a first reading, that both should lie on the table until the Commissioner received instructions from the queen concerning the former, and, that being done, the house might reassume the debate.[15]

And now I must tell you, that the Courtiers, being all along perswaded of their power to carry through the succession, with a few limitations granted · in lieu thereof, had not made any demands, or required instructions, concerning the Act of Security. But now that they were fully satisfied of their mistake they were obliged to inform the queen that, their measures being quite broke, matters were come to that height she must allow her Commissioner to grant the royal assent[16] to the Act of Security, or resolve to prorogue the Parliament without obtaining money to pay her troops. The queen and her ministers of England, considering what a noise these animosities betwixt her two kingdoms would make in the world, thought it better to satisfy the desires of the people by allowing that act the royal assent, than, by refusing it, to increase the divisions and be obliged to disband the army. And thereupon, the Commissioner having acquainted the house that he had obtained the queen's consent to pass the Act of Security into a law, it was soon read, approven and touched with the royal scepter. But the Marquis of Annandale having, in a former sessions [*sic*], protested against that clause in the said act, which secluded the king or queen of England in such cases, and without such concessions as were therein particularly specified, and being then adhered to by the Earls of Crawford, Lauderdale, Leven, Kintore and Hyndford, the Lord Elphinstone, William Morison of Prestongrange, Sir Gilbert Elliot of Minto, Archibald Douglass of Cavers, Mr Francis Montgomery of Giffin and Sir James Campbell of Auchinbreck, barons; Sir Patrick Johnston, Walter Stuart and Hugh Montgomery, burrows; they did all again renew their protestation against the said clause.[17]

After this the Parliament granted the queen six months cess, payable in twelve months time, and then went upon the report of the committee appointed last sessions for examining the accounts of the publick funds. In the mean time several good laws were presented as overtures, such as an act for a further representation of the state of barons in regard of the late increase of peers, an act for freedom of voting in Parliament excluding all officers of the army and others any ways concerned in Her Majesty's revenue from electing or being elected members of Parliament and three or four other good laws for regulating abuses, but none of them were finished this sessions.[18]

It was a great pity this Parliament did not proceed to name the commissioners for treating with England, which was a necessary consequence of the resolve. It was often moved, and, as I observed before, once so far advanced that a day was set apart for the same.[19] But the misfortune was the Cavaliers could not agree among themselves,[20] and this occasioned its being wholly put off this sessions. But had the two Dukes of Hamilton and Athol been prevailed upon to lay aside their picques, and allowed the Duke of Queensberry and the Earl of Seafield to have been two of the number, their friends were willing to have joined with the Cavaliers in all the rest, by which means there would have been twenty-two of the twenty-four treaters on their side and party. But the two dukes, notwithstanding all the solicitations and arguments used by their friends to the contrary would not hear of it, but vowed and protested if it were done they would never more concern themselves. So that the Cavaliers, to satisfy those two persons' ambitious designs, and in compliance with their private animosities and quarrels, were constrained to lay aside the nomination during this session though they plainly saw they would never again have such an opportunity of placing honest men in it. The Parliament, having thus gone through the most considerable affairs before them, was prorogued on the twenty-eighth of August 1704.

Immediately after, the Courtiers went away to London where the Marquis of Tweedale was made Chancellor, the Earls of Seafield and Roxburgh Secretaries, the Earl of Rothes Privy Seal, the Earl of Cromarty Justice General, Mr Baily of Jerviswood Treasurer Depute, the Earl of Selkirk, Lord Belhaven and Sir John Home Lords of the Treasury, and Sir W[illiam]. Hamilton of Whit[e]law Justice Clerk (but he lived not to enjoy that office many months, and was succeeded by Adam Cockburn of Ormistoun).

The first of these [Hamilton of Whitelaw] was bred a lawyer, and, after the Revolution, raised to the bench upon account of his whiggery and disloyalty. He soon displayed a froward, haughty mind. Betwixt man and man, wherein he had no particular concern, he was just, but extremely partial where his friend or his own politicks interfered. He had a sound, solid judgment, but all his actions were accompanied with so much pride, vanity, ill nature and severity that he was odious to every body. He gloried in his malice to the royal family and was a great promoter of the Hanoverian succession.[21]

People were generally well satisfied that he slipt the head, but they had small reason to brag of the change, for the other [Cockburn of Ormistoun] was a zealous Revolutioner and bigotted Presbyterian, which recommended him to King William. He was a man of good understanding and wanted not abundance of application to business, but of so hot, virulent, turbulent and domineering a temper that he was uneasy even to his own party. Of all that were concerned in the government there was none equalled him in vindictive persecution of all that he thought enemies to the established government of either church or state, having upon that score regard for neither sex, age or quality, but, Jehu like, drove always most furiously on, and by these means preserved his interest at Court [by] serving as a scarecrow to terrify others.[22]

A new commission of Council was likewise sent down, by which most of the Cavaliers and all the Duke of Queensberry's friends were cashiered and the Council entirely made up of their own gang. And thus was the government lodged in the hands of a sett of men that had nothing to recommend them besides their cheerful concurring with the designed ruin of their native country, and that by deserting and betraying, under trust, those by whom, as above narrated, they were commissioned and sent to London - contrary to their most sacred oaths and solemn vows, all rules of honour and common notions of integrity and ingenuity. But few and evil were their days. And indeed they behaved themselves as if they had known so much from the beginning, and were resolved to make best use of their time. For it is not to be imagined how much they were exalted, and how arbitrarily they demeaned themselves.

After the posts and employments were, as above, disposed of, all the Courtiers, excepting the two Secretaries, the Earls of Seafield and Roxburgh, returned to Scotland and took upon them the administration of affairs, in which they not only disobliged many, but gained the contempt of all the world by their indiscreet, haughty behaviour and the frequent blunders they daily committed, especially the Marquis of Tweedale, who was altogether incapable to exercise his office. Now the people of England began to enquire into the state of Scotland, they saw the Marquis of Tweedale and his party were so insignificant that they were trampled upon and despised through the whole nation. Yet nevertheless the Lord Godolphin favoured them because their scheme for settling the succession by the concession of a few deluding limitations would, as he thought, be safest for England, and afterwards easily repealed by a subsequent Parliament if once the monarch were fixed on the throne. But the Dukes of Queensberry and Argyle, on the other side, applyed themselves with so much success to the Whigg lords (now the prevailing party in England)[23] that they undertook for them.

The two dukes represented to them that the Duke of Queensberry had been laid aside for no crime, and no reason given, but what testified [to] his firmness and resolution in opposing every thing that was disagreeable and inconvenient to England. That the Marquis of Tweedale and his party had been zealous promoters of the Act of Security, both in framing it in Parliament and afterwards in procuring the royal assent to it. That they were so insignificant they could do nothing, but granting they should prevail, and carry the Succession by these limitations, of what dangerous consequence must even that prove, since thereby a great part of the chief means England had to continue Scotland under its obedience was removed and perhaps never to be recovered! These and the like considerations had the desired effect with the Whigg lords, who prevailed so far with Queen Anne and her ministers, as to lay aside this moteley ministry in Scotland (as they termed it in England)[24] and lodge the government again in the duke's hands.

Since I have made mention of the Duke of Argyle, and he is to make a great figure in what follows, it will not be amiss to say somewhat more particularly of him. John, Duke of Argyle, succeeded his father not only in his estate, honours and employments, but likewise in his lewdness and disloyalty, and, if it was possible, exceeded him in them both. He was not, strictly speaking, a man of sound understanding and judgment. For all his natural endowments were sullied with too much impetuosity, passion and positiveness, and his sense rather lay in a sudden flash of wit than a solid conception and reflexion. Yet, nevertheless, he might well enough pass as a very well accomplished gentleman. He was extremely forward in effecting what he aimed at and designed, which he owned and promoted above board, being altogether free of the least share of dissimulation, and his word was so sacred that one might assuredly depend on it. His head ran more upon the camp than the court, and it would appear nature had dressed him up accordingly, being altogether incapable of the servile dependency and flattering insinuations requisite in the last, and endowed with that cheerful, lively temper and personal valour necessary in the other. In Scotland he affected and gained the leading of the presbyterians, as his father had done before him, and was upon that and other accounts a very significant member.[25]

The great difficulty and question at London was [over] what measures were to be taken to make the new-designed ministry successful. They foresaw the other party, when laid aside, would oppose them. And being convinced that it was impossible to carry the succession in Scotland unless England and she were on better terms, resolved to authorize the queen to set a treaty on foot and nominate and appoint commissioners to meet and treat with those of Scotland for that effect.[26] And accordingly an act for that purpose was framed and passed in Parliament, but withal so imperious and haughty that the like treatment was never given by one nation to another. For in the very act itself they direct the Scots Parliament after what manner the Scots commissioners were to be chosen, expressly prohibiting their own commissioners (whom they allowed the queen to name) to meet and treat with those of Scotland unless the Parliament of Scotland did allow the queen the naming and appointing of them. And further to frighten the Scots into a compliance, they declare all Scotsmen to be aliens and incapable to enjoy the liberties and privileges of Englishmen, prohibit the importation of Scots cattle and linen cloth into England and exportation of horses and arms into Scotland and ordain that ships should be appointed to disturb and molest the Scots trade; with several other prohibiting clauses, all which were to take place about eight months thereafter, viz. Christmas 1705. Then they addressed the queen that she would grant the royal assent to the abovementioned act and give orders to send down troops to the borders and put the towns of Newcastle, Tinmouth, Berwick, Carlisle and Hull in a posture of defence.[27]

This was a strange preamble and introduction towards an agreement. First to propose an amicable treaty to remove grudges and animosities betwixt the two nations, but at the same time threaten the Scots with their power and vengeance if they did not comply with what was demanded of them. And truly all true Scotsmen looked upon it as a gross invasion on their liberties and sovereignty, and an insolent behaviour towards a free and independent people. And it was odd so wise a nation as England should have been guilty of so unpolitick a step, for they could not have proposed a more effectual way to irritate the Scots nation (when I say Scots, I exclude the Courtiers and mercenary members of Parliament from the category), and I look upon it as the first rise and cause of the general, I may say universal, aversion that appeared afterward to the Union. Nor ever could I hear a satisfying reason given for it, saving once I was assured by a pretty good hand that the English would not have presumed or ventured upon it had not our statesmen proposed it to them as what would effectually frighten us to yield to what was demanded by them. Vile, ungrateful, rapacious vultures, thus to tear their own vitals! Little did they consider the rock upon which they ran the queen when, by advising her to consent to a deed depriving her subjects of her protection, and declaring them aliens, she at the same time absolved them of their allegiance to her. Especially since it was a received, orthodox maxim at and since the Revolution that protection and allegiance are reciprocal.[28] Or it seems they had not advised with the learned Bacon or Coke,[29] who would have taught them it was the constant unanimous opinion of all the judges and lawyers of England since the union of the two crowns that the *post nati*, that is those born in the other kingdom after the accession of the same monarch to be king of both kingdoms were, by the laws of nature and customs of all nations, freemen, and had an uncontroverted natural right to enjoy the privileges of the natural free-born subjects of the other kingdom. However, the English stood at nothing to promote their design, and were encouraged by having so many Scotsmen to assist them in it.

Now the time the Parliament was to meet approached, the abovementioned alterations in the ministry were effected. The Marquis of Tweedale, the Earls of Rothes, Roxburgh and Selkirk, the Lord Belhaven, Baily of Jerviswood and Mr Johnstoun were cashiered.[30] The Duke of Argyll declared Commissioner to the next Parliament, the Earl of Seafield reinstalled Chancellor, the Marquis of Annandale and the Earl of Leven made Secretaries of State, the Duke of Queensberry Privy Seal and Sir James Murray of Philiphaugh Register. And all the Councellors that were laid aside by the last ministry (except Sir James Foulis of Colingtoun[31] and Mr Lockhart of Carnwath), restored.

Now that we have discussed this sett of ministers, let me compleat the characters of the leading men of that party by acquainting you that the Earl of Haddington was entirely abandoned to Whiggish and Commonwealth principles, and one of Cockburn of Ormistoun's beloved pupils. He much affected, and his talent lay in a buffoon sort of wit and raillery. [He] was hot, proud, vain and ambitious.[32]

John, Lord Belhaven, was a man that could not be fixed to any party or principle, being a mighty projector and still plodding [sic] how to advance himself, and for that end steered his course to many opposite shores. By which means he became distrusted by both Cavaliers and Revolutioners. It was avarice and ambition moved him to desert the Country party and go over with the Marquis of Tweedale. But as soon as he found them going down the hill he left them altogether and returned to his old friends, though, I am afraid, there is too much reason to believe he acted a double part. In Parliament he affected long, premeditated harrangues, wherein, having a prodigious memory, he used to be very full in citing such passages of history as made for what he advanced, driving parallels betwixt preceeding and present times. He was a well-accomplished gentleman in most kinds of learning, well acquainted with the constitution of this kingdom, very dextrous in chusing the proper seasons and means of managing a debate in Parliament, and a forward, useful member of in a party.[33]

The Cavaliers applyed to the Marquis of Tweedale and his party (who were henceforward called the *Squadrone Volante*[34] from their pretending to act by themselves and cast the balance of the contending parties in Parliament), that they would again unite with them in defence of their country.[35] But they positively refused to treat or concert with the Cavaliers, resenting to the greatest height the disappointments they met with last year.[36]

The Duke of Queensberry did not think fit to come down to the beginning of this session of Parliament, being desirous to see how affairs would go before he ventured himself in a country where he was generally hated and abhorred. And therefore he sent the Duke of Argyle down as Commissioner, using him as the monkey did the cat in pulling out the hot roasted chesnuts. The Duke of Hamilton, before the Parliament met, had been often conversing, and in private, with the Earl of Mar, and a great familiarity and confidence appeared to be betwixt them.[37]

John, Earl of Mar, was descended from, and the representative of, a family noted for its loyalty on many occasions both ancient and modern, and much beholden to the bounty of the crown. It is true indeed his father embarqued with the Revolution, but if all be true that is reported, his lordship gave a particular, though fatal, sign of his remorse and repentance.[38] This present gentleman's fortune being in bad circumstances when he came to age, he devoted himself to the Duke of Queensberry, and the Court measures, to which he always stuck close, till, in the year 1704, he headed such of the Duke of Queensberry's friends as opposed the Marquis of Tweedale and his party's designs, and that with so much art and dissimulation that he gained the favour of all the Tories, and was by many of them esteemed an honest man and well inclined to the royal family. Certain it is he vowed and protested so much many a time, but no sooner was the Marquis of Tweedale and his party dispossessed than he returned as the dog to the vomit and promoted all the Court of England's measures with the greatest zeal imaginable. He was not a man of a good *coram vobis*,[39] and was a very bad, though very frequent, speaker in Parliament. But his great talent lay in the cunning management of his designs and projects, in which it was hard to find him out when he aimed to be *incognito*. And thus he shewed himself to be a man of good sense but bad morals.[40]

The Duke of Hamilton no doubt expected, and was in hopes, to have drawn him over from the Duke of Queensberry. But his lordship found a way to insinuate himself so much into his grace, and bubbled him so far, that I have good reason to attribute his grace's appearing with less zeal and forwardness in this ensuing than in former Parliaments, to some agreement that passed betwixt them two.[41] And particularly I was told by a person of knowledge and integrity that he knew the Duke of Hamilton did promise not to oppose the queen's affairs, and chiefly her having the nomination of the commissioners to the then designed treaty, provided he himself should be one of the number; which was agreed to. But more of this hereafter.

Notes

1. *APS*, xi. 125–6: 11 July 1704. The queen's letter insists on the need to secure the Protestant succession but nowhere mentions the house of Hanover.
2. Sitting.
3. *Seafield Letters*, p. 154: Earl of Leven to Godolphin, Edinburgh, 18 July [1704], suggests that the Court party was so perplexed by this resolution that it was still in confusion on 17 July, when it passed with a large majority.
4. *APS*, xi. 127; *Crossrigg Diary*, pp. 138–9: 13 July 1704.
5. James VI and I in 1603.
6. Commissioner for Kincardineshire and a Lord of Session; *PS*, i. 236.
7. The member in question may have been GL himself.
8. *APS*, xi. 127–8; *Crossrigg Diary*, pp. 139–40: 17 July 1704.
9. Two of the semi-mythical heroes of the medieval *chansons de geste*.
10. *Crossrigg Diary*, pp. 151–4: 8 Aug. 1704.
11. *APS*, xi. 152.
12. The Tory majority in the Commons had been angered by the Lords' (where there was a narrow Whiggish majority) defeat of the 2nd occasional conformity bill (a measure designed to exclude Protestant Nonconformists from public office) in December 1703, and in April 1704 Parliament had had to be prorogued to break the deadlock between the two houses over the *Ashby v White* case (E. Cruickshanks, 'Ashby v. White: the case of the men of Aylesbury, 1701–4', in, *Party and Management in Parliament, 1660–1784*, ed. C. Jones (New York, 1984), pp. 87–103).
13. This was when the Commons deliberately amalgamated a supply bill, which the Lords traditionally did not amend, with an extraneous

bill (such as the third occasional conformity bill in December 1704). Thus the ministry of the day would be forced to support the passage of the measure through the Lords or lose the supply attached to it.

14. GL's chronology is awry here. The debate he is referring to in fact took place on 25 July, for which see, *Crossrigg Diary*, pp. 145–8.

15. *APS*, xi. 130: 3 August 1704; HMC *Laing*, ii. 83–5: memorial by Tweeddale, Seafield and Johnston, 26 July 1704.

16. The monarch at this time still retained the right to veto legislation of which s/he disapproved by witholding the royal assent.

17. *APS*, xi. 70, 133: 26 July 1703 and 5 August 1704.

18. *APS*, xi. 133, 174, 197, 204, App. p. 59.

19. *APS*, xi. 129: 21 July 1704.

20. Nor, indeed, with their allies: HMC *Portland*, iv. 121: News Letter, Edinburgh, 24 Aug. 1704.

21. *PS*, i. 327–8.

22. Cf. *PS*, i. 131; *DNB*, xi. 177.

23. The English general election of May 1705 was a triangular contest between the Whigs, ministerialist Tories, and High Tories or 'Tackers'. The Whigs gained substantially, and though they did not enjoy a majority in the Commons were able to capitalise on the ministerialist Tories' inability to get legislation past their embittered High Tory colleagues without Whig support.

24. I.e. a ministry composed of rival parties or factions.

25. Cf. P. Dickson, *Red John of the Battles; John, 2nd Duke of Argyll and 1st Duke of Greenwich* (1973). It is worth recalling that GL had known Argyll since they were both children, and considered him a personal friend.

26. *Seafield Letters*, p. 49: Seafield to Godolphin, Edinburgh, 8 June 1705.

27. GL's account of the legislation passed by the English Parliament is somewhat garbled, but preserves its basic thrust: *Journals of the House of Commons* (henceforth *CJ*), xiv. 477: 11 Jan. 1705; HMC, *Manuscripts of the House of Lords. Volume VI, 1704–1706*, vi. 230–2: 16 Dec. 1704. It is not clear from the wording if the English Parliament did mean to stipulate, as GL states here, that only Scottish Commissioners nominated by the queen were to be acceptable negotiating partners (see clause 1, p. 230).

28. A reference to the Hobbesian dictum: 'The obligation of subjects to the soveraign, is understood to last as long, and no longer, than the power lasteth, by which he is able to protect them' (*Hobbes's Leviathan. Reprinted from the Edition of 1651*, repr. (Oxford, 1943), p. 170).

29. Lord Chancellor Bacon (1561–1626) and Sir Edward Coke (1552–1634), the touchstones of eighteenth-century Common Law jurisprudence.
30. *Seafield Letters*, p. 52: Seafield to Godolphin, Edinburgh, 12 June 1705.
31. Commissioner for Edinburghshire and Lord Redford of the Court of Session; *PS*, i. 261.
32. Cf. *DNB*, xxiv. 212–13.
33. Cf. *DNB*, xxiv. 197–8.
34. The flying squadron; a sardonically military simile.
35. *Lockhart Letters*, p. 18: GL to Hamilton, Dryden, 12 Apr. 1705.
36. *Baillie*, p. 98: Roxburgh to Baillie, Floors, 28 May 1705; p. 121: Baillie to Roxburgh, [Edinburgh] 8 Sept. 1705.
37. And the Earl of Seafield: *Seafield Letters*, p. 46: Seafield to Godolphin, Edinburgh, 24 May 1705.
38. This reference is obscure, since it seems certain that the 5th Earl was solidly behind the Revolution at the time of his death: P. Hopkins, *Glencoe and the End of the Highland War* (Edinburgh, 1986), p. 137.
39. Presence.
40. There is no modern biography of Mar, but see: E. Gregg, 'The Jacobite career of John Earl of Mar', in, *Ideology and Conspiracy: Aspects of Jacobitism, 1689–1759*, ed. E. Cruickshanks (Edinburgh, 1982), for an excellent sketch of the man and his career.
41. HMC *Portland*, iv. 171: James Graham to Harley, Preston, 30 Mar. 1705.

[The Parliamentary Session of 1705]

At the opening of this session of Parliament, which met the twenty-eighth of June 1705, there appeared three different parties, viz: the Cavaliers, the *Squadrone*, or outed Courtiers, and the present Courtiers—which last consisted of true-blue presbyterians and Revolutioners and such as enjoyed pensions and civil or military posts. The Duke of Queensberry, as I said before, pretended sickness, and [made] one excuse after another to avoid being present at the beginning of the session, that he might see how affairs were like to go and whether or not he might venture himself in Scotland. And likewise let the world see that though the Duke of Argyle was Commissioner, yet he was not able to oppose the Cavaliers unless he [Queensberry] came down and by his presence and influence assisted and supported him. And indeed, while he was absent, such of his friends and followers who were left to follow their own inclinations and join the Cavaliers last sessions, still continued in that way. And so the Court measures were baffled in every thing that came before the Parliament. But no sooner was his grace amongst them than, one way or another, he perswaded them every one to return again to his beck and act as he proposed and directed, though against their own inclinations and judgments.[1] And here I cannot but wonder at the influence he had over men of sense, quality and estates. Men that had, at least many of them, no dependence upon him, and yet were so deluded as to serve his ambitious designs, contrary to the acknowledged dictates of their own conscience. For at the same time they knew and owned they were in the wrong and would not, some of them, stand to say that though they voted so and so themselves, yet they wished the Cavaliers might carry all the votes.[2]

This being matter of fact, clearly demonstrates the Cavaliers were mistaken in their measures and politicks when they postponed the more material affairs and trifled away the beginning of the Parliament on some acts that related to trade and other matters of no great importance. For had they immediately called for the queen's letter (which, and likewise the Commissioner's and Chancellor's speeches, chiefly insisted on the necessity and advantage of treating with England) in order to return an answer to it, the treaty would have naturally fallen under consideration.[3] And then, the Duke of Queensberry's friends and party not being gone off from them, they might easily have either rejected it altogether, or at least framed and clogged it as they pleased, and chosen such members as they had a mind to be commissioners for meeting and treating with the commissioners from England. Besides, I have always observed if anything for the country's interest was to be attempted in a Scots Parliament it must be in the beginning of the session, for in a little time the zeal and fervour of the members go off, they become weary with attendance and steal home to their country houses. And lastly, the Court, who had the purse and the power, were still gaining upon the Country, who has [sic] no arguments or perswasives to induce members to stand firm and attend, besides those of generosity and honour, which, though indeed the strongest of all motives, have not a like effect with all men.

It is to no purpose to spend so much time as to narrate the particulars of what passed whilst the Parliament had the state of the nation, in relation to its trade, under consideration. It is sufficient to say that several good acts were presented for that purpose, some of which passed and others were rejected in the house, and that the Court, according to their laudable custom, opposed them all.[4]

It is fit, however, particularly to mention that a Council of Trade was appointed with power to put the laws in relation to trade in execution. And it was recommended to them to bring the export and import of the nation to a balance, and lay the same before the house next sessions.[5] This indeed was very necessary, for the merchants met with no encouragement, and trade was carried on without any regard to the methods prescribed by law and the interest of the nation. There were likewise several proposals made for supplying the nation with money by a paper credit, particularly one offered by Dr Hugh Chamberlain and another by John Law. The first had, with his projects in England, broke,[6] and spent so great a part of his own money that he was necessitated to fly out of that kingdom.[7] The other was the son of a goldsmith in Edinburgh, who, being left a small estate which he had several years ago spent, had ever since lived by gaming and sharping, and, being a cunning fellow and expert in all manner of debaucheries, found a way quickly to get into my Lord Duke of Argyle's favour. And in confidence of his and the Squadrone (with whom he was very intimate) their assistance, he presented a very plausible scheme, and the Court and the Squadrone (except some that were monied men) espoused the same because it was so contrived that in process of time it brought all the estates of the kingdom to depend on the government.[8] But the house rejected the motion, and passed a resolve that the establishing any kind of paper credit so as to oblige it to pass, was an unproper expedient for this nation.[9]

This being over, let us now come to the more materiall proceedings of the Parliament. About twenty days after the Parliament met, the Cavaliers thought it proper, come of other things what will, to prevent the succession's being established. For the Court's chief design was to procure an act for a treaty with England.[10] Yet they designed to pass a few inconsiderable limitations, that in case they were disappointed in their designs concerning the act of treaty they might reassume the affair of the succession according to the old proverb, *catch geese if they cannot gazelings*.[11] The Cavaliers, I say, to prevent this after-game, had recourse to the measure they took last sessions by proposing the same resolve, viz.:

> Resolved. That the Parliament will not proceed to the
> nomination of a successor till we have had a previous treaty
> with England in relation to our commerce, and other

concerns with that nation. And further resolved. That this Parliament will proceed to make such limitations and conditions of government, for the rectification of our constitution, as may secure the liberty, religion and independency of the kingdom before they proceed to the said nomination.[12]

The Court and the Squadrone both united against this resolve although it advanced their respective projects, viz. the treaty and limitations, for the Squadrone were no ways now inclined for the Union, and both favoured and promoted the limitations only in so far as they might serve to advance the succession.[13] However, the Cavaliers insisted vigorously upon it, and by the assistance of the Duke of Queensberry's friends carryed it by a great majority.[14]

It was odd that the Marquis of Montrose could be so far seduced as not only to vote, but even reason with heat and passion, against this resolve.[15] But why should I say that it was odd? What could be expected from him who had ratified the Presbyterian government [of the Kirk] and Revolution in the first session, and in the last went every length with Johnstoun the Register, who was the son of the chief persecutor of his glorious great-grandfather,[16] and himself head of the Hanoverian, Republican, Whiggish faction in Scotland, and lastly, had several times of late received the sacrament from the presbyterian ministers, which, in honest men's opinion, inferred necessarily his owning the validity of their excommunication of his great-grandfather? For, if they had a power of administring sacraments, it must likewise be allowed that they had a power of excommunication.

When he first appeared in the world he had enough to recommend him to the love and affection of the nation [simply] by being the representative of that noble, loyal and worthy family. And his interest increased to so great a degree by his good behaviour after he came from his travels and in the first sessions of this Parliament, that, had he continued in these measures, he had the fairest game to play of any young man that ever was in Scotland, since undoubtedly he would have been acknowledged and followed as the head and leader of the Cavaliers. But being of an easy, mean-spirited temper, governed by his mother[17] and her relations (the family of Rothes) and extremely covetous, he could not resist the first temptation the Court threw in his way, and from the time he first engaged with them he adhered closely to their interest, and with the greatest vehemency prosecuted their measures notwithstanding all the friends of his father's family remonstrated to him against it, and that he lost the esteem and favour of them and the Cavaliers. He was a man of good understanding, yet was led by his nose by a set of men whom he far surpassed and never, in all his by-past life, did one material action that was prudent and discreet. His courage, upon some certain accounts, was much questioned, but his unsincerity and falseness allowed by all.[18]

But to return to the Parliament. The day this resolve past, the inclinations of the people were seen by their mirth and rejoicings. On the twentieth of July the Marquis of Tweedale presented a draught of a letter, in answer to the queen's, which was read next *sederunt*, but a motion being made that the house should, preferable to the said letter, take the acts in relation to trade under consideration, it was agreed to.[19] It was unaccountable in the Squadrone to be promoters of such a piece of strange stuff, and to expose their party by pushing what they knew was not agreeable to the house, and that it was certain the Court would join with the Cavaliers in opposing every motion that came from them. Their design was to shew that though the resolve against the succession had passed in the house, it was none of their fault and that they had still no other view but to obtain the same. The letter contained little save intimations of their readiness to establish the same successor with England, begging Her Majesty would grant them such limitations on her successors as were necessary for that purpose, and, lastly, assuring Her Majesty that, if this were once done, they would cheerfully set about the work.

This being over, the Cavaliers inclined to proceed upon the limitations, proposing thereby, first, to obstruct the succession's being established in case the projected treaty should fail, for they knew the Court would not grant them the royal assent, and that the succession would be rejected; next, to make the best they could of an ill bargain by clogging the monarch, in case the house of Hanover should come to the crown; and lastly, to ingratiate themselves with the people, who groaned exceedingly under the oppression of England and were extremely fond of every thing that seemed to free them of it.[20] And a motion being made to grant a first reading to an act and commission for a treaty with England, the Duke of Hamilton in opposition thereto moved that the house would proceed to the enacting of limitations. And a vote being stated in these terms: 'proceed to consider the act for a treaty, or limitations?', the latter carried.[21] And in the subsequent *sederunts* of Parliament several acts for that purpose were presented (in which the Squadrone joined against the Court), the most considerable of which are as follows. Act for Regulating the Chusing [of] the Officers of State; enacting that from and after Her Majesty's decease without heirs of her body all officers of state and Privy Counsellors, and Lords of Session, should be chosen and appointed by the Parliament, and in case of the decease of any of them during the vacancy of Parliament the office to be supplyed by one nominated by the Council, who should continue in the same till next session of Parliament, and that all the said officers of state and Privy Counsellors should be accountable to the Parliament. The Court offered a clause giving the power of chusing officers of state, etc (which by this act was solely lodged in the Parliament), to the king, with consent of Parliament, which was carried by a vote. But a motion that there should be three Presidents of the Session, to preside *per vices* each two months, was rejected. And then the whole act was approven.[22]

Then an act for a triennial Parliament was offered in these terms:

> Our sovereign lady, being willing to restore to her ancient kingdom their ancient custom and right to frequency of Parliaments, does therefore, with the advice and consent of Parliament, statute and ordain that there shall be a new

Parliament called and indicted to meet, sit and act. And that once every third year, after the first of August, in the year _____. And Her Majesty does hereby declare, with consent aforesaid, that this present Parliament shall not continue and endure any longer than the first of August aforesaid. And this without prejudice of Her Majesty and successor's royal prerogative and power to dissolve Parliaments sooner than the said term of three years, as shall be thought fit. And further, with the advice aforesaid, statutes and ordains that from and after the first day of August aforesaid, no farmer or collector of Her Majesty's customs and excise, or any other branch of her revenue, shall be capable to be a member of Parliament, nor to sit and vote therein, after the date aforesaid. And it shall be a sufficient objection against any member that he is concerned, directly or indirectly, as a farmer or collector, in any part of Her Majesty's revenue, to remove him from his place and vote in Parliament.

The Court saw it was to no purpose to oppose this act. Therefore, being deadly afraid of a new Parliament, they only proposed that this act should not take place during Her Majesty's life. The Cavaliers proposed it should commence immediately, but many members, who were afraid of their own interest to be elected a-new, proposed a medium betwixt the two, viz. that it should take place three years after the date, that is, the first of August 1708, with which the Court, [viewing it] as being the least of two evils, joined and carried it, and then the whole act was approven.[23]

Several other overtures were made that came not the length of being ingrossed into acts. And though the house did approve the abovementioned acts none of them obtained the royal assent, though the Court promised it often to many of the members and thereby wheedled over several to follow the Court in framing the act of treaty, they thinking themselves in a tolerable good state by these acts of limitations, and never imagining the treaty would terminate as it did.[24] But Mr Fletcher of Salton having, in a long discourse, set forth the deplorable state to which this nation was reduced by being subjected to English councils and measures, while one and the same person was king of both kingdoms, did conclude these above-mentioned acts of limitation were not sufficient. And therefore presented a scheme of limitations which he proposed should be ingrossed into an act and taken under the house's consideration. And though they did not pass in the house, yet it will not be amiss to set them down here.[25]

I. That elections shall be made at every Michaelmas head court for a new Parliament every year, to sit the first of November next following, and adjourn themselves from time to time till next Michaelmas. That they chuse their own president and that every thing be determined by balloting in place of voting.

II. That so many lesser barons shall be added to the Parliament as there have been noblemen created since the last augmentation of the number of the barons. And that in all time coming for every nobleman that shall be created there shall be a baron added to the Parliament.

III. That no man have a vote in Parliament but a nobleman or elected member.

IV. That the king shall give the royal assent to all laws offered by the estates, and that the President of the Parliament be impowered by His Majesty to give the royal assent in his absence and have ten pounds sterling a day of salary.

V. That a committee of thirty-one members, of which nine [are] to be a quorum, chosen out of their own number by every Parliament under the king, have the administration of the government, be his Council and accountable to the Parliament, with power, on extraordinary occasions, to call the Parliament together. And that, in the said Council, all things be determined by balloting instead of voting.

VI. That the king, without consent of Parliament, shall not have the power of making peace and war, or that of concluding any treaty with any other state or potentate.

VII. That all places and offices, both civil and military,

and all pensions formerly conferred by our kings shall ever after be given by Parliament.

VIII. That no regiment, or company of horse, foot, or dragoons, be kept on foot, in peace or war, but by consent of Parliament.

IX. That all the fencible men in the nation betwixt sixty and sixteen be armed with bayonets and firelocks, all of a calibre, and continue always provided in such arms, with ammunition suitable.

X. That no general indemnity or pardon for any transgression, shall be valid without consent of Parliament.

XI. That the fifteen senators of the College of Justice shall be incapable of being members of Parliament, or of any other office or any pension but the salary that belongs to their place, to be increased as the Parliament shall think fit. That the office of President shall be in three of their number, to be named by the Parliament, and that there be no Extraordinary Lords, as also that the Lords of the Justice Court shall be distinct from those of the Session and under the same restrictions.

XII. That if any king break in upon any of these conditions of government he shall, by the estates, be declared to have forfeited the crown.

Then he at large insisted on every particular article, demonstrating that the first eight were necessary to prevent English influence over our affairs by rectifying our constitution, the ninth to enable the nation to defend its rights and liberties and the tenth to terrify the ministers of state from presuming to give the king bad advice and doing things contrary to law. And here I must mention that the Earl of Stair having spoke against this scheme, Mr Fletcher, in answer thereto, when he came to justify this article, said it was no wonder his lordship was against it, for had there been such an act his lordship had long ere now been hanged for the advices he gave King James, the murder of Glenco and his conduct since the Revolution.[26] The eleventh, he said, was necessary to preserve the judicatories from corrupt judges, and

added, 'if the twelfth be not approven, sure I am this house must
own they treated King James most barbarously and unjustly'.

Another material point under the consideration of this session
was the plot. The preceding session had addressed the queen to
transmit, against the next sessions, such persons as were
evidences in, and such papers related to, that affair. In the
beginning of the session the Dukes of Hamilton and Athol were
very desirous to prosecute it to the greatest height, but the
Cavaliers were not so forward. Because, first, they were under a
kind of engagement, as above narrated, to the Earl of March and
Sir James Murray of Philiphaugh, that if the Duke of
Queensberry's friends did oppose the Marquis of Tweedale and
his party in the former sessions, not to insist on that affair.
Besides, it would irritate them to so great a degree that many of
them would not concur in opposing the designed act for a treaty
and this would ruine all. Next they were afraid they might well
show their teeth but could not bite, the edge of many people's
indignation against it being blunted by its lying so long dormant.
Had it indeed been entered upon while the horror of it was fresh
in their minds, and whilst the Duke of Queensberry and the other
conspirators were in disgrace and had not the government in their
hands, there were many would have pushed it violently enough.
But the case was altered, and, as matters stood then, they were
afraid they should be baffled in the attempt. But after the Duke of
Queensberry came down and seduced such of his friends as had,
in the last and beginning of this sessions, stood for the Country,
the Cavaliers did not so much oppose the two Dukes' desire of
prosecuting the plotters, but were resolved to stand, as it were,
neutral, till they saw if they and the Squadrone could prove
anything against the contrivers of it.

It being therefore moved that the house might know what
answer the queen had given to the abovementioned address from
the last session,[27] my Lord Commissioner acquainted the house
he had received some of the papers that were before the English
House of Lords, which he had put in my Lord Secretary
Loudoun's hands, and expected the rest in a little time. But when

the house went upon the consideration of these papers they were found to be no more than copies, for none of the principal papers, nor the persons that were evidences and remained in London (such as Sir John Maclean, Mr Keith and others) were sent to Scotland.[28] And those who lived in Scotland, such as Campbell of Glenderruell[29] and Captain Maclean, were sent out of the way, by which it was plain the queen and her ministry did not design a fair and full trial, since the Parliament could not proceed unless the persons that were evidences, and the original papers, were at their command, whereupon to have founded their accusation and proven the same. However, the Dukes of Hamilton and Athol, the Lord Belhaven, Baily of Jerviswood and some others, made several speeches on this subject wherein they vindicated themselves and asserted that the accusation against them, in the discovery of the said pretended plot, was false and calumnious. And the Duke of Athol particularly, in a long discourse, very handsomely narrated the beginning, progress and conclusion of the whole affair, illustrated the design of it, whence it had its rise, and who were the promoters of it, and accused the Duke of Queensberry of endeavouring to give the queen bad impressions of her good subjects [by] producing copies of letters from him to her, affirming the whole Cavaliers were concerned in the plot, or at least enemies to her, and that he had, the better to carry on his design, employed and held correspondence with and furnished passports and money to Frazer, and insisted upon many other particulars which rendered the affair and promoters of it, most odious.[30]

And though his grace did several times term the design (of which he asserted the Duke of Queensberry by name and surname, and several others, to be the authors and abettors) villanous, dishonourable, false and scandalous and not to be tolerated in a well-governed kingdom, yet the Duke of Queensberry and his accomplices made no answer, suffering all these and the like reproachful epithets, being conscious of their own guilt and glad to escape at so easy a rate.[31] And this was all that was done in expiscating that villanous design, in which the lives and fortunes of many of the chief families of the kingdom were levelled at.

Now we come to narrate what was done in relation to the act of treaty. The Earl of Mar in the beginning of this session had presented the draught of an act for appointing commissioners to treat with the commissioners from England upon an union of the two kingdoms of Scotland and England, which lay upon the table till most of the overtures in relation to trade and the limitations were discussed, but, these being now over, was reassumed.[32] Both it and the English act were much of the same nature, both empowering commissioners to meet and treat with one another of an union of the two kingdoms, and restricting them from treating of any alterations of the church government and discipline as established by law in the respective realms. Only, as I said before, the English act gave the nomination of their commissioners to the queen, and even required the same of the Scots, without which they discharged their commissioners to meet and treat. But the draught presented by the Earl of Mar left the power of the nomination blank, and we shall see afterwards how that affair was managed.[33]

Mr Fletcher of Salton, in a pathetick[34] discourse, represented the scurrilous and haughty procedure of the English in this affair and exhorted them to resent this treatment as became Scotsmen, by throwing out the motion of a treaty, until it were proposed in more civil and equal terms, out of the house with indignation.[35] But the house, rejecting the motion, called for the draught and the English act, and both were read. The Cavaliers and Country parties, observing that there was a great inclination in the house to set a treaty on foot, thought it improper to oppose it any longer in general terms, and therefore resolved to endeavour to clog the commission with such restrictions and provisions as should retard the treaty's taking effect. And for that end the Duke of Hamilton presented a clause to be added to the act, in these terms, viz.: 'That the Union to be treated on should no ways derogate from any fundamental laws, ancient privileges, offices, rights, liberties and dignities of this nation.' This the Court vigorously opposed, seeing it secluded them from treating on an entire or incorporating union of which the abolishing our Parliaments and subversion of our constitution was a necessary consequence. And it was this kind of union England designed and desired because it rivetted the Scots in perpetual slavery, depriving them of any legal method to redress themselves of the injuries they might receive from them by keeping them poor and under their chains. On the other hand, the Duke of Queensberry, Earl of Stair and all that were thoroughly on a Revolution foot were inclined the same way because they were conscious of their own guilt, and afraid, some time or other, a Scots Parliament (if reserved even under a federal union) might take them to task and punish them as they deserved. Whereas, if it were out of their power, and the Scots representation stifled and suppressed by the much greater majority of the English representation in one and the same Parliament, they expected to be protected against the just resentments of an injured and exasperated nation.

For these and such reasons, I say, the Court opposed this clause, and the arguments they adduced for rejecting it were to this purpose. That since Scotland and England were under the same sovereign, who did here mediate betwixt her two kingdoms, and that England had given ample powers to their commissioners, it would be unbecoming in Scotland to restrict their commissioners, and inferred a jealousy of Her Majesty. That it might occasion a stop to the treaty, since it was to be believed that England would expect our commissioners should meet and confer with as full powers as theirs. And lastly, [that] there would be no hazard in not restricting our commissioners since it was expressly provided that no matter or point treated of, and agreed to, should take place and be of force, unless it be first reported to and obtain the approbation of the Parliaments of both kingdoms. And that when this report was made, then was the proper time to consider whether they would agree to that scheme of union which the commissioners had projected, or reject it.

To this it was answered, that Scotland and England's being under one sovereign was the reason why this clause was necessary, since woful experience taught us, and it had been often complained of in this house, that our sovereign was under English influence and subject to the councils of her English ministers, who regarded the interest and honour of Scotland no farther than was consistent with that of England. That the adding of this clause could never infer the least mistrust of the queen's inclinations towards her ancient kingdom, since all that could be made of it was that the Scots Parliament, being sensible that the queen was not in a capacity to know the interest and circumstances of Scotland so well as that of England, had taken care to prevent any inconveniencies that might arise from thence. That there were some things so sacred that the least innovation or alteration, far less abrogating or suspending of them, was never to be tampered with, or the subject of any treaty. And the particulars of this clause, such as sovereignty, independency and freedom of the nation, being of this nature, ought to be added, and that England could not take it amiss seeing they themselves had, before they advised with us, restricted their own commissioners from treating on any alteration of the church government of that kingdom.

But whether that had been or not, we were a free, independent people, and had a power to give what instructions, powers and restrictions we pleased to our commissioners. Neither was it to be imagined that England, upon the account of this clause, would refuse to treat, because the very same clause, in the same express words, was inserted in the act of treaty in the reign of King James VI, and to the same purpose in most of the subsequent acts of treaty. And yet neither that king (who would have had good reason to be offended at any disrespect or distrust shown towards him, who was known by the Scots, acquainted with their humours and constitutions and had given signal proofs of his affection to his native country and subjects), nor his successors, nor the Parliament of England, made any scruple upon that account to meet and treat with the commissioners of Scotland.[36]

These and many other arguments were adduced for and against this clause, and the question being put, 'Add the clause or not?', it carried in the negative by a plurality of two voices.[37] And here I must observe and lament the woful fate of this nation, for though it was well known that the house was to be that day upon this grand affair, and the Court had mustered together every individual of their party, yet seven or eight of the Cavaliers and Country parties were absent, and thereby lost this clause, which, had it passed, would have proved a mortal stroke to the Court, they being resolved to have laid aside the treaty of union and prorogued the Parliament, by which means the nation had been free of that fatal thraldom to which it is since subjected. Nor must I omit that the Earl of Aberdeen turned tail to the Cavaliers in this important affair. It is not easy for me to determine the cause, but it is matter of fact that his lordship did not behave, on many occasions during this session, as might have been expected of one of his principles and circumstances, and (though this is not the proper place) could not be perswaded to be present at, and assisting against, the Union in the next sessions. Nay, the Cavaliers at last, being informed of his inclinations towards it, were glad to compound with him to stay away.[38]

This being over, another clause was presented in these terms:

> Provided always, that the said commissioners shall not go forth of this kingdom to enter into any treaty with those to be appointed for England, until there be an act passed by the Parliament of England, rescinding that clause in the English act by which it was enacted that the subjects of Scotland shall be adjudged and taken as aliens after the twenty-fifth of December 1705.

The Cavaliers enlarged upon this clause, as necessary to vindicate the honour of the nation from the injustice of the English in that act, believing, if it were added, the English would not comply with it, and so the treaty come to nothing.

The Courtiers, upon the same grounds, opposed it. But, observing it took with the house, they did not presume to do it openly but by a consequential motion to this purpose: that the clause should be approven, though not, as was proposed, be ingrossed into the body of the act for a treaty, but a resolve of the house pass, that after the foresaid act is finished the house will immediately proceed to consider whether the clause should be by a particular act, or by an order of the house. And the question being stated: 'Add the clause to the act, or by a separate way?', the latter branch carryed it.[39]

And now the Court thought themselves secure of having a treaty, for if the clause was turned into an act at the close of the session (when they had no more to require of the Parliament at this time) they might grant the royal assent to the act of treaty, and refuse it to this, as they should be directed from England. And in case the clause was turned into an order of the house, then they might dissolve the Parliament (their lawyers assuring them that no orders of a Parliament were valid and in force after its dissolution), by which means the act impowering commissioners to treat remained and the order ceased, and so the treaty might go on whether the Parliament of England did or did not repeal the act, which was so unjust in relation to Scotland, and notwithstanding the Parliament of Scotland did so expressly require it. But before the vote was stated upon the act for a treaty, the Duke of Athol entered his protestation in these terms:

> In regard that by an English act of Parliament, made in the last sessions thereof, entituled, An Act for the Effectual Securing England From the Dangers That may Arise From Several Acts Lately Passed in Scotland, the subjects of this kingdom are adjudged aliens, born out of the allegiance of the queen, as Queen of England, after the twenty-fifth day of December 1705, I do protest for my self, and in the name and behalf of all such as shall adhere to this my protestation, that, for saving the honour and interest of Her Majesty, as Queen of this kingdom, and maintaining and preserving the undoubted rights and privileges of her subjects, no act for a treaty with England ought to pass in this house unless a clause be added thereto prohibiting and discharging the commissioners that may be nominated and appointed for carrying on the said treaty to depart the kingdom in order thereto, until the said act be repealed and rescinded in the Parliament of England.

To which most of the Cavalier and Country parties, and all the Squadrone (these last, as I observed before, being inclined to go along with every motion that they thought would obstruct the treaty's taking effect at that time) did adhere, making in all twenty-four peers, thirty-seven barons and eighteen burrows.[40]

While the rolls were calling upon this vote (it being by this time late, and having been a long *sederunt*), many of the members, after they had given their votes, went out of the House, expecting the Parliament would not have proceeded to any more business that night. When, instantly after the last name in the roll was called, the Duke of Hamilton, addressing himself to the Chancellor, moved, that the nomination of the commissioners for the treaty should be left wholly to the Queen.[41]

This, you may be sure, was very surprizing to the Cavaliers and Country party.[42] It was what they did not expect would have been moved that night, and never at any time from his grace, who had, from the beginning of the Parliament to this day roared and exclaimed against it on all occasions. And about twelve or fifteen of them ran out of the House in rage and despair, saying aloud it was to no purpose to stay any longer, since the Duke of Hamilton had deserted and so basely betrayed them. However, those that remained opposed it with all their might, and a hot debate arose upon it, wherein the Cavaliers used the very arguments that the Duke of Hamilton had often insisted on upon this and the like occasions.[43]

> What! Leave the nomination to the Queen? No—she is, in a manner, a prisoner in England, and the Estates of Scotland had taught us our duty in a case nearly related to this during the captivity of King James I. Our Queen knew none of us, but as introduced by her English ministry, and recommended by our inclinations to serve that kingdom. Our Queen never had an opportunity to know the true interest of our country; and though she did, yet, as she was circumstantiated, could not show her regard for it. And who then so proper to nominate Scots commissioners to treat on Scots affairs, as a Scots Parliament?

The Court, and the Duke of Hamilton (though he well enough saw these and many other speeches and motions, such as, that no person that had any estate in England should be of the number of the commissioners, were levelled at him) made few or no answers to the arguments against the motion.[44] But, insisting that the sense of the House might be known upon it, a vote was stated at last in these terms: 'Leave the nomination of the commissioners to the Queen , or to the Parliament?' And the former, by the unfortunate and unseasonable absence of twelve or fifteen members, did carry by a plurality of eight voices, of which his grace the Duke of Hamilton had the honour to be one.[45] Immediately after this was over, the whole Act impowering commissioners to meet and treat with England was voted and approven, the Duke of Athol, having protested against it in respect of the reasons contained in his former protestation, and being adhered to by twenty-one noblemen, thirty three Barons, and eighteen Burrows.[46]

From this day may we date the commencement of Scotland's ruine, and any person that will be at the pains to reflect upon the management of this affair must be the more enraged when he sees how easily it might have been, and yet was not, prevented. For, if the first restricting clause (which was lost by the unaccountable neglect of some members) had been carried, we should not have had one word more of the treaty. Or, had the nomination been left to the Parliament (which was lost by the unreasonable humours of such members as left the house in a hurry), those of the commissioners that represented the barons would have been so well chosen that they might easily have obstructed the treaty's being brought to such a conclusion as afterwards happened. For I may affirm (it consisting with my certain knowledge) that the English, knowing the backwardness of the Scots nation to enter into an incorporating union would, if there had been but two or three members in the Scots commission that opposed it, [have] been so far from pushing it as they did that the treaty would have been advanced no further than those others that had been set on foot formerly.[47]

But to consider the Duke of Hamilton's part in the affair a little more particularly, it is true some reports had been whispered about, from the beginning of the Parliament, that his grace's behaviour in this point would prove as it did, and many were uneasy at the great familiarity that appeared betwixt him and the Earl of Mar. But yet all were unwilling to believe any thing that was amiss of one who had stood so firm, and done such service to his country, especially in this point, whereupon he had so frequently, nay, not many days before it fell out, expressed and declared his opinion and resolution. But the following particular will make his conduct the more unaccountable. That very morning on which this affair was concluded, about forty or fifty of the Cavaliers being met together, had under consideration whether it would be most proper to chuse the commissioners in a full house, or that every estate should separate and chuse such as would represent themselves, and inclined to prefer the last because they were sure to carry what barons they pleased, but might run the hazard of losing all the other way. Yet such was their confidence in, and deference to, the Duke that before they would determine themselves positively in it, they dispatched the Earl of Strathmore, George Lockhart of Carnwath and George Home of Whitfield[48] to acquaint his grace of what had passed amongst them, and desire his opinion. But his grace being abroad when they came to wait upon him, the message was not communicated to him, till just as the Parliament sat down. Mr Lockhart meeting him accidentally in the outer house, delivered his commission, to which he gave this answer: 'Tell these gentlemen it will be time enough for us to consider on that affair, for it shall not be in this day.'

I never yet could hear of any reasonable excuse he made for this behaviour. It is true indeed he endeavoured to vindicate himself by alledging that after the Parliament had rejected the several clauses that were proposed to be added to the act he thought it to no purpose to strive any longer. For since the Court would have had a majority to give the nomination to the queen, he might be allowed to give her the compliment. And next, that he thought it better, because, if the commissioners that were named by the queen did what was not approven of in the subsequent Parliament, we might better and more severely take them to task than if we had named them ourselves.

But, with his grace's permission, this will not stand the test. For, to consider the last part of the argument first, it cannot be admitted that the leaving the nomination to the queen was preferable to the Parliament's having it, because it was obvious and plain that if the queen had the nomination she would take care to pitch upon such as would be very pliable and do what was desired of them. And since it was as plain that there was too great an inclination in the house to have a treaty, and accept of an union, there was the greater need to have some well-chosen persons upon it that would be an awe-band over others and represent matters fairly and fully, both at the treaty and in the subsequent Parliament. And next, his grace had no reason to imagine that the Court was able to carry it to the queen. For he knew that the absence of some of the Cavaliers was the only reason of losing the restricting clause, and that there were several others that voted all along with the Court formerly would have left them upon this occasion. And consequently, if those members I spoke of had not deserted the house the Cavaliers, instead of the Court, had carried the vote by eight voices, and then he might have been sure of having had all the barons, such as were his friends and would have been faithful and useful to the country.

But I am afraid the true matter was his grace had a great mind to be one of the treaters himself,[49] and, foreseeing he would not be named by the Parliament, he resolved to rely upon the Commissioner's and the Earl of Mar's promise of his being named by the queen, and therefore (whether by capitulation with these noble lords, or merely a thought of his own the better to recommend him to the queen on this occasion, I shall not determine) took upon him to make the motion, that it might appear he had indeed made the compliment, and been the promoter and advancer of leaving the nomination to the queen. And to confirm what I advance, let us remember that we never heard of any other reason for the Duke of Argyle's not being named upon the treaty than his having represented to the queen that he had engaged upon his honour to bring the Duke of Hamilton to be upon the treaty, or else that he would not be concerned in it himself. And the queen refusing to name the Duke of Hamilton as he had promised, he resented it so far that he would not suffer himself to be named and even threatened at that time to oppose the Union on that account, though ways and means were fallen upon afterwards to induce him to alter his mind.

But to return back to his grace's defences. Let us suppose them good. Yet I would fain ask, whence he got that new light, and that so suddenly? And why did he not communicate the same to his friends, that, if they had been of the same mind, all might have gone on that way and the compliment to the queen been the greater? Little did he consider their differing this time encouraged the Court, and occasioned a thousand false reports, which did a great deal of harm and, which was worst of all, was the foundation of that jealousy that, in some measure, contributed much to the bad success that attended the country's affairs afterwards.[50] I have dwelt the longer upon this subject because, as I said before, this fatal act was the first successful step towards Scotland's chains, and all I shall add concerning it is an old Scots proverb: 'that sitting betwixt two chairs often occasions a fall', which was the Duke of Hamilton's case at this time.

It is now high time to return to the Parliament. In consequence of a preceeding vote, an address was approven to the queen, craving she would use her endeavours with the Parliament of England to rescind the alienation clause in their late act. Then, an act being presented prohibiting the treaters to enter upon the treaty until the alienating clause in the English act was rescinded, a motion that the Parliament should proceed to it by an order of the house, and not by way of [an] act, was put in opposition to it by the Court, and approven. And then the order was unanimously agreed to in these words: 'That the commissioners to be named by Her Majesty should not commence the treaty of Union until the clause in the English act declaring the subjects of Scotland aliens be repealed.'[51] After this the Parliament continued to sit some few days upon private business and was at last on the twenty-first day of September prorogued.[52]

Immediately thereafter the Earl of Mar was made Secretary of State in the room of the Marquis of Annandale, who had enjoyed that office only during the time of the Parliament, and was turned out because it was thought he held a private correspondence with the Squadrone, being rather inclined to favour the succession without, than with, an union, and would not follow the Duke of Queensberry's, and his partisans' dictates further than he pleased. He was a man framed and cut out for business, extremely capable and assiduous. Of a proud, aspiring temper, and, when his affairs and politicks went right, haughty to a great degree. And, *vice versa*, the civillest, complaisantest man alive, and a great affecter of popularity. He had gone backwards and forwards so often, and been guilty of such mean, ungentlemanny compliances to procure the favour of that party which he designed to engage, that no man whatsoever placed any trust in him. Even those of the Revolution party only employed him as the Indians worship the devil,[53] out of fear. And as soon themselves strong enough without him, they kicked him out of doors. And though honest men welcomed a guest so capable to serve them, and willing to do their, and now his, adversaries all the prejudice he could, yet they were secretly glad to see one that had been so severe to them humbled. As it was plain his being turned out of the Secretary's office was the cause that induced him to oppose the Union, so, upon that account, he was much caressed, but little trusted, by the Cavaliers.[54]

During the short interval betwixt the Scots and English Parliaments, let us give [*sic*] a particular account of two or three worthy Scots patriots that have shown zeal for their country's service and made a great appearance in it. And these are the Earl of Errol, Earl Marishal and the Lord Balmerino.

Charles, Earl of Errol, begun his life with general applause, and, by a constant tract of honesty and integrity gained the esteem of all men. He did not make a great outward appearance at the first view, yet he was a man of good understanding, of great honour and loyalty, well-tempered, courteous and affable and deservedly much trusted by all that wished well to the royal family. His own family was always loyal, and had so great a concern in the welfare and prosperity of the kingdom (being these many years hereditary Constables of Scotland), that it was natural to expect he would prove a faithful subject and a good countryman.[55]

The Earl Marishal of Scotland was master of a quick and lively spirit, a great vivacity of wit, an undaunted courage, and, in short, of a soul capable of doing great things. But his misfortune was, he could not seriously, at least for any tract of time, apply himself to business, being loose and irregular in his measures and too bent upon his pleasures. However, being a man of honour and capacity, he was always faithful to his prince and country, did them both great service and merited much from them.[56]

Lord Balmerino did not take the oaths and comply with the government after the Revolution till the year 1704 that he was perswaded to it, merely to give his assistance to prevent the Court's designs of settling the succession of the crown on the family of Hanover. He was a man of excellent parts, improved by great reading, [and] being perhaps one of the best lawyers in the kingdom and very expert in the knowledge of the Scots constitution, he reasoned much and pertinently in Parliament. And testifying, on all occasions, an unshaken loyalty to his prince and zealous affection to his country, he gained the love and esteem of all good men.[57]

But [now] turning our thoughts to the Parliament of England (which met the twenty-eighth of October[58]), all men were anxious to know whether or not that house would repeal the clause in their act complained of by the Scots, upon the doing whereof the commencement of the designed treaty depended. This happened to be the first session of that Parliament, and the Court was afraid to propose this affair till once they knew a little of the temper of the members, of which this new house consisted. For which reason it was not moved till about the latter end of this year. But by that time it was evident enough by their proceedings that the Court and the Whiggs now conjoined together had a vast plurality of voices.[59] And so Mr Secretary Harley[60] moved that the clause of the act passed last session declaring the Scots to be aliens after the twenty-fifth of December should be repealed.

To which Mr Bromley[61] and several others of the Tories returned answer to this effect: that they had remonstrated against this act last session because they thought it a piece of unnecessary and unwarrantable injustice done to the Scots, and an irregular procedure towards perswading them to meet and treat in a friendly manner, and with a disposition of agreement, but since the house was then of another opinion they were obliged to submit. But they would gladly know what was the matter now and why these very people that proposed it last year, and told us it was absolutely necessary for the honour and security of England, are the first that propose the repealing of it now? To this little return was made, save that the Scots seemed to be of a better temper and more disposed towards an amicable agreement and a treaty of union, than formerly, and, in general, that it was necessary. And so it was at last found, and accordingly repealed by both houses. The Tories indeed gave little or no opposition to it, for they knew that the obstructing any measure that would promote a treaty of union with Scotland would be mighty displeasing to the people of England, who were very fond of it. And next they considered that if the projected union did not come to pass (and indeed there was not then, nor a long time after, ever a man in Britain expected it), they had a fair occasion to blame and attack the ministry for thus prostituting the honour of England by first promoting this act as so necessary for England and then repealing it to gratify the stubborn humour of the Scots, and no good following thereupon to England.

Notes

1. *Seafield Letters*, pp. 54–7, 62: Seafield to Godolphin, Edinburgh, 7 and 14 July and 1 Aug. 1705.
2. *Lockhart Letters*, p. 14: GL to Hamilton, [before 26 Mar.] 1705.
3. *APS*, xi. 213–14: 3 July 1705.
4. See for example, *APS*, xi. 215–17 and *Seafield Letters*, pp. 68–9: Seafield to Godolphin, Edinburgh, 11 Aug. 1705.

5. *APS*, xi. 218, 222: 26 July and 14 Aug. 1705.
6. Gone bankrupt. Chamberlen was one of the originators of the abortive Land Bank scheme backed by the English Tories in opposition to the Whiggish Bank of England in the mid-1690s.
7. *DNB*, x. 10–12.
8. John Law of Lauriston, subsequently the founder of the Banque Generale in France and the originator of the disastrous Mississippi scheme; R. Minton, *John Law, the Father of Paper Money* (New York, 1975).
9. *APS*, xi. 218, 27 July 1705.
10. Cf. Sir John Clerk's disagreement on this point: 'If the succession had been settled, there would not have been a word of the union', cited in, T. Somerville, *The History of Great Britain During the Reign of Queen Anne* (1798), p. 200 note 46. N.b. see p. 156 note 13, for the provenance of Clerk's comments on GL's *Memoirs*.
11. *Baillie*, p. 31: the Earl of Roxburgh to Baillie, London, 4 Jan. 1705, suggests some of the new ministry at least had exactly the reverse order of priorities.
12. *Seafield Letters*, pp. 61–2: Seafield to Godolphin, Edinburgh, 18 July 1705.
13. *Baillie*, pp. 107–8: Baillie to Roxburgh, [Edinburgh] 7 June 1705.
14. *APS*, xi. 216: 17 July 1705; *Seafield Letters*, p. 59: Seafield to Godolphin, Edinburgh, 18 July 1705.
15. *Crossrigg Diary*, p. 165: 17 July 1705; HMC *Portland*, iv. 211: Greg to Harley, Edinburgh, 19 July 1705.
16. The 1st Marquis of Montrose, commander of the Royalist army in Scotland 1644–5, who by the early eighteenth century was regarded by the Jacobites as the prime exemplar of patriotism and loyalty in the Great Civil War in Scotland—hence GL's disgust with his great-grandson; B. Lenman, *The Jacobite Risings in Britain 1689–1746* (1980), pp. 20–24.
17. Christian Leslie.
18. Cf. *DNB*, xxii. 322–3. GL had a personal agenda here, Montrose having proved difficult about paying for a horse GL had sold him at Montrose's own request (*Lockhart Letters*, pp. 4–5: GL to Mungo Graham of Gorthie, Dryden, 13, 14 and 15 Sept. 1704).
19. *APS*, xi. 217: 24 July 1705.
20. *Seafield Letters*, pp. 166–7: Adam Cockburn of Ormiston to Godolphin, Edinburgh, 1 Aug. 1705.
21. *APS*, xi. 218: 31 July 1705; *Crossrigg Diary*, p. 167: 31 July 1705; *Seafield Letters*, pp. 63–4, 65–6: Seafield to Godolphin, Edinburgh, 1 Aug. 1705.

22. *APS*, xi. 218, 223: 2 and 21 Aug. 1705; HMC *Portland*, iv. 227: Greg to Harley, Edinburgh, 21 Aug. 1705.
23. *APS*, xi. 219, 223: 7 and 22 Aug. 1705; HMC *Portland*, iv. 229: Greg to Harley, Edinburgh, 23 Aug. 1705. *Baillie*, p. 116: Baillie to Johnstone, 23 Aug. 1705 and *Seafield Letters*, p. 79: Seafield to Godolphin, Edinburgh, 26 Aug. 1706, suggest that the proposal for new elections to take place in 1708 was carried because the Court supported a proposal made by the Squadrone.
24. GL may be referring here to a specific case, that of his father-in-law the Earl of Eglinton: *Seafield Letters*, pp. 57, 66: Seafield to Godolphin, Edinburgh, 14 July and 5 Aug. 1705.
25. *APS*, xi. 222: 15 Aug. 1705; HMC *Portland*, iv. 224: Greg to Harley, Edinburgh, 16 Aug. 1705.
26. William Greg's account of this exchange, also eyewitness, is much less colourful than GL's: HMC *Portland*, iv. 224: Greg to Harley, Edinburgh, 16 Aug. 1705.
27. *Seafield Letters*, pp. 81–2: Seafield to Godolphin, Edinburgh, 26 Aug. 1705.
28. *APS*, xi. 224, 235, 245: 24, 30 and 31 Aug. and 11 Sept. 1705.
29. Colin Campbell of Glendaruel, Fraser's accomplice in the Scots Plot.
30. HMC *Portland*, iv. 236: Greg to Harley, Edinburgh, 30 Aug. 1705.
31. *Seafield Letters*, pp. 83–4: Seafield to Godolphin, Edinburgh, 3 Sept. 1705.
32. *APS*, xi. 216: 20 July 1705.
33. HMC *Mar and Kellie MSS*, p. 235: Mar to Lady Mar, Edinburgh, 30 Aug. 1705.
34. Moving.
35. *APS*, xi. 224: 28 Aug. 1705; HMC *Portland*, iv. 232: Greg to Harley, Edinburgh, 28 Aug. 1705.
36. Cf. HMC *Portland*, iv. 233–4: Greg to Harley, Edinburgh, 28 Aug. 1705.
37. *APS*, xi. 236: 31 Aug. 1705; *Seafield Letters*, p. 85: Seafield to Godolphin, Edinburgh, 3 Sept. 1705.
38. Sir George Gordon, 1st Earl of Aberdeen, formerly President of the Court of Session (as Lord Haddo) and Chancellor of Scotland under Charles II; *DNB*, xxii. 196–7.
39. *Seafield Letters*, pp. 85–6: Seafield to Godolphin, Edinburgh, 3 Sept. 1705; HMC *Portland*, iv. 239: Greg to Harley, Edinburgh, 1 Sept. 1705.
40. *APS*, xi. 236–7: 1 Sept. 1705. Those who adhered to Atholl's protest were: the Duke of Hamilton, the Marquesses of Montrose

and Tweeddale, the Earls of Errol, Marischal, Rothes, Home, Wigton, Strathmore, Roxburgh, Haddington, Selkirk, Aberdeen, Ruglen and Bute, Viscount Stormont, Lords Salton, Semple, Balmerino, Blantyre, Pitsligo, Belhaven, Colvill and Kinnaird; among the barons, Lockhart, Sir James Foulis of Colington, Sir Robert Sinclair of Longformacus, Sir John Swinton of that Ilk, Sir Patrick Home of Renton, George Baillie of Jerviswood, John Sinclair jr of Stevenston, Alexander Ferguson of Isle, John Brisbane jr of Bishopton, William Cochran of Kilmaronock, Sir Humphrey Colquhoun of Luss, Sir John Houston of that Ilk, John Graham of Killearn, James Grahame of Buchlivie, Robert Rollo of Powhouse, Sir Patrick Murray of Ochtertyre, John Murray of Strowan, Sir David Ramsay of Balmaine, Alexander Gordon of Pitlurg, John Udney of that Ilk, James Moir of Stonywood, Ludovick Grant of that Ilk, David Bethun of Balfour, Major Henry Balfour of Dunboug, Robert Douglas of Strahendry, Patrick Lyon of Auchterhouse, James Carnegy of Finhaven, James Halyburton of Pitcurr, David Grahame jr of Fintrie, James Ogilvy jr of Boynd, Alexander Duff of Bracoe, Alexander Mackghie of Palgoun, Sir George Sinclair of Clyth, James Sinclair of Stempster, Alexander Abercrombie of Tillibody, George Mackenzie of Inchculter and Aeneas Mackleod of Cadboill; among the burgh members, Alexander Robertson, Alexander Watson, Alexander Edgar, Patrick Bruce, Alexander Duff, Sir John Erskine, James Spittle, Francis Molison, Sir Peter Halkat, John Hutcheson, William Sutherland, John Lyon, Dougald Steuart, Sir Robert Anstruther, John Carruthers, George Home, James Bethun and Robert Fraser.

41. *APS*, xi. 237. Seafield had been advocating this since before the session opened: *Lockhart Letters*, pp. 17–18: GL to Hamilton, Dryden, 12 Apr. 1705.

42. The Court was apparently no less surprised at their success and Hamilton's conduct: HMC *Mar and Kellie*, p. 235: Mar to Lady Mar, Edinburgh, 7 Sept. 1705.

43. *Crossrigg Diary*, p. 171: 1 Sept. 1705.

44. HMC *Portland*, iv. 239: Greg to Harley, Edinburgh, 1 Sept. 1705.

45. *Seafield Letters*, pp. 86–8: Seafield to Godolphin, Edinburgh, 3 Sept. 1705. HMC *Portland*, iv. 239: Greg to Harley, Edinburgh, 1 Sept. 1705 states it passed by only 4 votes.

46. *APS*, xi. 237. Those adhering to Atholl's protest were as follows: for the peers, the Marquesses of Montrose and Tweeddale, the Earls of Errol, Marischal, Rothes, Home, Wigton, Strathmore, Roxburgh, Haddington, Selkirk, Aberdeen and Ruglen, Viscount Stormont,

Lords Salton, Semple, Balmerino, Blantyre, Pitsligo, Belhaven, Colvill and Kinnaird; among the barons, Lockhart, Sir Patrick Home of Renton, George Baillie of Jerviswood, John Sinclair jr of Stevenston, Alexander Ferguson of Isle, John Brisbane jr of Bishopton, William Cochran of Kilmaronock, Sir Humphrey Colquhoun of Luss, Sir John Houston of that Ilk, John Graham of Killearn, James Grahame of Buchlivie, Robert Rollo of Powhouse, Sir Patrick Murray of Ochtertyre, John Murray of Strowan, Alexander Gordon of Pitlurg, John Udney of that Ilk, James Moir of Stonywood, Ludovick Grant of that Ilk, David Bethun of Balfour, Major Henry Balfour of Dunboug, Robert Douglas of Strahendry, Patrick Lyon of Auchterhouse, James Carnegy of Finhaven, James Halyburton of Pitcurr, David Grahame jr of Fintrie, James Ogilvy jr of Boynd, Alexander Duff of Bracoe, Alexander Mackghie of Palgoun, Sir George Sinclair of Clyth, James Sinclair of Stempster, Alexander Abercrombie of Tillibody, George Mackenzie of Inchculter and Aeneas Mackleod of Cadboill; among the burgh members, Alexander Robertson, Alexander Watson, Alexander Edgar, Patrick Bruce, Alexander Duff, Sir John Erskine, James Spittle, Francis Molison, Sir Peter Halkat, John Hutcheson, William Sutherland, John Lyon, Dougald Steuart, Sir Robert Anstruther, John Carruthers, George Home, James Bethun and Robert Fraser.

47. The Scottish Parliament created commissions to negotiate a constitutional union of Scotland and England in 1604, 1668, 1670, 1689 and 1702–3. All of them had failed.

48. Commissioner for New Galloway; *PS*, i. 358.

49. Clerk endorsed this interpretation of Hamilton's behaviour: Somerville, *History*, p. 202 note 48. See also, *Baillie*, pp. 44–5: Roxburgh to Baillie, London, 5 Feb. 1705.

50. His fellow Cavaliers' suspicions of Hamilton were better founded than GL's trust. As early as February Secretary Johnstone reported home that: '[the Duke of Hamilton's] friends are so gross as to intimate to great men here that he is *chambre a louer*' (*Baillie*, p. 47: Johnstone to Baillie, London, 15 Feb. 1705).

51. *APS*, xi. 237–8: 4 Sept. 1705; HMC *Portland*, iv. 241: Greg to Harley, Edinburgh, 4 Sept. 1705.

52. Cf. HMC *Portland*, iv. 242, 243, 245–6: Greg to Harley, Edinburgh, 6, 8 and 11 Sept. 1705.

53. The American Indians were believed to worship the devil at this time.

54. Cf. *DNB*, xxx. 82–4. *Baillie*, pp. 158, 147–8: Annandale to Baillie, Craigiehall, 15 Jan. and 13 Sept. [1706], suggests the Cavaliers and the Court were right to be suspicious of the Marquess.
55. Charles Hay, 13th Earl of Erroll; *CP*, v. 99.
56. *CP*, viii. 484–5.
57. *CP*, i. 391.
58. GL is slightly inaccurate: the English Parliament met on 25 Oct. 1705.
59. This was not the case. Some 246 Whigs were returned as against 267 Tories, but about 24 Tories (led by Harley) adhered to the government notwithstanding their party allegiance, which gave the ministry a narrow majority of about 27.
60. Robert Harley, subsequently 1st Earl of Oxford and Mortimer and premier minister in the last years of Queen Anne; B. W. Hill, *Robert Harley. Speaker, Secretary of State and Premier Minister* (1988).
61. William Bromley of Baginton, M.P. for Oxford University and the leading anti-ministerial Tory in the Commons; *DNB*, vi. 403–4.

[Negotiations for Union, Spring 1706]

The Parliaments of both kingdoms having thus passed acts impowering the queen to appoint commissioners to meet and treat with commissioners of the other kingdom, and all obstructions being removed that could impede the treaty's commencement, in the month of March 1706 Her Majesty issued out commissions (one for Scotland and another for England) appointing the following persons to be commissioners for treating of an union betwixt the two kingdoms of Scotland and England.

For Scotland: the Earl of Seafield (Chancellour), the Duke of Queensberry (Privy Seal); the Earls of Mar and Loudoun (Secretaries of State), Sutherland,[1] Morton,[2] Weemys,[3] Leven, Stair, Roseberry and Glasgow; Lord A[rchibald]. Campbell (since Earl of Ilay),[4] the Viscount of Dupplin,[5] the Lord Ross;[6] Sir Hugh Dalrymple (President of the Session), Adam Cockburn of Ormiston (Justice Clerk), Robert Dundass of Arnistoun, Mr Robert Stuart of Tillicultry,[7] Sir Alexander Ogilvy of Forglen[8] ([all] Lords of the Session); Mr Francis Montgomery of Giffin,[9] Sir David Dalrymple, Sir Patrick Johnston (Provost of Edinburgh),[10] Sir James Smollet,[11] George Lockhart of Carnwath, William Morison of Prestongrange,[12] Alexander Grant younger of Grant,[13] William Seton younger of Pitmedden,[14] John Clerk younger of Pennycuick,[15] Hugh Montgomery (Provost of Glasgow);[16] Daniel Campbell[17] and Daniel Stuart (taxmen of the customs).

For England: the Archbishop of Canterbury;[18] the Archbishop of York;[19] W[illiam]. Cowper (Keeper of the Great Seal);[20] Lord Godolphin ([Lord] Treasurer); the Earl of Pembroke (President of the Council);[21] the Duke of Newcastle (Privy Seal);[22] the Dukes of Devonshire,[23] Somerset[24] and Bolton;[25] the Earls of Sunderland,[26] Kingston,[27] Carlisle[28] and Orford;[29] Viscount Townshend;[30] the

Lords Wharton,[31] Grey,[32] Powlet,[33] Somers[34] and Hallifax;[35] John Smith (Speaker of the House of Commons);[36] W[illiam]. Cavendish, Marquis of Hartington,[37] J[ohn]. Manners, Marquis of Granby;[38] Sir C[harles] Hedges[39] and R[obert]. Harley (Secretaries of State); H[enry]. Boyle (Chancellour of the Exchequer);[40] Lord Chief Justice Holt,[41] Lord Chief Justice Trevor;[42] Sir E[dward]. Northey[43] (Attorney General); Sir Simon Harcourt (Solicitor-General);[44] Sir J[ohn] Cooke (Advocate-General);[45] and Stephen Waller, doctor in law.

All these were of the Court or Whig interest except Mr Lockhart in the Scots, and the Archbishop of York in the English, commission. This last, as was reported, was named merely out of respect to the dignity of the office he bore, but would not be present so much as once at the treaty. The other because, being my Lord Wharton's nephew, they expected to carry him off, and as he was surprized at his being named, so he had no inclination to the employment and was, at first, resolved not to have accepted it. But his friends, and those of his party, believing that he might be serviceable by giving an account how matters were carried on, prevailed with him to alter his resolution.[46]

He, however, foreseeing that several things would occur during the treaty that were contrary to his principles, [such] as the business of an incorporating union and in consequence thereto the succession of the house of Hanover to the crown, convened together the Earls of Home and Southesk,[47] the Viscount Stormont, Mr Cochran of Kilmaronock, Mr Fletcher of Salton and Mr Henry Maul of Kelly[48] (who were the chief instruments of perswading him to attend the treaty) and wrote to the Duke of Hamilton, who was then in Lancashire. And, having communicated to them his difficulties, he desired their advice and direction how he should behave, and particularly whether or not he should protest and enter his dissent against those measures, being resolved to receive instructions from them as a warrant for his procedure and to justify his conduct.

To whom they all unanimously returned this answer, that if he should protest he could not well continue longer to meet with the other commissioners, and if he entered his dissent it would render him odious to them, and that they would be extremely upon the reserve with him, so as he would be utterly incapable to learn any thing that might be useful afterwards in the opposing the design. Whereas if he sat quiet and concealed his opinion as much as possible, they, expecting him to leave his old friends and party, would not be so shy and he might make discoveries of their designs and thereby do a singular service to his country. Therefore they agreed in advising him neither to protest nor dissent, nor do any thing that might discover his opinion and design unless he could find two or three more to concur and go along with him (which was not to be expected), but to sit silent, making his remarks of every thing that passed, and remain with them as long as possibly he could. And then at last, before signing of the result of the treaty, to find out some pretence or other of absenting himself.[49]

Mr Lockhart having thus accepted of his employment only to gratify the desire of those of his party, and that he might serve them, and having regulated his conduct as they directed, having exactly done all, and nothing more, than they required of him, and it being evident that upon this account he drew upon himself the displeasure and malice of the Court in a particular manner, it was hard that the Cavaliers likewise should have objected against him. 'What!', said they, after he came down to Scotland from the treaty, and continued so saying till they saw him as keen as any in Scotland against the Union when under the Parliament's consideration, 'he of the Country party and suffer an incorporating union to be agreed without opposing it? What! He a well-wisher to the royal family and hear the succession of the crown given to Hanover without protesting against it?' These and suchlike were their sayings of him. I believe they did not, and there are but few still, that know the grounds upon which he went. But these gentlemen were to blame (though it is what they often fall into), and it is very discouraging to censure and condemn the actions of those that they have no reason to distrust. It is impossible, at least improper, to discover all the secret springs and motives that induced such and such measures to be taken by all that are well-wishers to that cause. And if they have observed the persons doing things for which they do not understand the reasons to have formerly behaved honestly, they ought to rest some time in suspence before they give their judgment. However, Mr Lockhart was so well warranted for what he did, and his constant behaviour since he came to be a Parliament man so unblameable, that he has no cause to be uneasy at so rash and unreasonable censures, and might rather have expected from the Cavaliers their kindness than displeasure. But to waive this digression, which I thought necessary because of the unjust censures of some upon that gentleman's behaviour,[50] let us proceed to the matter we are upon.

Yet before we come to give an account of the treaty itself, let us enquire more narrowly whence it had its rise, what was designed by it and who were the promoters of it. By all the accounts I could ever yet learn, the Treasurer of England[51] and [the] Court party there did not at first design the Treaty of Union should have gone the length it afterwards did, it being a mighty stroke to the power of the monarchy, and consequently to them, who advised and directed the queen in all matters. But the Treasurer being extremely blamed for allowing the queen to pass the Scots Act of Security and [that] concerning peace and war, into laws, knew the Tories, who waited only for a proper time, designed to lay hold on this as a handle wherewithal to pull him down. And therefore to save himself, by amusing England with the hopes of an entire union, he set this treaty on foot with a design to have spun it out as long as he was in hazard of the attempts and malice of his enemies. But the Whigg party joined most sincerely in the measure of an incorporating union.[52]

They knew the Scots would not settle the succession of their crown as it was in England without either such limitations upon their sovereign as would secure them and their interests from the influence of English councils, or good terms from England in relation to trade and commerce (the first of which did not suit their designs, and the other they had no mind to bestow that way).

And therefore preferred this of an entire, or incorporating, union to all the measures that had been proposed for reducing Scotland to England's beck and obedience. For they thought it not only secured England from the dangers that might arise from thence, but made likewise for their own private designs and projects. For if that party had only projected the security and interest of England a foederal union (which would have been more acceptable to Scotland) would have done that as effectually as an entire one, for they had the same baits of communication of trade and other advantages wherewithall to tempt the Scots to yield to them the one way as the other. And after having perswaded them on the faith of this foederal union to settle the succession of that crown as it was in England, all fears of a separate interest and a Pretender to the crown vanished. And in a little time thereafter, when once affairs were settled, they might easily, by an act of the English Parliament, deprive the Scots of such privileges as they thought tended too much to their own disadvantage by virtue of their enjoying this communication of trade (as they did formerly by their Act of Navigation in King Charles the Second's reign[53]), and by these means gain their ends of reducing the Scots to their measures and at the same time continue them (their old enemies, whom they still do and ever will heartily hate and abhor) under the bonds of slavery they have been exposed to these hundred years by past.

But the Whigs had somewhat in view besides the general interest and security of England, or establishing the succession of the house of Hanover on the two thrones of this island (all monarchs and race of kings being equally odious to them) their design being sooner or later to establish a Commonwealth, or at least clip the wings of the royal prerogative and reduce the monarch to so low an ebb that his power should not exceed that of a Stadthouder of Holland or a Doge of Venice.[54] And it was plain and obvious such designs could be more easily executed when the legislative authority of Scotland was abrogated by reducing the representation of that nation to a small and inconsiderable number, incorporated with a much greater and subjecting her to [the] laws, regulations and government of another kingdom of which they had the chief management and direction, than if the Scots nation and Parliament remained a distinct and independent people and judicature, and were thereby in a capacity to assist their sovereign in maintaining his just rights and prerogatives in that as well as his other kingdoms. They remembred how the Scots in the reign of King Charles the Second did cast the balance and defeat their design of secluding the Duke of York[55] from succeeding to the crown,[56] and were resolved by this incorporating union to remove that obstacle to their future projects and designs.

Thus, the Court and Whig parties in England agreeing (though upon different topics and views at first) in the measure of a treaty of union betwixt the two kingdoms, the latter prevailed to have a plurality of their own party in both commissions, particularly the Scots, who so frankly yielded to the demands of the English, and prostituted the honour and surrendred the interest of their country, that the terms of the treaty proved so advantageous for England and destructive to Scotland that the Treasurer and Court party could not, without giving a greater handle against them than what they proposed to evade by this measure, so much as connive at or countenance any person that endeavoured to obstruct the Union's taking effect. On the other hand, the Scots statesmen and Revolutioners were so sensible (as was remarked somewhere else) of their own guilt in betraying their country and acting contrary to its interest these many years by-past, that they thought themselves in no security from being called to account for their actions, unless they removed the Parliament and rendered the nation subservient and subject to a people whom they had served, and from whom they looked for protection.[57]

The treaty being now brought to its commencement, before we enter into the detail of it let us a little cast our eyes upon the temper and disposition of the Scots nation, and observe how much the interest of the distressed royal family[58] increased in that kingdom. It being apparent that four parts of five of the nobility and gentry even in the western shires, and many more than half of the commons over the whole kingdom, did on all occasions express their inclination and readiness to serve that cause, accounts of which were from time to time transmitted to France.[59] And the French king, being much straitened by the success of the confederated arms against him, seemed more sincere in promoting the interest of the royal family than formerly, when his affairs went clearly on. Whether this proceeded from his regard to them or his own particular interest, I leave it to the charitable reader to determine, after he has called to mind this prince's behaviour to King Charles the Second during his exile[60] and what little he has done, besides the giving of a yearly pension, for the late King James since the Revolution [of] 1688.[61]

But sure it is, he gave out as if he were in earnest to do something at this time for the royal family's interest, though perhaps the true design was to give the English arms a diversion at home. And for this end he dispatched one Hookes,[62] who arrived at Edinburgh in the month of August or thereby, 1705, with letters from the French king and King James to the Duke of Hamilton, the Earl of Errol, the Earl Marischal and the Earl of Home, exhorting them to stand up and act for the interest of the distressed royal family, and promising to assist the Scots (his dearly beloved ancient allies) in so good a design as the restoring their king to his thrones, impowering Hookes to receive proposals and desiring them to send over to France one fully instructed to treat, and conclude with him for that effect.[63]

This Hookes was one of the Duke of Monmouth's chaplains when he invaded England. Whether he was taken prisoner and pardoned, or made his escape after the defeat of that rebellious enterprize, and when it was he turned Roman Catholick and entered the French service, I cannot tell, but at this time he was actually a Colonel, and commanded a regiment of foot in the French army. And being a mettle-pragmatical fellow (as is easily to be credited by his raising himself to such a post), he had gained credit at the court of France and was pitched upon to manage the correspondence with Scotland. In conversing with him it appeared he was a man of good enough sense, but extremely vain and haughty, and not very circumspect in the management of so great a trust, being rash and inconsiderate. Which will appear from a proposal he made of being admitted to the meeting of the Cavaliers and Country party in Patrick Steel's (the place where they rendezvoused to concert their measures every day before the Parliament met) to propose their owning the king's interest and moving his restoration in Parliament. And it was with difficulty he was perswaded to refrain from it, and likewise from his informing the Duke of Argyle, when he was prisoner next year after the siege of Menin, that he had been the year preceding in Scotland treating with the king's friends, and saw his grace when he was commissioner to the Parliament.[64] In all his proposals he shewed a great deal more concern to raise a combustion in the kingdom, and so give a diversion to his master's enemies, than what did really and solidly tend to the advancement of the king's affairs.[65]

However, the Cavaliers, to whom his letters and message were delivered, not being then in a condition to give a positive answer to his demands, told him in general terms that they were willing to do every thing that could in reason be demanded of them for advancing the king's service, and would, as they were desired, send over one in a little time to confer with King James and the king of France.[66] With which answer he returned to France.

The Cavaliers resolving, as they had engaged, to send one over to see what offers of assistance the French king would make, unanimously made choice of Captain Henry Straton,[67] being a person of entire honour and honesty, and every way well qualified for such an imployment. And accordingly, next day, after Mr Lockhart returned from the treaty, which was some time about the latter end of July 1706, Straton (having waited till he came down to get a full account of what had passed there) set sail from Leith in Captain James Tait his ship, and arrived safely in France.[68] Mr Lockhart, besides what concerned the treaty, was desired to pump the Tories in England and see how they stood affected and what they would do in case the king came over and the Scots declared for him. And accordingly, having found means to understand the Duke of Leeds,[69] the Lord Granville[70] and

several other of the Tories' sentiments on that point, he informed
Captain Straton that they were much more cautious and not near
so forward in England as in Scotland, all there being of opinion
no attempt was to be made during Queen Anne's life.

Captain Straton was kindly received, but could bring nothing
to a conclusion, the battles of Ramillies and Turin[71] having so
disconcerted the French king's measures that he was not in a
capacity to afford either men or money, at that time, for our
king's service. However, King James told him he longed
extreamly to be amongst his Scots friends, and obliged him to
give in writing and signed, a character of every man in the Scots
Parliament as they stood affected to him and were capable to
serve him.[72] And then he was dismissed, with fair promises from
the French king of doing all that could be expected at another
time, and with letters from King James to the Duke of Hamilton,
Earl of Errol, Earl Marishal and Viscount of Stormont.[73] Which
last had likewise two letters inclosed in his, one to the Duke of
Athol and the other to the Marquis of Montrose, to be delivered
as he saw proper. The first was delivered, and kindly received, but
the other person was turned such an obstreperous renegado that it
was to no purpose to make any attempt on him. Besides, there
was a visible danger of his discovering all to the ministers of
state, who, though they knew that Captain Straton had been in
France, took no notice of it, he having been furnished with
credentials from honest merchants in Edinburgh to act as
supercargo in the ship which transported him, wherein was a
considerable quantity of lead, and by these means sufficiently
able to give an account of the occasion of his voyage. However,
they did not doubt but this his first voyage concerned something
more than trade, but having no proof they did not prosecute him.
And thus these two negotiations came to no effect at this time. In
the interim the people's inclination towards King James still
increased, and his interest prevailed daily more and more over all
the kingdom.

But it is high time to reassume the treaty, the first meeting of
which was on the sixteenth of April, when the Lord Keeper of

England and Lord Chancellor of Scotland made the following introductory speeches:

My Lords, We the commissioners appointed by Her Majesty and authorized by the Parliament of England to consult and treat with your lordships, as impowered in the like manner by Her Majesty and Parliament of Scotland, concerning an union of the two kingdoms, and such things as we the commissioners on both parties shall think convenient and necessary for the honour of Her Majesty and the common good of both kingdoms, do apprehend there never was in any assembly of this nature so little reason as at present for the commissioners of England to give any verbal assurances of their zeal to promote and complete (so far as in their power) the great and good design we are met about, since it cannot be doubted but we bring along with us the same sentiments which so lately appeared in the Parliament of England, where they took care to manifest by a solemn act that they did postpone all other considerations to their evidencing a good and friendly disposition towards Scotland. The Parliament of England, in making that unexpected advance, seeming resolved, if possible, to attain that union which has so long been thought necessary by all that wish well to the prosperity of both kingdoms. And we most sincerely assure your lordships we do accordingly meet your lordships with hearts fully resolved to use our utmost endeavours to remove all difficulties in this treaty, to prevent all misunderstandings and cherish and improve the good dispositions to one another, and to have the general and joint good of both kingdoms solely in our view, and not the separate of either, but to act as if we were already united in interest and had nothing left but to consider what settlements and provisions are most likely to conduce to the common safety and happiness of this whole island of Great Britain. Which measures, if pursued on both parts, we hope may enable us to prepare such terms of union as may prove satisfactory to Her Majesty and the Parliament of both kingdoms.

My Lords, The Lords Commissioners for Scotland have
desired me to assure your lordships that they meet you on
this occasion with great willingness and satisfaction, to treat
of an union betwixt the two kingdoms, and of such other
matters and concerns as may be for Her Majesty's honour
and the maintaining a good understanding between the two
kingdoms. We are convinced that an union will be of great
advantage to both. The Protestant religion will be more
firmly secured, the designs of our enemies effectually
disappointed and the riches and trade of the whole island
advanced. This union hath often been endeavoured both
before and since the kingdoms were united in allegiance
under one sovereign, and several treaties have been set on
foot for that end, though without the designed success. But
now we are hopeful that this shall be the happy opportunity
of accomplishing it. Her Majesty hath frequently signifyed
her good inclinations towards it, and we are the more
encouraged to expect success in this treaty by the good
disposition which appeared in the Parliament of Scotland to
it, and by the friendly proceedings of the Parliament of
England, which give general satisfaction. We have a great
confidence in your lordships' good intentions, and we shall
be ready on our parts to enter into such measures with you
as may bring this treaty to such a conclusion as may be
acceptable to Her Majesty and the Parliament of both
kingdoms.

The English, before they opened their pack to shew the golden
ware the Scots were to get from them, first proceeded to demand
and secure what they wanted of the Scots, and for that end made
the following proposal:

That the two kingdoms of England and Scotland be for ever
united into one kingdom, by the name of Great Britain. That
the united kingdom be represented by one and the same
Parliament and that the succession to the monarchy of the
united kingdom (in case of failure of heirs of Her Majesty's
body) be according to the limitations mentioned in the Act

of Parliament in England in twelfth and thirteenth years of the reign of King William, entituled: 'An Act for the Limitation of the Crown and the Better Securing the Liberties of the Subject.'

The Scots demanding time to consider of a reply, and being convened together for that end, there was not any that appeared against this proposal, all of them (except Mr Lockhart, who, as was before observed, had orders from his friends to sit silent and make his observations) positively declaring for this scheme of an entire (as the English termed it) or incorporating union (as the Scots termed it). But, because they knew the Scots nation was rather inclined for a foederal than this kind of union,[74] and that the clause proposed to be added to the Scots act of Parliament impowering the queen to nominate commissioners—which would have restricted the commissioners from treating on any subject that should any ways derogate from any fundamental laws, ancient privileges, offices, rights, liberties and dignities of the nation—was rejected by a plurality of only two voices, they all agreed, and thought it necessary once to make a proposal for a foederal union. And having accordingly agreed upon the draught of the proposal, ordered the Chancellor to give it in to the Board in name of the Scots commissioners. But, lest the English commissioners should be offended at their not giving a direct answer to their first proposal, and to let them understand the true cause of their proceeding after this manner, and that they did not design to reject what was proposed by the English, they ordered the Chancellor, after the proposal was read, to make the following discourse:

> My Lords, I am commanded to acquaint your lordships there is nothing in this proposal (of a foederal union) but what the Scots had always claimed as their right and privilege as being under the same allegiance with England. But that by making this proposal they did not reject the other proposal (of an entire union) made by your lordships, but are of opinion this scheme would be most effectuall to facilitate the English succession's being established in Scotland.

Now let God and the world judge if the making this proposal
after such a manner was not a bare-faced indignity and affront to
the Scots nation and Parliament. It is true indeed they did it out of
regard to them. And it was the only regard they shewed during
the whole treaty for them. But it proceeded more from fear of,
than love to, them. Else, since they knew it would be so much
more acceptable than the other scheme, why did they propose it
with a design, and actually afterwards, upon the English
commissioners telling them in a saucy manner they did not
incline so much as once to take it into consideration (their very
words), resile[75] pittifully and meanly from it without saying one
word to enforce it? For even if there had been no previous
agreement betwixt the two sets of commissioners, and both had
met on equal terms, without any dependence the one upon the
other for places, pensions, etc, yet this preliminary step was
sufficient to encourage the English to have proposed and
expected such conditions from the Scots as they pleased, and
thought convenient for England. And the Scots commissioners
were so sensible of the meaness [sic] of this proposal, and so
fearful of informing the world how little regard they had for the
honour and interest of their country in a matter whereupon her
future misery or happiness depended, that they concealed this
discourse which they ordered the Chancellour to make in their
names, and did not, as usual in all other occasions, record and
ingross it in their minutes. However, I found a way to get a copy
of it in these very words, as I have set it down.

The English commissioners, as I said before, having refused to
take this proposal under their consideration, the Scots made no
further delay but agreed to the proposal of an entire union, as
contained in the proposal made first by the English commissioners.[76] Which being the main game the English were in
quest of, and the groundwork upon which all the structure was to
be built, the Lords Commissioners of both kingdoms set about
the regulation of the trade, respective laws, taxes and debts of the
two kingdoms, wherein the Scots commissioners agreed to and
accepted of such terms as the English commissioners were

pleased to allow them.[77] It is needless to recapitulate all the articles and heads of this treaty, they having so often been published in print, and canvassed upon by people of all persuasions and professions, that none can be ignorant of them.[78]

It will suffice here to make some few remarks upon the behaviour of the commissioners at the treaty. In doing of which I crave leave once more, in the first place to observe, how pitifully they abandoned their proposal of a foederal, and accepted of an incorporating, union, basely betraying and meanly giving up the sovereignty, independency, liberty, laws, interest and honour of their native country, in defence whereof their fathers had chearfully exposed their lives and fortunes and gained immortal praise and glory throughout all the world, bravely maintaining and defending the same against all attempts of the Britons, Romans, Saxons, Danes, Normans and English, and all other foreign and domestic enemies for the space of above two thousand years. But from the commencement unto the conclusion of this treaty it was as plain as two and three make five that the Scots commissioners were resolved (for the reasons already mentioned) to agree to and accept of a scheme of union, though upon never so unequal and unreasonable terms. For at the separate meetings of the Scots commissioners, if a difficulty was at any time started or an objection made to what they were concluding, all the answer you received was to this purpose, 'It is true it had better be so and so, but we must not be too stiff. The English will not agree otherwise, and I am sure you would not break the treaty for this'. And thus they proceeded all along, without having any regard for the true interest of their country, endeavouring only as much as possible to palliate their own knavery and hoodwink the nation from discerning the same.

For which end sometimes they pretended to differ from the English commissioners, and reports were industriously noised abroad, that the treaty would break up without concluding on any scheme, particularly when the Scots did insist to obtain a greater abatement of taxes and the English by piecemeal, and as with reluctancy consented to it. And in regulating the number of the

Scots representatives in Parliament, the English propose thirty-eight Commoners, the Scots make a great noise about it and a solemn conference must be appointed to debate on that subject, whereas all this was contrived to deceive the world with a belief that both sides stood zealously for their respective countries, and that this was no packed up commission, but consisted of persons upon an equal footing who had no dependency upon, nor secret correspondence and project with, one another. It consisted with my certain knowledge[79] that the English did design from the beginning to give the Scots forty-five Commoners, and a portionable number of peers, but had the Scots stood their ground I have good reason to affirm that the English would have allowed a much greater number of representatives and abatement of taxes, for the English saw too plainly the advantage that would accrue to England by an union of the two kingdoms upon this scheme and would never have stuck at any terms to obtain it. And indeed they cannot be blamed for making the best bargain they could for their own country, when they found the Scots so very complaisant as to agree to every thing that was demanded of them, managing all matters in a private club, so that when the Scots commissioners met amongst themselves a paper containing an answer to the last demand of the English commissioners was presented by the Chancellor or one of the two Secretaries, which being read was immediately approved of and then given in to the general meeting without being discoursed upon (as matters of such weight and importance require), or the commissioners allowed copies or the least time to consider what was contained in it.

And thus they drove on headlong to a conclusion, which they effectuated on the [22] day of [July] 1706. Many were the handles to bubble over the Scots to it, such as repeated assurances from the leading merchants in London of erecting manufactories and companies for carrying on the fishery. The communication of trade was magnified to the skies, and the East and West India gold was all to terminate in Scotland. But the Equivalent[80] was the mighty bait, for here was the sum of three hundred ninety-one thousand eighty-five pounds sterling to be remitted in cash to

Scotland, though the Scots were to pay it and much more back again in a few years by engaging to bear a share of the burthens imposed on England and appropriated for payment of England's debts. This was a fund, say they, sufficient to put Scotland in a capacity for prosecuting trade, erecting manufactories and improving the country, as it accordingly proved; for to it we may chiefly ascribe that so many of them agreed to this union. The hopes of recovering what they had expended on the African company,[81] and obtaining payments of debts and arrears due to them by the Scots government (it being articled in the treaty that it should be expended this way) prevailed with many to overlook the general interest of their country.

The treaty being thus brought to a period, the Scots statesmen and true blue Revolutioners, and the English ministry and Whigs, upon the same considerations that moved them first to enter upon this measure and thereafter conclude it in those terms, resolved with their utmost vigour to prosecute, in their respective Parliaments of both kingdoms, the design of uniting the two nations according to the articles agreed to by the commissioners, though I know they were very diffident of success and did not expect to have carried it through at the time the Scots Parliament met. And had it not been for some very particular unexpected accidents they would not have come off as they did, of which we will hereafter have occasion to give a more particular account. Only let me remark at this time, that there seemed to have been a chain of accidents all tending directly to the ruin and overthrow of this poor people, among which none of the least was the death of Charles, Earl of Home.

One cannot imagine how great a loss the royal family and Country party sustained by it, for though he was one that did not express himself with any tolerable share of eloquence, yet he was master of a sound judgment and clear conception, and had a particular talent of procuring intelligence of his adversaries' most secret designs, so that generally he informed his friends of them, and thereby gave them an opportunity to thwart them. This proceeded from his being esteemed by people of all parties, on account of his eminently unbyassable honesty and integrity in both private and publick matters. And the want of this intelligence was an unspeakable disadvantage to those that opposed the Union in the ensuing Parliament. He had given evident proofs that no temptation could seduce him in the least from prosecuting and adhering, with the utmost vigour, to what he owned to be his principle and opinion, and was so zealous for the interest of his country that he never deserted it, though he might, more than once, have made his own terms with the Court. He was so faithful to the royal family that he suffered much upon that account and was more relyed upon than any other. And so well was his reputation established that he proved an awe-band over others, and frequently obliged the Cavaliers to suspend their private grudges and joyn cordially in one measure.[82]

Before the Parliament met in Scotland the statesmen returned hither from London and took all imaginable pains to give false glosses and representations of what was agreed to in the treaty, and put such a face upon, and gave such accounts of, it (though the articles themselves were kept a mighty secret, no copies being allowed of them and in England a proclamation emitted prohibiting all books and wagers on that subject), that at first it took generally with the Scotchmen. But no sooner did Parliament meet and the articles appear in publick, but the nation, seeing how different they were from the accounts they first had of them, became universally averse to the project, as will be seen in the sequel.[83]

The Squadrone likewise about this time pretended as much as any to dislike the Union. But as they never scrupled to serve their own interest, though at their country's cost, no sooner was the Marquis of Montrose made President of the Council (which place had been vacant from the time the Marquis of Annandale was removed from thence and made Secretary of State, and which he had often refused to accept of again after he was laid aside from being Secretary of State to make way for the Earl of Mar), I say, no sooner was the Marquis of Montrose invested with that office, and a letter come down from the Duchess of Marlborough to the

Earl of Roxburgh, assuring them of being taken into favour, and intrusted with the government, if they would concur with the measures of promoting the Union, than they struck in with the Court and forwarded the Union with the greatest heat and zeal of any in the Parliament.[84]

A gentleman on a certain occasion, having privately argued with my Lord Roxburgh, and answered all his arguments for the Union, concluded that posterity would curse his memory if he concurred with measures which so infallibly brought his country to ruin. To which his lordship replyed, that he did not value what was to come after he was gone provided he could obtain his ends now and be revenged of the Duke of Queensberry, which he had reason to believe would be more easily attained if the Union had once taken effect.

I have mentioned this story as a sample of the motives which induced the venerable Squadrone to enter into this measure. The presbyterians appeared most zealously against the Union. The ministers were every where apprehensive of the Kirk government, and roared against the wicked Union from their pulpits, made resolves and sent addresses against it from several presbyteries and the Commission of the Assembly, as we shall hear by and by.[85] But no sooner did the Parliament pass an act for the security of the Kirk than most of their zeal was cooled, and many of them quite changed their notes and preached up what not long before they had declared anathemas against. Yet with no effect, for their auditories[86] stood firm, and the clergy lost much of their reputation by shewing so much selfishness and little regard for the interest and honour of their country.

The differences likewise, and envy, that arose betwixt the two Dukes of Hamilton and Athol contributed not a little to the obstructing the opposition the Court party would have met with. But nothing so much saved the Union from being totally demolished as the season of the year. For had not the Parliament met and sat in the winter, and the weather proved very rainy and tempestuous, it would have been impossible to have kept the country people from coming to a head from all parts of the kingdom and tearing in pieces all those that promoted it. This by the by, but when we come to the Parliament itself we shall have these particulars more under our consideration, and then it will evidently appear that though the articles of the Union were approved of in Parliament, yet the whole nation was altogether averse to them.

Notes

1. John Gordon (or Sutherland), 16th Earl of Sutherland; *DNB*, xxii. 217.
2. James Douglas, 12th Earl of Morton; *CP*, ix. 298.
3. David Wemyss, 4th Earl of Wemyss; *DNB*, lx. 246–7.
4. Subsequently 3rd Duke of Argyll; *DNB*, viii. 341–2.
5. Thomas Hay of Balhousie, heir-apparent to the Earl of Kinnoull; *CP*, iv. 558, vii. 321.
6. William Ross, 12th Lord Ross; *DNB*, xlix. 279–80.
7. Commissioner for Bute; *PS*, ii. 672–3.
8. Commissioner for Banff; *PS*, ii. 551.
9. Commissioner for Ayrshire; ii. 505.
10. Commissioner for Edinburgh; *PS*, i. 384.
11. Of Stainflett and Bonhill, Commissioner for Dumbarton; *PS*, ii. 650.
12. Commissioner for Peebleshire; *PS* ii. 510.
13. Commissioner for Inverness-shire; *PS*, i. 296.
14. Commissioner for Aberdeenshire; *PS*, ii. 629.
15. Commissioner for Whithorn; *PS*, i. 124.
16. Of Busbie, Commissioner for Glasgow; *PS*, ii. 505.
17. Of Shawfield, Commissioner for Inveraray; *PS*, i. 100–1.
18. Thomas Tenison; *DNB*, lvi. 57–60.
19. John Sharp; *DNB*, li. 408–11.
20. Subsequently Baron, then Earl, Cowper; *DNB*, xii. 389–93.
21. Thomas Herbert, 8th Earl of Pembroke; *DNB*, xxvi. 217.
22. John Holles, 1st Duke of Newcastle-upon-Tyne; *DNB*, xxvii. 170–1.
23. William Cavendish, 1st Duke of Devonshire; *DNB*, ix. 370–5.
24. Charles Seymour, 5th Duke of Somerset; *DNB*, li. 297–9.
25. Charles Paulet, 2nd Duke of Bolton; *DNB*, xliv. 84–5.
26. Charles Spencer, 4th Earl of Sunderland; *DNB*, 343–9.
27. Evelyn Pierrepont, 5th Earl of Kingston-upon-Hull (subsequently Marquess then Duke); *DNB*, xlv. 262–3.
28. Charles Howard, 3rd Earl of Carlisle; *DNB*, xxviii. 7–8.
29. Edward Russell, 1st Earl of Orford; *DNB*, xlix. 429–31.

30. Charles Townshend, 2nd Viscount Townshend; *DNB*, lvii. 109–17.
31. Thomas Wharton, 5th Baron, subsequently Earl and then Marquess, Wharton (and GL's uncle); J. Carswell, *The Old Cause. Three Biographical Studies in Whiggism* (1954), pp. 27–130.
32. Ralph Grey, 4th Baron Grey of Warke; *CP*, vi. 170.
33. John Poulett, 4th Baron, subsequently Earl, Poulett; *DNB*, 230–1.
34. John Somers, 1st Baron Somers; *Lord Somers: a Political Portrait* (Madison, Wisconsin, 1975).
35. Charles Montagu, 1st Baron, subsequently Earl of, Halifax; *DNB*, xxxviii. 218–23.
36. M.P. for Andover; *DNB*, liii. 77.
37. Subsequently 2nd Duke of Devonshire; *CP*, iv. 344.
38. Subsequently 2nd Duke of Rutland; *CP*, xi. 266–7.
39. M.P. for West Looe; *DNB*, xxv. 362–3.
40. M.P. for Westminster, subsequently 1st Baron Carleton; *DNB*, vi. 110.
41. Sir John Holt; *DNB*, xxvii. 202–5.
42. Later 1st Baron Trevor of Bromham; *DNB*, lvii. 228–9.
43. *DNB*, xli. 200.
44. M.P. for Bossiney; *DNB*, xxiv. 322–5.
45. *DNB*, xii. 90–1.
46. *Lockhart Letters*, pp. 26–30: GL to Loudon, Mar and Hamilton, 9 and 16 Mar. 1706.
47. James Carnegie, 5th Earl of Southesk; *CP*, xii (2). 145–6.
48. Subsequently titular 5th Earl of Panmure; *DNB*, xxxvii. 85–6.
49. *Lockhart Letters*, pp. 23–5, 24–5, 28–30: GL to Hamilton, 1 and 25 Jan. and 16 Mar. 1706.
50. Though GL did not know it, one of his most influential traducers (despite having no apparent cause to be so) was Hamilton, for an example of which see: Scottish Catholic Archives, Edinburgh, Blairs Letters 2/159/13: Fr James Carnegy to the Scots College, Edinburgh, 11 Mar. 1710.
51. Lord Godolphin.
52. *Miscellany of the Abbotsford Club. Volume First* (Edinburgh, 1837), p. 391: George Ridpath to Robert Wodrow, London, 27 Apr. 1706.
53. The Navigation Acts barred ships with anything but predominantly English crews and English masters from trading with England's colonies, and were an abiding source of resentment in Scotland.
54. Both of these were notorious in early eighteenth-century Europe for being elective and hence merely ceremonial heads of state, though

in fact the Stadthouderate was *de facto* hereditary and retained considerable military authority.

55. The future James II and VII.

56. This is a somewhat fanciful interpretation of Scotland's role in the Exclusion Crisis of 1679–81, for which see: R. Hutton, *Charles the Second. King of England, Scotland and Ireland* (Oxford, 1989), pp. 381–403.

57. Cf. *Stair Annals*, i. 210–11: Stair to Mar, 3 Jan. 1706.

58. The exiled (catholic) Stuarts.

59. *Correspondence of Colonel N. Hooke, Agent From the Court of France to the Scottish Jacobites, in the Years 1703–7* (henceforth *Hooke Correspondence*), ed. W. D. Macray, 2 vols, *Roxburghe Club* (1870), i. 424–6.

60. Charles II was maneuvred into leaving France in 1654 as the prelude to an alliance between France and the Cromwellian Protectorate.

61. GL appears to be overlooking, or disregarding, the French expeditionary force sent to Ireland 1689–91 and two serious attempts at surprise invasions of England (in 1692 and 1696) which were thwarted in equal parts on both occasions by the Royal Navy and the premature discovery of the plan. See: D. Szechi, *The Jacobites. Britain and Europe 1688–1788* (Manchester, 1994), pp. 41–57.

62. Colonel Nathaniel Hooke.

63. *Hooke Correspondence*, i. 206, 208–9, 209–10, 211, 213–14. The fact that none of the letters referred to by GL refer to anything more precise than Louis XIV's desire to restore the ancient liberties of Scotland (at no point do they refer to the exiled Stuarts) suggests that he never actually saw one of them.

64. Hooke's own account of his encounter with Argyll after the surrender of Menin is at variance with GL's (which probably derived from Hamilton's brother, the Earl of Orkney). See, *Hooke Correspondence*, ii. 75.

65. GL is nowhere mentioned in Hooke's report on his 1705 mission to Scotland, but the Duke of Hamilton had a number of prolonged discussions with him. Hence Hamilton is likely to have been GL's source of information regarding Hooke and his negotiations. Since the Duke clearly did not impress Hooke, and if, as seems likely, Hamilton was seeking to prevent any agreement between the Cavaliers and the French on plans for an uprising, an obvious way to do this would have been to traduce Hooke to those, such as GL, Hamilton knew were likely to favour such schemes. See, *Hooke*

Correspondence, i. 376–418 *passim*. Cf. also, J. S. Gibson, *Playing the Scottish Card. The Franco-Jacobite Invasion of 1708* (Edinburgh, 1988), ch. 1.
66. Cf. *Idem*.
67. The resident Jacobite agent in Edinburgh.
68. GL seems here to be unaware that an emissary (Charles Fleming) had been sent by the Cavaliers to negotiate French assistance for a rising in Scotland in December 1705 (*Hooke Correspondence*, i. 414, 477–8).
69. Sir Thomas Osborne, the former Earl of Danby and premier minister of Charles II's reign; A. Browning, *Thomas Osborne, Earl of Danby and Duke of Leeds, 1632–1712*, 3 vols (Glasgow, 1944–51).
70. John Granville, 1st Baron Granville of Potheridge; *CP*, vi. 88.
71. Ramillies, won by the Duke of Marlborough on 23 May 1706, and Turin, won by Prince Eugene on 7 September 1706, were two of the worst defeats suffered by French arms in the eighteenth century.
72. Unfortunately lost.
73. *Hooke Correspondence*, ii. 289–90: Errol to Charles Fleming, 9 June 1707 ns.
74. *Seafield Letters*, p. 169: Cockburn to Godolphin, Edinburgh, 22 Sept. 1705.
75. Draw back.
76. GL's account of the attitude of the Scots Commissioners to the question of whether the Union should be federal or incorporating is supported by the Courtier Sir John Clerk's recollections of the negotiations, for which see, *Memoirs of Sir John Clerk of Penicuik*, p. 60.
77. *Lockhart Letters*, pp. 31–6: GL to Harry Maule of Kellie, London, 9 and 26 May and 4 June 1706.
78. G. Holmes, *The Making of a Great Power. Late Stuart and Early Georgian Britain 1660–1722* (1993), p. 430.
79. This may be a reference to information GL gained access to through his uncle, Lord Wharton, who was on the English Commission.
80. The annual remittance of Scotland's contribution to the Treasury's 'take' of existing English taxation levied to service the English national debt. Since pre-1707 Scotland had not incurred the debt, it was agreed Scotland's input would be refunded.
81. I.e. the Darien venture.
82. *CP*, vi. 558.
83. *Memoirs of Sir John Clerk*, pp. 58, 64–5.

84. *Seafield Letters*, p. 94: Seafield to Godolphin, Edinburgh, 14 Oct. 1706. *Baillie*, pp. 137–9: Roxburgh to Baillie, 28 Nov. 1706, suggests the Squadrone's attitude to the Union may have been more principled than GL allows.
85. HMC *Mar and Kellie*, pp. 274–5: John Logan to Mar, Alloa, 27 Aug. 1706.
86. Congregations.

[Scotland and the Union – I: The Treaty in Parliament]

We come now to the Parliament itself, on which all men's eyes were fixed, expecting to learn the fate of the nation. Whether it were to remain free and independent, or under the colour and pretext of an union be altogether at the discretion of another, stronger and richer, people, its avowed enemies, and be rendered altogether incapable to exert itself and defend its liberties as became a free people. These considerations brought together an unprecedented number of people of all ranks, sexes, ages and persuasions, from all corners of the land to Edinburgh, and everyone now pretended to understand the politicks [*sic*] and give their opinions freely and avowedly of state affairs.[1]

The Parliament met the third of October 1706, to which the Duke of Queensberry was appointed Commissioner. The queen's letter and the Commissioner and Chancellor's speeches consisted chiefly in setting forth the advantages that would accrue to the nation by being united with England, and therefore recommended the treaty as agreed to by the commissioners and craved subsidies. The Court prevailed in the first *sederunt* to have the articles of union read, and proceeded immediately to the consideration of them. And it was not without some struggle obtained that all records relating to former treaties betwixt both kingdoms should be laid before the house, and that in the intervals of Parliament they might be seen by all that called for them in the lower Parliament house, where the Lord Register should order some of his servants to attend.[2]

On the fifteenth the Court moved that in terms of the resolve past the twelfth, the house should proceed to the consideration of the articles of union.[3] There were many opposed this as too hasty a procedure in so momentous an affair, and craved liberty, now

141

they had seen the articles, to consider and advise with their constituents concerning them. From whence arose a hot debate, whether or not the Parliament, without particular instructions from their constituents, could alter the constitution of the government. The courtiers alledged the affirmative, since the members had ample commissions to do all things for the good of the country, and that one of the reasons assigned in the proclamation for summoning this Parliament was to consider on ways and means to unite the two kingdoms.[4]

To which it was replyed, it was true the commissions were ample, but the very nature of them bound up the commissioners from overturning the constitution of the kingdom or disposing of what did not belong to them, viz. the representatives of the shires and boroughs. The design of sending them there being to preserve their constituents' rights and privileges and give advice to the sovereign in making laws and supporting and upholding that constitution, by virtue of which they first received their commissions and accordingly met and acted. And as for the reasons alledged from the summons of Parliament, everybody knew the nation had nothing of the Union in their view at the time this Parliament was chosen. Besides, it was so long ago that it was not strange the barons, freeholders and burghs expected their representatives should advise with them. And since they were not allowed to have a new election, that thus their sense of this weighty affair might be known in Parliament, that it would tend much more to the honour of the commissioners of the treaty if it was approved of in a Parliament called for that purpose, or by members who had received the fresh instructions and opinions of the nation, than by a Parliament which had continued so long, and thereby so many of its members corrupted by bribes, pensions, places and preferments.[5]

A great deal more to this purpose was urged and insisted upon, but at length a vote was stated in these words, 'Proceed to consider the articles of the treaty or delay?' But it carried in the affirmative by a plurality of sixty-four voices,[6] and all that the Country party could obtain was that the house should not proceed to vote and approve any of the articles until they were all once read and discoursed on by the members.[7] After which the house proceeded to, and in a few days finished, the reading of them. The Country party, particularly the Dukes of Hamilton and Athol, the Marquis of Annandale, the Lords Belhaven and Balmerino, Mr Fletcher of Salton and Sir David Cunningham of Milncraig, took a great deal of pains to expose the unreasonableness of the several articles as they went through them, but the Courtiers very seldom made any reply, having resolved to trust to their number of led-horses and not to trouble themselves with reasoning.

During this time the nation's aversion to the Union increased. The Parliament Close and the outer Parliament House were crowded every day when the Parliament was met with an infinite number of people, all exclaiming against the Union and speaking very free language concerning the promoters of it. The Commissioner as he passed along the street was cursed and reviled to his face, and the Duke of Hamilton huzzaed and conveyed every night with a great number of apprentices and younger sort of people from the Parliament House to the Abbey, exhorting him to stand by the country, and assuring him of being supported.[8] And upon the twenty-third of October, above three or four hundred of them being thus employed did, as soon as they left his grace, hasten in a body to the house of Sir Patrick Johnston (their late darling Provost, one of the commissioners of the treaty, a great promoter of the Union in Parliament where he sat as one of the representatives of the town of Edinburgh), threw stones at his windows, broke open his doors and searched his house for him, but he having narrowly made his escape prevented his being torn in a thousand pieces. From thence the mob, which was increased to a great number, went through the streets threatning destruction to all the promoters of the Union, and continued for four or five hours in this temper till, about three next morning, a strong detachment of the Foot Guards was sent to secure the gate called the Netherbow Port and keep guard in the Parliament Close.[9]

It is not to be expressed how great the consternation was that seized the Courtiers on this occasion. Formerly they did, or pretended, not to believe the disposition of the people against the Union,[10] but now they were thoroughly convinced of it and terribly affraid of their lives, this passage making it evident that the Union was crammed down Scotland's throat.[11] For not only were the inclinations of the elder and wiser known by the actions of the rasher and younger, but even the very soldiers, as they marched to seize the Port, were overheard saying to one another, 'It is hard we should oppose those that are standing up for the country; it is what we cannot help just now, but what we won't continue at.'[12] The mob being once despatched, guards of regular forces were placed in the Parliament Close, Weigh-House and Netherbow Port, and the whole army,[13] both horse and foot, was drawn together near Edinburgh and continued so all the session of Parliament. Nay, the Commissioner (as if he had been led to the gallows)[14] made his parade every day after this, from the Parliament House to the Cross (where his coaches waited for him, no coaches, nor no persons that were not members of Parliament being suffered to enter the Parliament Close towards the evening of such days as the Parliament was sitting), through two lanes of musqueteers, and went from thence to the Abbey the Horse Guards surrounding his coach, and if it was dark for the greater security a part of the Foot Guards likewise.[15]

This mob was attended with bad consequences to the Country party. For, falling out before the nation was equally informed of the state of affairs and equally inflamed with resentment, it was the easier dissipated and discouraged others from making any attempts for the future, and gave occasion to the Courtiers here to represent to the ministry of England not to be alarmed for it consisted of a party of rascally boys, no other being concerned in it, though the chief of the Country party had encouraged and hired them out. Besides, the placing of these guards overawed many both in and out of the house.

Though it was plain to all unbyassed people that this mob had its rise very accidentally, yet the government was not fond of any such amusements, and therefore the next day after it happened the Privy Council met and ordained these guards to be continued and emitted a proclamation against tumultuous meetings, wherein they commanded all persons to retire off the streets whenever the drum should beat and give warning, ordered the guards to fire upon such as would not obey and granted an indemnity to such as should on that occasion kill any of the leidges.[16] And next day the Chancellor acquainted the Parliament with what had happened, and what the Council had done on that occasion, and then, the motion being read, a motion was made that the Council should have the thanks of the house for providing for the safety of the Parliament, and that it be recommended to them to continue their care therein.[17] Nobody pretended to justify, on the contrary everyone condemned, mobs, but it was alledged that since the mob was dispersed, and no further fear of it, there was no need of those guards being continued, especially in the Parliament Close, which seemed an overawing the Parliament and was never practised in any kingdom save by Oliver Cromwell when he designed to force the Parliament of England to his own ends.[18] That it was the town of Edinburgh's privilege to maintain the peace within its own districts and that the inhabitants were willing to undertake it. And that the sole privilege of commanding and placing guards about the Parliament House belongs to the Earl of Errol as High Constable, and to the Earl Marishal as Marshal of Scotland.[19]

However, the Courtiers, being deadly afraid of their bones, gave no ear to decency, reason, or justice, but pressed a vote, and the motion was approved, reserving, nevertheless, the town of Edinburgh's right to their privileges on other occasions. But before voting the Earl of Errol protested,

> That the continuing of standing forces within the town of Edinburgh, and keeping guards within the Parliament Close and other places within the town in the time of Parliament (as is done at present), is contrary to the right of his office as High Constable, by which he had the only right of guarding the Parliament without doors as the Earl Marishal had within doors, and was an incroachment on the rights and privileges of Parliament and on the particular rights and

privileges of the town of Edinburgh. And if any vote should pass contrary to his right, or the Earl Marishal's right, or the Parliament or town of Edinburgh's rights and privileges, that it should not in any time thereafter prejudice the same, or be any ways drawn in consequence.

And he desired this protestation might be inserted in the minutes and recorded in the books of Parliament. To which protestation adhered the Dukes of Hamilton and Athol; the Marquis of Annandale; the Earl Marishal; the Earls of Wigton, Strathmore, Selkirk and Kincardine; [the] Viscounts of Stormont and Kilsyth; the Lords Semple, Oliphant, Balmerino, Blantyre, Bargeny, Belhaven, Colvil, Duffus and Kinnard; George Lockhart of Carnwath, Sir James Foulis of Colingtoun, Andrew Fletcher of Salton, John Brisbane of Bishopton, William Cochran of Kilmaronock, John Stuart of Kilquinlock, John Graham of Killearn, James Graham of Bucklivy, Robert Rollo of Powhouse, Sir Patrick Murray of Auchtertyre, John Murray of Strowan, Sir Thomas Burnet of Leys, Alexander Gordon of Pitlurg, James More of Stonywood, Patrick Lyon of Auchterhouse, David Graham of Fintree, James Ogilvy of Boyn, Alexander Mackie of Palgown, James Dunbar of Hemprigs and George Mackenzie of Inchcoulter, Barons; Alexander Robertson, Alexander Edgar, Alexander Duff, Francis Molison, Robert Kelly, William Sutherland, Archibald Shields, John Lyon, John Carruthers, George Home, James Bethune, John Bain and Robert Frazer, Burrows.[20]

Notwithstanding this precaution of the government, and that several boys were incarcerated as being accessory to the late mob and a committee of Parliament appointed to make enquiry after such as had, or should be guilty of, such tumultuous meetings, or of shewing any disrespect towards my Lord Commissioner, yet his grace was constantly saluted with curses and imprecations as he passed through the streets. And if the Parliament sat till towards evening then to be sure he and his guards were well pelted with stones, some whereof even entered his coach and often wounded his guards and servants. So that often he and his retinue were obliged to go off at a top gallop and in great disorder.[21]

If now we leave the town and make a tour through the country, though the badness of the season prevented their coming together and proceeding to acts of violence, yet there we shall find the same, if not a greater, aversion to the Union, which amongst other things appears from the addresses that were presented during this session of Parliament from several shires, stewartries, burghs, towns and parishes situated in all corners of the land, Whig and Tory, Presbyterian and Episcopal, south and north, all agreeing against the Union.[22] I know very well that the author of the *History of Europe for the Year 1706*,[23] and that vile monster and wretch Daniel Defoe, and other mercenary tools and trumpeters of rebellion,[24] have often asserted that these addresses and other instances of the nation's aversion to the Union, proceeded from the false glosses and underhand dealings of those that opposed it in Parliament, whereby the meaner sort were imposed upon and deluded into those jealousies and measures.[25]

I shall not deny but perhaps this measure of addressing had its first original, as they report. But it is absolutely false to say that any sinister means were used to bring in subscribers. The contrary is notoriously known, for the people flocked together to sign them and expressed their resentments with the greatest indignation. Neither was it from a mobbish humourish fit that this proceeded, for the barons and freeholders, being denied the liberty of giving instructions to their representatives, entered into this measure as the most proper to signify their inclinations to them, and it is not to be expressed what a value, I may say veneration, the commons shewed for the soveraignty [*sic*], which they expressed by exclaiming against the taking away the crown and the laws of the land. But I would ask these haukney[26] scriblers, if they reckon the barons and freeholders of the nation among the number of these led horses? If they do, what shall become of the *vox populi*, will it continue *vox Dei*?[27] I would further ask them, since these addresses were carried on, as they alledged, why did not the promoters of the Union bring counter-addresses to the Parliament?[28] Sure it will not be said that they wanted inclination, interest, or reason on their side? This measure had taken away the argument of the nation's dissatisfaction from the anti-Unioners and justified the promoters of the Union – that they did what was agreeable to the nation, at least to so many as should address for it.

But the truth of the matter lies here: they did attempt it, but could prevail in no place but the town of Ayr, where they got one subscribed, but by so pitiful and small a number that they thought shame to present it, especially when one a little thereafter, against the Union, was signed by almost all the inhabitants of that town. Neither did they omit any thing in their power to obstruct the addresses against the Union, but without success, except in the shire of Ayr, where the Earls of Loudoun, Stair and Glasgow prevailed with most of the gentlemen to lay it aside (though otherwise they expressed themselves as opposite to the Union as in any other place), and in the town of Edinburgh, where, after an address was signed by many thousands, they prevailed with the magistrates to prohibit it by threatning to remove the Parliament and Judicatories from thence.[29] And lastly, in those shires where the great men that were promoters of the Union had their estates and interests (such as Argyleshire, Bute, Sutherland, etc) and are, as it were, petty sovereigns themselves. Yet they could not, though they endeavoured to, persuade their vassals and tenants to sign an address for the Union, and were obliged to compound with them not to sign against it.[30]

Having said so much of these addresses·it will not be improper to insert a copy of one of them which was for the most part made use of everywhere, excepting that some of the western parishes added the inconsistency of the Union with the National and Solemn, League and Covenants,[31] and likewise the name of the places from whence these addresses came. And then it will appear that all those places of the nation that were not under the dominion of some Highland powers who promoted the Union,[32] did shew their aversion and unwillingness to enter into it.

To His Grace, Her Majesty's High Commissioner and [the] Right Honourable the Estates of Parliament, the Humble Address of_____ Humbly Sheweth,

That we, undersubscribing, have seen the articles of the Union agreed upon by the commissioners nominated in behalf of Scotland, and the commissioners nominated in behalf of England, in which they have agreed that Scotland and England shall be united in one kingdom, and that the united kingdom shall be represented in one and the same Parliament. And seeing it does evidently appear to us that such an incorporating union as contained in these articles is contrary to the honour, fundamental laws and constitutions of this kingdom, Claim of Right and rights and privileges of the barons and freeholders and burrows of this kingdom and church, as by laws established, and that the same is destructive to the true interest of the nation. Therefore, we humbly beseech your grace and Honourable Estates, and do confidently expect, that you will not allow of any such incorporating union, but that you will support and preserve entire the soveraignty and independency of this crown and kingdom, and the rights and privileges of Parliament, which have been so valiantly maintained by our heroick ancestors for the space of two thousand years, that the same may be transmitted to succeeding generations as they have been conveyed to us. And we will heartily concur with you for supporting and maintaining our soveraignty and independency and church government with our lives and fortunes, conform to the established laws of the nation.

This draught being framed so as to comprehend everybody's wish, was heartily approved and signed by the far greater majority of the barons, freeholders, heretors, farmers and others of the shires of Edinburgh, Dunbarton, Stirling, Renfrew, Fyfe, Aberdeen and Kincardine; the barons and freeholders of the shires of Perth, Forfar, upper and nether wards of Lanark, Roxburgh, Berwick and Linlithgow and stewartries of Annandale and Kircudbright [sic]; the inhabitants of the burghs of Dysart,

Dumferling [sic], Linlithgow, Forfar, Crail, Air, Ruglen, Glasgow, St Andrews, Culross, Stirling, Inverkeithing, Annan, Lochmaben, Dunbar, Burntisland, New Galloway, Lauder and Perth; the inhabitants of the towns of Dunkeld, Falkland, Hamilton, Borristounness, Paisly, Maybole and Peterhead; the masters of families and others in the parishes of Tullyallan, Blantyre, Evandale, Cambusnethan, Cambuslang, Kilbryde, Bothwell, Old and Easter Muncklands, Stonehouse, Dalserf, Covingtoun, Symingtoun, Libertoun, Carstairs, Quothquan, Dunsire, Carnwath, Crawford, Crawford John, Out-barony of Glasgow, Carnoch Force, Saline, Lesmahagoe, the four Glenkenns, Douglas, Carmichaell, Pettinane, Capuch, Lethendy, Alith, Kinloch, Errol, Kilspyd, Kinnard, Inchtane, Longformacus, St Maldoes, Kinfauns, Logie, Airth, Tarbet, Dunnipace, Dennay, Chainhilkirk, Calder, Kirk-Michael, Girvan, Kirkoswald, Barr, Clackmannan and Biggar.

Such a number of addresses so unanimously signed, was, as I said before, a sufficient indication of the nation's aversion to the Union. But its progress must not stop on that account. Such as had at first contrived it, or were since bribed or bubled[33] over to it, must not be affrighted at the scarecrows of reason, justice, laws, rights, privileges, inclinations of the people, instructions of constituents, or the advice of even an angel from heaven. For, as the poet says,

> Rebels like witches, having signed the rolls,
> Must serve their masters, though they damn their souls.[34]

For the Parliament had no more regard to these addresses, which contained the inclinations and earnest supplications of the people, than if they had indeed served for no other use than to make kites, which was the use my Lord Duke of Argyle was pleased to assign them publickly in Parliament. Nay, the Earl of Marchmont had the impudence to oppose their being allowed a reading in Parliament, alledging they were seditious. Which was accordingly for some time denied, till that worthy gentleman Sir James Foulis of Colington ended the debate by acquainting the house that if the addresses were not received from those members

that were entrusted with them, he did not doubt but those that
subscribed them would come and own them at the door of the
house, and crave liberty to deliver them out of their own hands.[35]

Besides these addresses already mentioned, there were
likewise addresses presented from the Commission of the Royal
Boroughs in relation to trade, from the Commission of the
General Assembly in relation to the Church and from the Council
General of the Company Trading to the East and West Indies
(once the darling of the nation) in relation to its particulars, and
all of them met with the usual reception.[36] But because each of
them did give an account wherein they were lesed[37] by this union,
and best explain their own concerns, I shall insert them at large:

> The Humble Address of the Commissioners to the General
> Convention of the Royal Burrows of this Ancient Kingdom
> Convened the Twenty-Ninth of October 1706, at Edinburgh,
> Upon the Great Concern of the Union Prosposed Betwixt
> Scotland and England, for Concerting Such Measures as
> Should be Esteemed Proper for Them to Take, With
> Relation to Their Trade or Other Concerns, Humbly
> Sheweth,
>
> That, as by the Claim of Right, it is the privilege of all
> subjects to petition, so at this time being mostly impowered
> by our constituents, and knowing the sentiments of the
> people we represent, it is our indispensible duty to signify
> to your grace, and [the] Honourable Estates of Parliament
> that, as we are not against an honourable and safe union
> with England, consisting with the being of this kingdom
> and Parliaments thereof, without which we conceive neither
> our religious nor civil interests and trade, as we now by law
> enjoy them, can be secured to us and our posterity, far less
> can we expect to have the condition of the people of
> Scotland, with relation to these great concerns, made better
> and improved without a Scots Parliament. And seeing by
> the articles of union now under the consideration of the
> Honourable Estates it is agreed that Scotland and England
> shall be united into one kingdom, and the united kingdom

be represented by one and the same Parliament, by which
our monarchy is suppressed, our Parliament extinguished
and in consequence our religion, character, Claim of Right,
laws, liberty, trade and all that is dear to us daily in danger
of being encroached upon, altered, or wholly subverted by
the English in [a] British Parliament, wherein the mean
representation allowed for Scotland can never signify in
securing to us the interests reserved by us, or granted to us
by the English, and by those articles our poor people are
made liable to the English taxes, which is a certain,
insupportable burden considering that the trade is uncertain,
involved and wholly precarious, especially when regulated
as to export and import by the laws of England under the
same prohibitions, restrictions, customs and duties. And
considering that the most considerable branches of our trade
are differing from those of England, and are and may be yet
more discouraged by their laws, and that all the concerns of
trade and other interests are after the Union subject to such
alterations as the Parliament of Great Britain shall think fit,
we therefore supplicate your grace and Honourable Estates
of Parliament, and do assuredly expect, that you will not
conclude such an incorporating union as is contained in the
articles proposed, but that you will support and maintain the
true reformed Protestant religion and church government, as
by law established, the soveraignty and independency of
this crown and kingdom and the rights and privileges of
Parliament, which have been generously asserted by you in
some of the sessions of this present Parliament. And do
farther pray that effectual means may be used for defeating
the designs and attempts of all Popish Pretenders
whatsoever to the succession of this crown and kingdom,
and for securing this nation against all the attempts and
encroachments that may be made by any persons
whatsoever upon the sovereignty, religion, laws, liberties,
trade and quiet of the same. And we promise to maintain
with our lives and fortunes all these valuable things in

opposition to all Popish and other enemies whatsoever, according to our laws and Claim of Right.

Signed by order, and in presence of the Convention,

by Samuel McLellan, Praeses.

Thus the trading part of the nation were either (as some would have it) such knaves, or such blockheads, as not to see the great advantages that would arise from this union. Let us now see what was the opinion of those concerned in the Church.

The Humble Representation and Petition of the Commission of the General Assembly of this National Church,

Humbly Sheweth,

That besides the general address made by us for securing the doctrine, worship, discipline and government of this Church, and now under your consideration, which with all gratitude we acknowledge, there are some particulars which, in pursuance of the design of our said address, we do with all humility lay before your grace and lordships.

1. That the sacramental test[38] being the condition of access to places of trust and to benefits from the crown, all of our communion must be debarred from the same, if not in Scotland, yet through the rest of the dominion of Britain, which may prove of the most dangerous consequence to this church.

2. That this church and nation may be exposed to the further danger of new oaths from the Parliament of Great Britain unless it be provided that no oath, bond or test, of any kind, shall be required of any minister or member of the Church of Scotland which are inconsistent with the known principles of this church.

3. There being no provision in the Treaty of Union for the security of this national church by a coronation oath, to be taken by the sovereigns of Britain, they be engaged to maintain the doctrine, worship, discipline and government of this church, and the rights and privileges of it, as by law are now established.

4. That in case the proposed union be concluded the church will suffer prejudice unless there be a commission for plantation of kirks, valuation of teinds[39] and making the registers of that court that were burnt, and a judicatory in Scotland for redressing of grievances and judging causes which were formerly judged by the Privy Council, such as the growth of popery and other irregularities, and with which judicatory the church might correspond about thanksgivings and fasts.

5. Likewise we do humbly represent that in the second part of the oath of abjuration in favour of the succession in the Protestant line there is reference made to some acts in the English Parliament which everyone in this nation who may be obliged to take the said oath may not so well know, and therefore cannot swear with judgment. As also there seems to us to be some qualifications required in the successor to the crown which are not suitable to our principles.[40]

6. And in the last place, in case this proposed treaty of union shall be concluded, this nation will be subjected in its civil interest to a British Parliament wherein twenty-six prelates are to be constituent members and legislators. And lest our silence should be constructed to import our consent or approbation of the civil places and power of churchmen, we crave leave in all humility and due respect to your grace and [the] Honourable Estates of Parliament, to represent that it is contrary to our known principles and covenants that any churchmen should bear civil offices, or have power in the Commonwealth.

These things we humbly beseech your grace and lordship[s] to consider, and provide suitable remedies thereto, and we shall ever pray, etc.

Signed in the name, in presence, and at the appointment of the foresaid commissioners of the General Assembly,

William Wisheart, Moderator.

When this address was framed there were several of the ministers did sincerely promote this and every other measure against the Union,[41] judging it against the interest and honour of the nation, [and] particularly Mr John Ballantyne, minister at Lanark. Yet, as I observed elsewhere, no sooner did the Parliament pass an act for the security of their Kirk, wherein the danger that might arise from what was included in the second, third and fourth articles of their address was provided against, than most of the brethren's zeal cooled – thereby discovering that provided they could retain the possession of their benefices they cared not a farthing what became of the other concerns of the nation.[42] When the Commission of the General Assembly first met, the ministers to one man, excepting some few in or about Edinburgh,[43] did declare against the Union, but could do nothing effectually and to purpose because the ruling elders (who were for the most part dependers on the government, none of the Cavaliers ever desiring such an employment) thwarted and overruled them in everything, but at last the above-mentioned representation was made.[44] After which the ministers dwindled away in their number, most of them that came from the country returning thither. And little besides the representation was done by the Commission in this critical juncture, only some few presbyteries, such as Lanark, Hamilton, Dumblain and some others addressed the Parliament against the Union. But the brethren for the most part were guilty of sinful silence,[45] which so enraged the populace against them that they did not stand to tell them to their faces that they were selfish and time-servers.

I come next to:

The Humble Representation of the Council General of the Company Trading to Africa and the Indies.

Finding by the fifteenth article of the treaty of union, agreed upon by the commissioners appointed by Her Majesty on behalf of Scotland with those appointed likewise on behalf of England, that upon payment of such a proportion of the equivalent therein mentioned as will answer the principal stock advanced by us and our constituents, with interest thereof at five percent *per annum*, our company is to be dissolved, we think ourselves bound not to be silent on this occasion, and therefore, though it be not necessary to trouble your grace and Right Honourable the Estates with a recital of the many valuable rights, powers, privileges and immunities granted, ratifyed and confirmed to and in favour of our company by several acts of Parliament, nor with a recapitulation of the many injuries and discouragements which we have met with and the just demands we have by the laws of nations for reparation of the great losses and damages which we sustained by means thereof, nor with a repetition of the several publick assurances given during the last and present reign of a hearty concurrence in repairing our losses and maintaining our rights. All these having been on former occasions fully represented to your grace and Right Honourable the Estates, yet, as being matters of great concern to us and our constituents, we humbly crave leave at this extraordinary juncture, to put you in mind thereof in general, and withall to make the following remarks upon that part of the said article which doth more immediately relate to the concerns of our Company.

1. We humbly conceive that the sum proposed to be paid to us out of the said equivalent is not adequate to the great losses and damages already sustained by us, and to the taking away likewise so many valuable privileges as we now enjoy, the benefit of which must accrue to the English East India Company.

2. It may be thought hard, that we should not be allowed the full interest of our money, when in the computation of the equivalent all the interest is stated at six percent and the payment thereof yearly. Whereas our interest is computed only at five percent, though the most part of our stock has been advanced without any profit upwards of ten years ago.

The third and fourth articles, consisting chiefly of the security of being paid that sum in case the company be dissolved, it is [sic] needless to insert them here.

5. We do not find that any provision is made for the security or safe-conduct of any persons, ships or effects belonging to

our company, or to such other persons as do, or may, trade by virtue of permissions already granted by the Court of Directors of our company before the real dissolution thereof.

Lastly. It is humbly conceived that the subsisting our company upon the same foot with the East India and other trading companies in England is no ways inconsistent with the trade of the united kingdom.

All which premisses being matters of great concern to us and our constituents, we do therefore in all humility and with great earnestness recommend the same to the serious consideration of your grace and Honourable Estates of Parliament.

Having dwelt so long on these addresses, it is now time to leave them and turn our thoughts unto the Parliament. Only allow me once more to remark, that as the addresses are a sufficient indication of the nation's aversion to enter into this union, so they contain the reasons and motives that induced the several interests, persons and communities to it.

The Parliament (as I have already narrated) having in a very superficial manner given the articles a reading, the Court resolved now to do something to purpose. But before we enter upon their proceedings, let us remark that, as during the first reading of the articles the Courtiers were not at the pains to solve the doubts and answer the objections raised by the Country party, so they continued the same method throughout the whole remaining part of the session, allowing the Country party to argue some little time upon the matter under the house's consideration, and then moving a vote upon it. If it was objected that the affair was not sufficiently understood and ripe for a vote, the answer was: 'the house is best judge of that', and so proposed a vote whether they should proceed to vote the matter under debate or delay it? The first branch whereof being sure to carry, away they drove on by their majority of voices, carrying everything after what manner they pleased.[46]

And to tell the truth of it, their designs would not stand the test if canvassed upon, and therefore those modest gentlemen chose rather to carry on their work by the power of numbers than that of reason. And as this unprecedented method made their game more sure, by not exposing the weakness of their arguments, so likewise it proved a very expeditious way — which they much affected, their guilty consciences suggesting that all delays were dangerous. Thus discovering that though they did not value, yet they were conscious of, the great prejudice which would arise to the nation from the measures they were then pursuing.

Which puts me in mind of what happened two years thereafter, when my Lady Orkney[47] came to Scotland. The Earl of Selkirk, speaking to her of the town of Edinburgh, was pleased to say she could make no judgement of what Edinburgh was, for he could not, had he not seen it, have believed that the effects of the Union would have been so soon seen to its prejudice. Impudent or imprudent wretch, thus to acknowledge his own villainy! It was a pity the nation should be altogether undone so soon, and that there is no more mischief for him and his partizans to accomplish. And it will be as great a pity if sooner or later he and they be not as high erected on a gibbet as the honour and interest of the nation are by their means dejected.[48] This being premised, my reader will not be surprized to find so great a work accomplished in so short a time, and serves to inform him how fairly matters were managed. Sure I am, since the creation of the world never was there so much partiality, disorder and folly in any meeting that pretended to a legal establishment.

To return now to the Parliament. On the first of November a motion was made that the house should proceed to the further and more particular consideration of the articles. Against which a delay was proposed by the Country party till once the sentiments of the English Parliament were known, they having once before rejected the terms of union which the commissioners of both kingdoms had agreed to and the Scots Parliament approved,[49] and till the members had consulted their constituents, which was urged as more necessary now than formerly when the motion was made since several shires and boroughs had already addressed, and many more were preparing to address, and did shew an utter aversion to the Union.[50]

But, this delay being refused, the next resource to postpone the ratification of any of the articles was to begin at the security of the church.[51] But that not doing either, the last of all was to urge the unreasonableness of agreeing to a union of the two kingdoms till once they had gone through and found that the terms thereof were for the interest of this kingdom, of which being once perswaded, all the rest would go glibly down. Besides, if they should in the first place agree to the union of the two kingdoms, subverting the monarchy and sinking the Parliament (which was [sic] the contents of the first article), who knew but the royal assent might be given thereto and the Parliament adjourned, and so the nation be united upon no terms, or at best upon such as England of themselves should condescend to give us afterwards, which was compared to a young maid's yielding upon a promise of marriage, which was seldom performed.

There being so much reason in the motion, the Courtiers knew not how to get over it, and the House generally inclined to it by taking the terms of the Union previously into consideration before they approved of the union itself. But the Lord Register found a back door whereby to make their retreat by presenting a resolve in these terms:

> That it be agreed that the house in the first place proceed to take the first article of the treaty into consideration, with this proviso: that if all the other articles be not adjusted by the Parliament, then the agreeing to and approving of the first article shall be of no effect.

Which, after a long debate being put to the vote, was approved.[52]

And next day[53] the consideration of the first article being resumed, many learned discourses were made, proving to the conviction of all unbyassed persons (nay, of the Courtiers themselves, who did not, as I observed before, make any answers besides calling for a vote upon the question), that this and every scheme of an incorporating union was altogether inconsistent with the honour of this nation and absolutely destructive to its

interest and concerns, both civil and religious.[54] Nay, some
affirmed that this scheme would infallibly be a handle to any
aspiring prince to undertake and accomplish the overthrow of the
liberties of all Britain, since, if the Parliament of Scotland could
alter, or rather subvert, its constitution, it afforded an argument
why the Parliament of Britain might do the same. And that the
representatives of this country being reduced to a poor, miserable
condition, must and would hang upon and obey those who had
the power of the purse, and, having shewed so little regard for the
support of their own constitution, it was not to be expected they
would much regard that of any other.

The Duke of Hamilton outdid himself in his patheticall
remonstrance: 'What?', says he,

> shall we in half an hour yield what our forefathers main-
> tained with their lives and fortunes for many ages? Are none
> of the descendents here of those worthy patriots who
> defended the liberty of their country against all invaders,
> who assisted the great King Robert Bruce to restore the
> constitution and revenge the falshood [sic] of England and
> usurpation of Baliol? Where are the Douglasses and the
> Campbells? Where are the peers; where are the barons,
> once the bulwark of the nation? Shall we yield up the
> sovereignty and independency of the nation, when we are
> commanded by those we represent to preserve the same,
> and assured of their assistance to support us?

Thus, and with a great deal more to this purpose, he
endeavoured to rouse up the pristine courage of the Scots
Parliament, and drew tears from many of his auditors' eyes, nay
from some who were resolved, and actually did, vote for the
article, particularly the Lord Torphicen.[55] But all would not do.
Quos Deus vult perdere, prius dementat.[56] The leopard may
change his spots and the Ethiopian his colour, but it is impossible,
at least very rare, that anything will alter a rebel and traitor. And
accordingly, a question being stated, 'Approve the first article or
not?', it carried in the affirmative by a plurality of thirty-three
voices. But before the vote was stated it was agreed that the state

of this and all other votes, and a list of the members as they voted upon the question, should, if demanded, be printed, that the nation might know who were for and against the Union.[57]

And likewise the Duke of Athol protested for himself and all that should adhere to him that an incorporating union of the crown and kingdom of Scotland with the crown and kingdom of England, and that both nations should be represented by one and the same Parliament, as contained in the articles, is contrary to the honour, interest, fundamental laws and constitution of this kingdom, the birthright of the peers, the rights and privileges of the barons and boroughs and is contrary to the Claim of Right, property and liberty of the subject, and [the] third act of Her Majesty's Parliament [of] 1703, wherein it is declared high treason to quarrel, or endeavour by writing, malicious and advised speaking, or other open act or deed to alter or innovate the Claim of Right or any article thereof. And he craved that he and such as adhered to him might renew their protestations against further proceedings in this matter and adjoin their reasons for the same, and that this be inserted in the minutes and recorded in the books of Parliament.

And the Duke of Hamilton; the Marquis of Annandale; the Earl of Errol; the Earl Marishal; the Earls of Wigton, Strathmore, Selkirk and Kincardine; the Viscounts of Stormont and Kilsyth; the Lords Semple, Oliphant, Balmerino, Blantyre, Bargeny, Belhaven, Colvil and Kinnard; George Lockhart of Carnwath, Sir James Foulis of Colingtoun, Andrew Fletcher of Salton, Sir Robert Sinclair of Longformacus, Sir Patrick Home of Renton, John Sinclair of Stevenson, John Sharp of Hoddam, Alexander Ferguson of Isle, John Brisbane of Bishopton, William Cochran of Kilmaronock, Sir Hugh Colquhoun of Luss, James Graham of Bucklivy, John[58] Sharp of Houston, Sir Patrick Murray of Strowan,[59] James More of Stonywood, David Beaton of Balfour, J.[60] Hope of Rankeiller, Patrick Lyon of Auchterhouse, James Carnegy of Phinhaven, David Graham of Fintrie, James Ogilvy [jr] of Boyn and George Mackenzie of Inchcoulter, barons; Alexander Robertson, Walter Stuart, Alexander Watson,

Alexander Edgar, John Black, James Oswald, Robert Johnson, Alexander Duff, Francis Molison, William Scot, George Smith, Robert Scot, Robert Kellie, John Hutchison, William Sutherland, Archibald Sheilds, John Lyon, George Spence, William Johnstoun, John Carruthers, George Home, John Bain and Robert Frazer, burrows, did all adhere to this protestation.[61]

But now I must not omit to remember that just when the vote was to be called, the Marquis of Annandale offered a resolve in the following terms:

> Whereas it is evident since the printing, publishing and considering the articles of treaty now before this house, this nation seems averse to this incorporating union in the terms now before us, as subversive of the sovereignty and fundamental constitution and Claim of Right of this kingdom, and as threatening ruin to this church as by law established. And since it is plain that if an union were agreed to in these terms by this Parliament, and accepted of by the Parliament of England, it would in no sort answer the peacable and friendly ends proposed by an union, but would on the contrary create such dismal distractions and animosities amongst ourselves, and such jealousies and mistakes between ourselves and our neighbours as would involve these nations in fatal breaches and confusions. Therefore [we are] resolved that we are willing to enter into such an union with our neighbours of England as shall unite us entirely and after the most strict manner in all our and their interests of succession, wars, alliances and trade, reserving to us the sovereignty and independency of our crown and monarchy and immunities of the kingdom, and the constitution and frame of the government both of church and state, as they stand now established by our fundamental constitution, our Claim of Right and the laws following thereupon.

Or, if the house did not relish this resolve, he proposed another in these terms, continuing the same narrative as the former:

Resolved this house will proceed to settle the same succession with England upon such conditions and regulations of government within ourselves as shall effectually secure the sovereignty and independency of this crown and kingdom and indissolvable society of the same, with the fundamental rights and constitutions of the government, both of church and state as the same stands established by the Claim of Right and other laws and statutes of this kingdom.[62]

When my lord presented this resolve he knew well enough the Court would not go into it, and therefore did not press it in opposition to the article, lest it had been rejected and thrown out of doors. But, having read it to the house, he enforced it with a few arguments and moved it might lie upon the table as a motion, his design being to let England see that though this nation did not incline to enter into an incorporating union in the terms of the articles, yet some advances had been made, which shewed a disposition of adjusting and agreeing matters with them.[63] And we shall hereafter see of what use this might have been, had measures been duly concerted, or after they were concerted, adhered to.

The first article of the Union being now over, the house immediately took under consideration an act for the further security of the Kirk, which, being ingrossed into the articles of Union, it is to no purpose to transcribe it here.[64] All that I shall say of it is that many additional clauses for its better security were offered and rejected, being opposed by the Earl of Marchmont, the Justice Clerk and others, whose greatest glory was to have been zealous sufferers for the good old cause. These and the other Courtiers being affraid to give the Church of England too much cause of jealousy if greater and better terms were demanded for the Church of Scotland than the Church of England.[65] And though many of the well-meaning brethren were, or seemed, satisfyed with this act, yet it did by no means please those of more mettle and understanding, so that the bulk of the ministry were picqued, though they bore it quietly and made not so much noise as at the beginning.[66]

The house thereafter went upon the second article of the treaty (whereby the succession of the crown of Scotland was established as in England), upon which arose a hot debate, the Country party insisting that before the succession was settled the limitations upon the crown of England ought to be taken previously under the house's consideration, that it might be known how they suited with the circumstances of this nation, and if any others were fit to be added.[67] The Courtiers would by no means allow of this, for now they were in a fair way of carrying through the Union, the fewer clogs upon the sovereign so much the better for them who esteemed themselves worthy of, and expected, great rewards and marks of favour should be poured down upon them, which restrictions on the sovereign might have prevented. They argued that the Parliament of Great Britain would be more competent judges of what was necessary for the united kingdoms than this house, and were clear for leaving it wholly to them. But it was replyed, that any limitations by the Parliament were alterable by a subsequent Parliament, but if the articles of union would be so punctually observed during future ages as was alledged by some, that not the least pin of them could or would be altered without demolishing the whole structure, then it followed that it was the general interest of all Britain to have such limitations as were necessary to be put upon the successors of the crown inserted and stipulated in the articles. And as to what concerned Scotland in particular, the general objection against the whole scheme of an incorporating union, viz. that its representation could but act precariously in the Parliament of Great Britain was as pat on this occasion as any other.

While this subject was warmly debating, a motion was thrown in, that since the different sentiments of people were like to run so high, a short recess might be granted to inform the queen of the present state and temper of the nation in respect to the Union, and beg Her Majesty, through her great wisdom, would be pleased to consider upon ways and means to prevent the fatal consequences that might thereupon ensue.[68] This of all proposals was most disagreeable to the Courtiers, for they had heretofore been at great pains to conceal the true state and inclinations of the people from their friends in England, lest while they were engaged in a bloody war abroad, the fears of raising a civil one at home might divert them from prosecuting the Union, which project had so exasperated the nation against them that they knew they had lost all their interest, and, if it miscarried, could not expect safety at home. For these reasons they all opposed this motion, and most eagerly demanded a vote upon the article, not allowing the members to speak their thoughts and give their arguments in behalf of the motion, but called out in mobbish disorderly manner, 'a vote, a vote', which was at last stated and the article approven.[69]

The Earl Marishal (in the terms of the Act of Security) protested that no person could be designed successor to the crown of this realm after the decease of Her Majesty, and failing heirs of her body, who is successor to the crown of England, unless that in this or any ensuing Parliament during Her Majesty's reign there be such conditions of government settled and enacted as may secure the honour and sovereignty of this crown and kingdom, the freedom, frequency and power of Parliaments, [and] the religion, liberty and trade of this nation from English and foreign influence. And he thereupon took instruments, and the adherers thereto were as follows: the Dukes of Hamilton and Athol; the Earls of Errol, Wigton and Strathmore; the Viscounts of Stormont and Kilsyth; the Lords Semple, Oliphant, Balmerino, Blantyre, Bargeny, Colvil and Kynnard; of the barons, George Lockhart of Carnwath, Andrew Fletcher of Salton, Alexander Ferguson of Isle, John Brisbane of Bishopton, William Cochran of Kilmaronock, John Graham of Killearn, James Graham of Bucklivy, Robert Rollo of Powhouse, John Murray of Strowan, James More of Stonywood, [Thomas] Hope of Rankeiller, Patrick Lyon of Auchterhouse, James Carnegy of Phinhaven, David Graham of Fintrie, James Ogilvy of Boyn, James Sinclair of Stemster and George Mackenzie of Inchcoulter; of the burrows, Alexander Edgar, James Oswald, Alexander Duff, [Francis] Molison, George Smith, Robert Scott, Robert Kellie, John

Hutchison, Archibald Sheilds, John Lyon, John Carruthers, George Home, John Bain and Robert Frazer.

Then the third article (which appoints both kingdoms to be represented by one and the same Parliament) falling under consideration, the Country party did all that men could do to shew what destruction this alone, supposing there was no more, would bring infallibly upon this nation.[70] That it was unequall for us to sink our own constitution when the English would not allow the least alteration in theirs, which was an example to teach us how sacred all who value their liberty esteem the smallest point in their fundamental constitution, and of how dangerous a consequence it is to allow the least alteration thereof. That it could not be expected that the small proportion which the members of this kingdom (even supposing the whole house was transplanted) did bear to the members of England would ever enable them to manage and carry affairs so as to provide for the several cases that might exist in this part of the island, since they were to be incorporated with a set of men who had even different interests among themselves and would much less regard the circumstances of us, to whom all factions bore a natural antipathy. That in all nations and under every form of government there were some things which could admit of no alteration by any power whatsoever, without which there could be no authority or durable establishment. That these were called fundamentals, or, according to the modern phrase, the original contract, whereof the constitution being rights and privileges of Parliament were the most valuable and considerable, and that accordingly no Parliament or power whatsoever could legally prohibit the meeting of Parliaments in all time coming, or deprive any of the three estates of its right of sitting and voting in Parliament.[71]

But by this treaty the Parliament of Scotland was entirely abrogated, the rights and privileges thereof surrendered, and those of England substituted in their place. That if the Parliament of Scotland can alter or dispose of their fundamentals, the British Parliament may do the same, and how then had we any security that what was stipulated in the treaty with respect either to the representation of Scotland in that Parliament, or any other privileges and immunities granted to Scotland might and would be continued and performed as England pleased? And how did we know but that for the utility of the united kingdom these privileges and immunities might be rescinded by this almighty power of Parliament and the Scots members be declared useless and sent a-packing home? That although Parliament had a power to make alterations of its fundamental rights and constitution, yet the same could not be done without the consent of every member. For though the legislative power is indeed regulated by majority of voices, yet the resigning or surrendering of the rights and privileges of the nation (which these of the Parliament may be justly stiled) was not subject to the suffrage, being founded on dominion and property, and could not be legally done without the consent of every member who had a right to vote, nay, of every person who had the right to elect and be represented in Parliament.

And that the representatives of shires and boroughs were at least[72] but delegates, impowered to meet and make laws for the good of the people they represented, and for preserving the rights and privileges and supporting and maintaining the constitution of that government, by which their constituents were united into one body and from whence their own authority to meet and act was derived, and therefore they could not alienate the rights and privileges of their own constituents without a particular warrant for that effect. But that by this treaty the constitution of Parliament in general was not only wholly altered, or rather surrendered, but the barons and burghs did suffer in their particular rights and privileges. For, supposing the twenty-second article (which restricted the quota of peers, barons and boroughs that were to sit in the Parliament to a certain number) should be rejected, yet nevertheless the barons and boroughs were forfeited of their judicative capacity, to which they had an undoubted right and title as ancient as the origin of this kingdom and Parliament, and of which they could not deprive their constituents without their own consent and allowance. Further, the barons urged, that though for their conveniency they consented to the settling a certain number to represent and act in their names in Parliament, yet they had as good a right to sit and vote and advise their sovereign when they pleased to reassume the same, as the peers.[73] Of which this and the twenty-second article deprived them. And it was also represented that the members being obliged to reside so long in London attending the Parliaments was of itself sufficient to drain and exhaust the whole specie of money in the nation.[74]

These, I say, and many other arguments, were insisted on to shew the dishonour, inequality and prejudice that would arise to the nation from this article, but all to no purpose. The Courtiers had ears and would not hear, hearts and would not understand, nay, mouths, but would not speak; few or no answers were to be made, but a vote required, whereby the sense of the house was to be known and the matter determined. And thus they drove furiously on to approve the article.[75] But, before voting, the Marquis of Annandale entered the following protestation upon the foot and in consequence of his last-mentioned motion, and bearing the same narrative:

> Whereas it is evident since the printing, publishing and considering the articles of treaty now before this house, this nation seems averse to this incorporating union in the terms now before us, as subversive of the sovereignty and fundamental constitution and Claim of Right of this kingdom, and as threatening ruin to this church as by law established. And since it is plain that if an union were agreed to in these terms by this Parliament, and accepted of by the Parliament of England, it would in no sort answer the peacable and friendly ends proposed by an union, but would on the contrary create such dismal distractions and animosities amongst ourselves, and such jealousies and mistakes between ourselves and our neighbours as would involve these nations in fatal breaches and confusions. Therefore, I do protest for myself, and in name of all those that will adhere to this my protestation, that an incorporating union of the crown and kingdom of Scotland with the crown and kingdom of England, that both nations

shall be represented by one and the same Parliament, as contained in the articles of the treaty of union, is contrary to the honour, interest, fundamental laws and constitution of this kingdom, is a giving up of the sovereignty, the birthright of the barons and boroughs and is contrary to the third act of Her Majesty's Parliament, 1703. As also that the subjects of this kingdom, by surrendering the sovereignty and Parliaments, are deprived of all security both with respect to such rights as are by the intended treaty stipulated and agreed, and in respect of such other rights, both ecclesiastical and civil, as are by the same treaty pretended to be reserved to them. And therefore I do protest that this shall not prejudge the being of future Scots Parliaments and conventions within the kingdom of Scotland at no time coming.[76]

To which the Dukes of Hamilton and Athol; the Earl of Errol; the Earl Marishal; the Earls of Strathmore and Selkirk; the Lords Salton, Semple, Oliphant, Balmerino, Blantyre, Bargeny, Belhaven, Colvil and Kinnard; George Lockhart of Carnwath, Sir James Foulis of Colingtoun, Sir John Lauder of Fountainhall, Andrew Fletcher of Salton, Sir Robert Sinclair of Longformacus, Alexander Ferguson of Isle, John Brisbane of Bishopton, William Cochran of Kilmaronock, James Graham of Bucklivy, Robert Rollo of Powhouse, John Murray of Strowan, James More of Stonywood, John Forbes of Culloden, David Beaton of Balfour, Henry Balfour of Dumbrog, [Thomas] Hope of Rankeiller, Patrick Lyon of Auchterhouse, James Carnegy of Phinhaven, David Graham of Fintrie, James Ogilvy of Boyn, Alexander Mackie of Palgowan and George Mackenzie of Inchcoulter, barons; Alexander Robertson, Walter Stuart, Alexander Watson, Alexander Edgar, James Oswald, Francis Molison, Robert Kellie, Robert Scot, John Hutchison, Archibald Sheilds, John Lyon, John Carruthers, George Home, John Bain and Robert Frazer, burrows, did all adhere.[77]

These three preceding articles (which comprehended the uniting the two kingdoms, the succession of the two crowns and representation of both kingdoms by one and the same Parliament) being approved, the other articles of the treaty fell under consideration, which did settle and regulate the taxes, trade and method of dispensing justice in this part of the island, with regard to the different civil laws, forms and constitutions of the two nations. But so many books and pamphlets were published, and have been collected and read on these subjects by people of all ranks and persuasions, that I may refer the reader to the articles of the Union and forbear resuming the several arguments that were *hinc inde*[78] alledged and adduced. It is sufficient to observe that the Parliament would not regard the intolerable burthen they laid upon the nation by subjecting it to the same taxes as in England (a few inconsiderable ones already imposed in England being only provided against), but no care was taken of what might and will come upon it, though it was made evidently appear to the conviction of all who had the least concern for their country that Scotland never was, nor ever would be in a condition to bear them, both because of the height and extensiveness, and likewise the nature of them, there being many species of trade and domestick commodities which, although indifferent with relation to the interest of England, yet were absolutely necessary to Scotland, such as salt, foreign and domestick, the last whereof the Scots proportionably make greater use of than in England, and the other was necessary for their fishing. But by taxing it the Dutch, who have no duty upon salt, can and will easily undersell them.

It is true indeed, a drawback was allowed for such fish, beef and pork cured with foreign salt, as should be exported. But it had been much better there had been no duty at all on the foreign salt. The high duties likewise upon tar, iron, lintseed, timber, etc (part of which the English stand not so much in need of as the Scots, or are provided with them at home) were downright ruin to Scotland. And the opening of a door, for importing English cloths and other goods, and the prohibition of exporting Scots wool, did all stand in a direct opposition to Scotland's welfare. In short, it was obvious that by these taxes, customs and prohibitions the nation parted with its own certain little, but improvable, trade,

upon the imaginary view of another which many asserted would
never answer the pretended expectations. And as to the laws and
dispensing of justice in the nation, all was lodged, with liberty
and power of cutting and carving, in the hands of the British
Parliament in which only a small, insignificant number could
know or have any regard for the Scots constitution and
circumstances. So that the College of Justice and other heritable
jurisdictions did all, notwithstanding the provisions made for
them, stand for the future upon a very precarious footing, all
being expressly provided to be under the regulations of, or
alterable by, the British Parliament when the utility of Great
Britain required it, which is a handle to be made use of upon any
occasion or for any design.

The example of the fate of Wales and Ireland was often
mentioned,[79] and many other examples illustrated, to shew the
inevitable confusion and destruction that must consequently
follow. But all to no purpose. For though such as undertook and
promoted the scheme of uniting the two kingdoms pretended to
see what none else saw, and not to see what everybody else saw,
and thus sold and betrayed the sovereignty, liberty, trade, wealth
and everything that is esteemed dear and sacred by a free people,
to be managed and disposed of by a people generous to none and
avowed enemies to our country, yet there was nothing alledged,
or could be alledged, as an argument to disprove the hardship and
unreasonableness of Scotsmen's engaging to subject themselves
to these burthens, which were appropriated for payment of
England's debts contracted before the union, save the sum of
money advanced by England which was called the Equivalent,
because it amounted to three hundred ninety-one thousand and
eighty-five pounds sterling, the sum computed to equal what
Scotland, by being subjected to those taxes which were
appropriated for payment of England's debts, would by its
customs and excise contribute thereto.

But if Scotland was to have had an equivalent for what she lost
by the Union, at least such particulars as redounded to England's
advantage, where was the equivalent for her sovereignty, the

removal of her Parliaments and seat of government, which kept the great ones, and consequently the money, at home? Was it the communication of trade? No. So far otherways, that this very particular (when restricted to the regulations of England) was of itself sufficient enough to ruin Scotland, being opposite to her interest in all points, excepting the liberty of trading to the plantations, and even that was said to be but precarious, and only as interlopers, the Companies monopolizing the same. And where was the equivalent for the dissolution of the Scots African Companies? Was there any reparation made for the barbarous treatment Scotland received from her neighbours of England and the ruin of her colony,[80] of which they were the principal cause? It is true indeed, part of the Equivalent was appropriated for paying the several sums of money that had been advanced by the subjects of this nation, for carrying on that great work, with five percent of interest. But no thanks to England for that. For Scotsmen by this means purchased their own company themselves, and made a present of it to the English, since the fund from whence this sum had its rise did flow from Scotland. But the truth of the matter lies here: a sum of money was necessary to be distributed amongst the Scots. And this distribution of it amongst the proprietors of the African Company was the cleanliest way of bribing a nation to undo themselves, and, alas, it had the designed effect.

Notes

1. For a thoughtful summation of the Court's thinking on the advantages and disadvantages of the treaty of Union, see: HMC, *Laing*, ii 125–35: memorial by Seafield [Aug. 1706].
2. *APS*, xi. 305–7: 3 and 10 Oct. 1706; HMC *Mar and Kellie*, p. 290: Mar to Nairne, Edinburgh, 13 Oct. 1706.
3. *APS*, xi. 307: 12 and 15 Oct. 1706; *Seafield Letters*, p. 95: Seafield to Godolphin, Edinburgh, 14 Oct. 1706.
4. A reference to the abortive treaty negotiations of 1702–3, for an account of which see: Riley, *Union of England and Scotland*, pp. 177–82.

5. *Seafield Letters*, pp. 96–7: Seafield to Godolphin, Edinburgh, 16 Oct. 1706.

6. The Squadrone by its support for the Court on this point signalled that it intended to back the Treaty of Union, effectively giving the pro-treaty position a guaranteed majority in the Scots Parliament: *Baillie*, p. 164: Baillie to Johnstone, [Edinburgh] 15 Oct. 1706; *Seafield Letters*, p. 97: Seafield to Godolphin, Edinburgh, 16 Oct. 1706 (n.b. Seafield puts the ministerial majority at 66).

7. Cf. HMC *Mar and Kellie*, pp. 292–3: Mar to Nairne, Edinburgh, 16 Oct. 1706.

8. HMC *Mar and Kellie*, p. 296: Mar to Nairne, Edinburgh, 23 Oct. 1706.

9. HMC *Portland*, iv. 340–1: Daniel Defoe to Harley, Edinburgh, 24 Oct. 1706; HMC *Mar and Kellie*, pp. 298–9: Mar to Nairne, Edinburgh, 26 Oct. 1706.

10. HMC *Mar and Kellie*, p. 281: Mar to Harley, Edinburgh, 21 Sept. 1706.

11. *Seafield Letters*, pp. 173–4: Lord Dupplin to Godolphin, Edinburgh, 25 Oct. 1706; HMC *Portland*, iv. 359–60: Earl of Stair to Harley, Edinburgh, 26 Nov. 1706.

12. HMC *Portland*, iv. 350: Defoe to Harley, Edinburgh, 13 Nov. 1706.

13. I.e. the forces available in Scotland.

14. It was customary for the condemned to be paraded through the streets on a cart on their way to the gallows, escorted by detachments of cavalry and infantry.

15. HMC *Mar and Kellie*, pp. 326, 327: Mar to Nairne, Edinburgh, 16 and 19 Nov. 1706.

16. The queen's Scottish subjects.

17. *APS*, xi. 309: 25 Oct. 1706.

18. Cromwell was usually (and probably erroneously) blamed for the purge of the Long Parliament carried out by the army in 1648, generally known as 'Pride's Purge', which secured a Parliamentary majority for the trial of Charles I.

19. *Crossrigg Diary*, pp. 176–7: 25 Oct. 1706; HMC *Mar and Kellie*, pp. 299–300: Mar to Nairne, 26 Oct. 1706.

20. *APS*, xi. 309–10: 25 Oct. 1706.

21. HMC *Portland*, iv. 352: Defoe to Harley, Edinburgh, 19 Nov. 1706.

22. *Seafield Letters*, p. 99: Seafield to Godolphin, Edinburgh, 3 Nov. 1706; pp. 176–7: Earl of Mar to Godolphin, Edinburgh, 26 Oct. 1706.

23. I have been unable to locate this publication.

24. I.e. Whigs.

25. HMC *Portland*, iv. 345: Defoe to Harley, Edinburgh, 5 Nov. 1706.
26. Hack.
27. A reference to what was popularly believed to be a Leveller/radical Whig doctrine, which translates as: 'the voice of the people is the voice of God'.
28. It is interesting to note that on the government side at this time Sir David Nairne (then resident in London) asked exactly the same question of the Earl of Mar (HMC *Mar and Kellie*, p. 320: Whitehall, 14 Nov. 1706), but never received any answer despite Mar's acknowledgement that he had received Nairne's letter.
29. HMC *Mar and Kellie*, p. 316: Mar to Nairne, Edinburgh, 7 Nov. 1706.
30. *Baillie*, p. 171: Johnstone to Baillie, London, 26 Nov. [1706].
31. These documents had assumed an unchallengeable, totemic importance among the militant presbyterians of southwestern Scotland after 1660, and hence could not be excluded from any formal consideration of opposition or support for any measure by them.
32. Such as the Duke of Argyll and the Earl of Sutherland.
33. Duped.
34. 'A Panegyrick, 1696–7', lines 25–6, from *Poems on Affairs of State* (London, 1697–1716).
35. *APS*, xi. 311: 1 Nov. 1706.
36. *APS*, xi. 315–16, 369: 6 and 8 Nov. and 26 Dec. 1706.
37. Lessened, infringed.
38. This was the provision by which officeholders, in order to qualify themselves for office in England, had to prove they had taken communion according to the rites of the Church of England at least once in the previous year.
39. A levy of c.10% on the agricultural produce of a parish designed to maintain the parish kirk and minister (tithes).
40. A reference to the requirement laid down in the English Act of Succession that Queen Anne's successor be a communicating member of the Church of England.
41. *Baillie*, p. 167: Baillie to Johnstone, [Edinburgh] 29 Oct. 1706.
42. *Seafield Letters*, pp. 99, 101 and fn 1: Seafield to Godolphin, Edinburgh, 3 and 7 Nov. 1706, imply that the government was most concerned by the Kirk's initial opposition to the Union.
43. Such as the influential Principal of Edinburgh University, William Carstares.
44. HMC *Portland*, iv. 339–40: Defoe to Harley, Edinburgh, 24 Oct. 1706.

45. The sin of omission.
46. Cf. HMC *Mar and Kellie*, pp. 308–9: Mar to Nairne, Edinburgh, 3 Nov. 1706.
47. Elizabeth Villiers, Selkirk's sister-in-law and former mistress of William III; *DNB*, lviii. 326.
48. GL's attack on Selkirk is somewhat puzzling as he appears to have consistently voted with his brother, Hamilton, against the Union (whatever his personal sentiments on the subject may have been).
49. The terms drawn up by the English and Scots Commissioners in 1604, and subsequently endorsed by the Scottish Parliament in 1607, were then rejected by the English Parliament.
50. *APS*, xi. 311.
51. *APS*, xi. 312: 2 Nov. 1706.
52. *APS*, xi. 312: 4 Nov. 1706. The wording here differs slightly from that given by GL.
53. It was in fact the same day: *APS*, xi. 312–13: 4 Nov. 1706.
54. Cf. *Baillie*, pp. 167–8: Baillie to Johnstone, [Edinburgh] 5 Nov. 1706.
55. James Sandilands, 7th Lord Torphicen; *CP*, xii (1). 781. Clerk noted of this oration: 'This speech was very handsomely expressed and a great many more to the same purpose; and yet, in all this, he plaid the mountebank entirely; for at the same time that he was caballing at the head of the Tory side, he was in secret with the Duke of Queensberry every night, or at least two or three times a week' (Somerville, *History*, p. 218 note 29).
56. 'Whom God would destroy, he first sends mad.'
57. *APS*, xi. 313–15.
58. *PS*, ii. 631–2, gives Sharp's first name as 'Thomas'.
59. Rect., Auchtertyre.
60. *PS*, i. 361, gives Hope's first name as 'Thomas'.
61. *APS*, xi. 313.
62. See *APS*, xi. 313: 4 Nov. 1706, for a slightly different version of these resolutions.
63. *Seafield Letters*, p. 102: Seafield to Godolphin, Edinburgh, 7 Nov. 1706.
64. *APS*, xi. 315.
65. *Seafield Letters*, p. 103: Seafield to Godolphin, Edinburgh, 11 Nov. 1706.
66. *Baillie*, p. 170: Johnstone to Baillie, London, 23 Nov. [1706].
67. *APS*, xi. 322: 14 Nov. 1706; *Seafield Letters*, pp. 105–7: Seafield to Godolphin, Edinburgh, 16 Nov. 1706.

68. *APS*, xi. 325: 15 Nov. 1706. The version printed here differs from that outlined by GL.
69. *Crossrigg Diary*, pp. 182–3: 14–15 Nov. 1706; HMC *Mar and Kellie*, pp. 323–5: Mar to Nairne, Edinburgh, 16 Nov. 1706.
70. *APS*, xi. 328: 18 Nov. 1706.
71. Here and in the paragraph below GL is assuming a Lockeian view of political rights and privileges as property stemming from an 'original compact' (J. Locke, *Two Treatises of Government*, ed. W. S. Carpenter (repr. 1986), pp. 164–5).
72. Rect., best.
73. This right had technically been abolished in 1587: *PS*, i. xviii.
74. This was already a serious problem in early eighteenth-century Scotland (see *Lockhart Letters*, pp. 7, 9, 13) and it was feared the Union would exacerbate it.
75. HMC *Mar and Kellie*, pp. 326–7: Mar to Nairne, Edinburgh, 19 Nov. 1706.
76. The version printed in *APS*, xi. 328, differs slightly from that given by GL.
77. *APS*, xi. 328–9.
78. From here to there (i.e. variously).
79. Wales was formally annexed to England, and the Welsh formally given representation in the English Parliament, in 1536; Ireland still retained its own Parliament (and was to continue to do so until 1801), but until 1782 it was constitutionally subordinate to the English, later British, Privy Council.
80 Darien.

[Scotland and the Union – II: Conspiracies and Protests]

Having traced the Parliament so far, let us now turn our thoughts again upon the temper and behaviour of the people of this nation. And there we shall find everybody enraged and displeased, especially the commons, who exclaimed against those of greater rank that they gave them not encouragement enough to come into Edinburgh in a body to raise the Parliament.

The first that made any formal appearance was the town of Glasgow, for the Provost and the town council opposing the subscribing of an address to the Parliament against the Union, great numbers betook themselves to arms, drove the magistrates out of town, insulted everybody that they thought favoured, or was so much as lukewarm in disclaiming, the Union, mounted guards, and rambled about for two or three days together. But a strong detatchment of dragoons being commanded thither surprised two of the chief leaders, Findlay and Montgomery (both mean artificers) and brought them prisoners to Edinburgh castle, and the mob soon thereafter dwindled into nothing.[1] About the same time the shires of Dumfries, Kirkcudbright, Galloway, Ayr and Clydesdale were all ready and keen to take up arms, and a considerable number, near to two or three thousand, of the commons came in arms to the town of Dumfries, where they publickly burned the articles of the Union and affixed upon the cross a paper entituled: 'An Account of Burning the Articles of Union at Dumfries', wherein they at large gave their reasons for protesting against this union. And because from this paper we may make an estimate of the opinion the inferior rank of people had of the Union, and thereby see it was noways such as has been industriously represented, I shall insert it word for word as it was affixed on the cross, and is as follows:

177

These are to notifie to all concerned what are our reasons
for, and designs in, burning the printed articles of the
proposed union with England, with the names of the Scots
commissioners, subscribers of the same, together with the
minutes of the whole treaty betwixt them and the English
commissioners there anent.

We have herein no design against Her Majesty, nor against
England, nor any Englishman. Neither against our present
Parliament in their acts or actings for the interest, safety and
sovereignty of this our native ancient nation, but to testify
our dissent from, discontent with, and protestation against
the twenty five articles of the said Union, subscribed by the
foresaid commissioners, as being inconsistent with, and
altogether prejudicial to, and utterly destructive of, this
nation's independency, crown rights and our constitute
laws, both sacred and civil. We shall not here condescend
upon the particular prejudices that do and will redound to
this nation if the said union should be carried on according
to the printed articles, but refer the reader to the variety of
addresses given into the present Parliament by all ranks,
from almost all corners of this nation against the said union.
Only we must say and profess that the commissioners for
the nation have been either simple, ignorant, or treacherous,
if not all three, when the minutes of the treaty betwixt the
commissioners of both kingdoms are duly considered, and
when we compare their dastardly yieldings unto the
demands and proposals of the English commissioners, who
on the contrary have valiantly acquitted themselves for the
interest and safety of their country. We acknowledge it is in
the power of this present Parliament, to give remissions to
the subscribers of the foresaid articles, and we heartily wish
for a good agreement among all the members of the
Parliament so as it may tend to the safety and preservation
of both church and state, with all the priviledges belonging
thereto within the kingdom of Scotland. But if the
subscribers of the foresaid treaty of union, with their

associates in Parliament, shall presume to carry on the said union by a supream power over the generality of this nation, then, and in that case, as we judge that the consent of the generality of the same can only divest them of their sacred and civil liberties, purchased and maintained by our ancestors with their blood.

So we protest that whatever ratification of the foresaid union may pass in Parliament, contrary to our fundamental laws, liberties and priviledges concerning church and state, may not be binding upon the nation now, nor at any time to come. And particularly we protest against the approbation of the first article of the said union before the priviledges of this nation contained in the other articles had been adjusted and secured.

And so we earnestly require that the representatives in Parliament, who are for our nation's priviledges, would give timeous warning to all corners of this kingdom that we and our posterity become not tributary and bondslaves to our neighbours without acquitting ourselves as becomes men and Christians. And we are confident that the soldiers now in martial power have so much of the spirits of Scotsmen that they are not ambitious to be disposed of at the pleasure of another nation. And we hereby declare we have no design against them in the matter.

Whoever is at pains to consider this paper may easily discern that it is of a rustick composition.[2] But yet it evidently shews what a regard those people had for the sovereignty of the nation, and that they were willing to lay aside their private differences and join for the common interest thereof.

There were none appeared with so much zeal against the Union as the western shires, where a vast number of people, and chiefly the Cameronians,[3] were willing to have ventured their all against it. And for this purpose they had several meetings among the ringleaders of them, divided themselves into regiments, chose their officers, provided themselves with horses and arms, mentioned the restoration of the king as the most feasible grounds to go upon to save their country, were so far reconciled to the northern parts (whom formerly they hated heartily upon account of their different principles of religion)[4] and episcopal party, that they were willing to join and concert measures with them for the defence of their common native country, and had appointed correspondents in all places, from whom, and to whom, they might receive and give intelligence and sent their emissaries throughout all the kingdom to strengthen and encourage their party and such as would joyn in defence of their country, particularly dispatching some on whom they did most rely, to try the pulses of those members of Parliament who were against the Union.[5]

There was one Cunningham of Eckatt[6] who had been very instrumental in promoting the late Revolution, but upon the late Peace of Ryswick the regiment whereof he was major being broke he went to Darien, and after the fatal ruine of that enterprize, returning to Scotland, he lived privately at his country house in none of the best conditions. He had often applied for a post, but, notwithstanding of the levies that were made after the war broke out again, could never obtain so much favour as to be provided for in the army, which he and everybody believed to proceed from his being faithful in the discharging of the trust the Company placed in him when he went to Darien. For thus did they treat all that were not inclined to betray this and every other project that tended towards Scotland's advantage.[7]

This gentleman, being a little disgusted at this treatment, and taking the ruine of his country mightily to heart, was soon known to these western negotiators, and (being altogether of the [sic] Presbyterian principles) entirely trusted by them. I know there are many do think that he was a creature of the Courtiers and employed by them as a spy, because about this time he was often with some of the leading men of the Court, and had, since the commencement of the Union a company of foot bestowed on him. But in my opinion he was sincere.[8] And for his being often at court, that, he told his friends, in the meantime he was obliged to do, because he understood they suspected him. And if he got this employment it has been by some interest that I cannot discover. But whether he was sincere or not in his heart is what I cannot determine, but sure I am by his actions it appeared he was, and he brought matters to such a consistency that, provided concerted measures had been kept, he had raised the Parliament with a vengeance.

But to go on with the story. This gentleman being well acquainted with Mr Brisbane of Bishopton,[9] discovered to him his earnest desire of doing something on this occasion to save his perishing country, and signalize himself, and told him that he was sure he could ingratiate himself with the western shires and be able to persuade them to rise in arms and march under his command to Edinburgh, he having thoroughly discoursed with the negotiators and found them of opinion (to which he likewise agreed) that there was no way to save the nation but first by raising the Parliament and then declaring for King James. Mr Brisbane having communicated what he had thus learned to Mr Cochran of Kilmaronock and Mr Lockhart of Carnwath, they desired him to encourage Cunningham to persevere in his design, whereupon he resolved to make a progress through the western shires to sound the people himself, and prepare them to draw together upon a proper occasion. For which cause they advanced him fifty guineas and gave him assurance if any misfortune befel him his wife and children should be taken care of and provided for, which was all he demanded as a recompense at that time.

But before he went off he was desirous of to know what part the two Dukes of Hamilton and Athol would bear if he should meet with opposition either before or after he had raised the Parliament, particularly if, as he marched towards Edinburgh from the west, the Duke of Athol would cause his Highlanders secure the pass of Stirling, and so open a passage for, and communication with, the northern parts. Mr Cochran was sent to acquaint the Duke of Hamilton, and Mr Lockhart told Murray of Strowan,[10] and he the Duke of Athol, of all that had passed and what Mr Cunningham desired. The former appeared somewhat shy in making any promise and engaging, but seemed to approve the measure and insinuated he would do everything that an honest man could desire. The other frankly undertook what was demanded and seemed very keen to have the project executed.

Of which Mr Cunningham being informed, thus fraughted and instructed, away he went from Edinburgh into the country, and, having soon obtained and gained the entire credit with the ringleaders, the first discovery he made was that the Court, fearing a storm from hence, had gained over Mr Hepburn (a mountain Cameronian minister and the darling of the people)[11] to their side, and he served them as a spy. And though he roared as much as any against the Union, did nevertheless oppose all their measures of appearing openly against it.[12] And Cunningham having acquainted several, particularly Mr Macmillan[13] (another Cameronian minister, who was sincere in his opposition to the Union) of Hepburn's villainy, they soon withdrew the people from Hepburn and Macmillan became the leading man and oracle.

Mr Cunningham having traversed through the country, and finding all as he wished, concerted that all should be ready to rise in arms on the first call, that he should have the chief command of them until they met with such other parts of the kingdom as should join for the preservation of their common liberties and that some person of most eminent quality and capacity should be pitched upon to command all. After this he returned to Edinburgh, and, having acquainted his three friends with his successful negotiations, they communicated it to such as they thought proper. To some particularly all that had passed and was concerted, and to others only in general terms that something would be done very soon. By this time the Parliament had advanced far, and approven several of the articles. And as it was plain such a desparate disease required a desparate remedy, Mr Cunningham goes again to the country with a design to put his formed enterprize in execution. And having dispatched his emissaries and appointed the precise day wherein they should all privately march and meet at the town of Hamilton, in order to march forward with all speed to Edinburgh, above seven or eight thousand men, well armed (all with guns and swords, five or six hundred with bayonets for the muzzles of their guns and twice as many of them on horseback) were on the wing and would without doubt have kept the tryst, had not the Duke of Hamilton a day or two before the prefixed time of their rendesvouz sent expresses privately (without acquainting any of those who he knew were conscious of the concert) through the whole country, strictly requiring them to put off their design at this time. And, his grace being entirely trusted, by these means so thwarted and broke the measure that not above five hundred, who were more forward than the others, came to the place appointed. Mr Cunningham returning soon to Edinburgh, gave a full account of all he had done and by what means he was disappointed, which at once both baulked and surprised a great many honest men.[14] And some indistinct accounts of this preparation and other rendesvouzes coming to the government's ears, the Parliament repealed that clause of the Act of Security which allowed and ordained rendesvouzes of the fensible men.

What induced the Duke of Hamilton to this measure I shall not determine. Some swore he was under capitulation with the Court. Others will tell you he was afraid to venture because of his estate in England. All I ever heard alledged on his behalf was that he thought the nation was by no means in a fit state for such an enterprize at that time, because the English had sent their troops to the borders and more forces would be wafted over from Holland, and so the nation be undone and all that joyned cut in pieces. But others said that by this argument all opposition to the Union was in vain, for if the English had a mind for it, why, it must be swallowed down. But, even supposing it were so, his grace ought to have advertised his friends of it, before he had counteracted what had been contrived by them. Others again maintained there was no such hazard in the attempt, because England, being engaged in a bloody war, would have dropped the Union rather than drawn on themselves a civil war.

But supposing it otherwise, they thought Scotland might have defended themselves for some time, till France had counteracted the troops that were to come from abroad, especially since the nation was unanimous and cordial in the cause and not seven thousand standing forces in all Britain, of which those that were in Scotland were so dissatisfied with the Union that everybody knew, and the officers had acquainted the government, that they could not be trusted, nine parts of ten being inclined to joyn with those that opposed it. But to pass over these things, this I may assert, that had not the Duke of Hamilton taken this course the Parliament had been at once se[n]t a-packing and the projected Union demolished. In which case all those that had appeared most forward for it would have fled, having horses laid and always ready to carry them off from the danger they had reason to dread and justly deserved.

The preceeding project being thus broke, the next measure the Country party in Parliament thought upon was (according to the precedent in the minority of James the fifth) to invite as many of the barons, freeholders and heretors as could possibly be got to Edinburgh,[15] that they might in a body wait upon the High Commissioner and by a prolocutor[16] intreat his grace to lay aside the designed union, [or] at least grant a recess until they had informed the queen of the present temper and disposition of the nation and obtained an order calling for a new Parliament to settle and provide for the calamities that were too likely to follow. And they resolved, whether his grace granted or refused this just and reasonable demand, that a national address representing the same things should be signed and forthwith sent to the queen.

This measure came first from the Duke of Athol and Mr Fletcher of Salton, and was relished and recommended by the Duke of Hamilton and generally approved of by everybody. So that all hands were set to work to acquaint their friends in the country of the design, and desire them to come privately to Edinburgh against a certain prefixed day. In the meantime, Mr Henry Maul (brother to the Earl of Panmure [and] a person of great honour and merit, and every way fit for such a task)[17] was pitched upon to be the prolocutor, and the form of an address to the queen concerted and agreed to by all who were upon the concert of carrying on the project, in the following terms:

We noblemen, barons, gentlemen, burgesses and other subscribers, your Majesty's most dutiful subjects of this your ancient kingdom, do beg leave to lay before your Majesty our deep concern and sorrow, and unexpressible regrate, that your Majesty seems to have been prevailed upon by misrepresentations which have been made to you of the nature of an incorporating union so far to favour the articles of the treaty now before the Parliament, that your signification of your approbation of them is like to bring that affair to a conclusion, which will not only be highly dishonourable to this nation by the suppressing the soveraignty and Parliaments, but sink the rents, destroy the trade and subject the people of this kingdom to intolerable taxes. And, considering the almost universal aversion to this treaty, is more likely to be the occasion of separating these kingdoms for ever than of uniting them in affections.

We do further beg leave, with all imaginable respect, to represent to your Majesty that an union so little founded in the affections of the people, and which consequently must be maintained by force, may be very dangerous to the liberty of Britain. For though we have nothing to apprehend from your Majesty's just and benign government, yet a designing prince may easily make use of that force which awes one end of this island, to subdue the other and so enslave the whole. Though, to obviate such a design, we hear there are many who make no bones of proposing to dissipate and destroy the people of this nation in a few years. Therefore, in order to prevent such a chain of miseries as is like to be the consequence of a forced union, we, your Majesty's most dutiful and loyal subjects, make our most humble supplication to your Majesty, that in consideration of these things you would be pleased graciously to yield to the most earnest prayers of your loving subjects in this your kingdom, by discountenancing this treaty and calling a new Parliament in this your ancient kingdom, according to our Claim of Right, by which we are entituled to frequent Parliaments, and likewise a General Assembly of the church of this kingdom. And we shall always pray for your Majesty's long and happy reign over us.

Against the time appointed above five hundred gentlemen were come actually to Edinburgh, and many more a-coming. But just as the business was ripe, and the next day appointed for execution, the Duke of Hamilton acquainted those in concert with him that unless they would add a clause to the address intimating their willingness to settle the succession in the house of Hanover he would by no means be concerned in the measure, alledging that without it the English Tories, who it was expected would oppose the Union in the English Parliament, could have no foundation to go upon. You may easily imagine it was no small surprize, after all things had been adjusted even to his grace's satisfaction, to find this objection thrown in the way. And it was generally believed that it was done a-purpose to break the design, since his grace and every other body could not be ignorant that the greatest part of those gentlemen who were come to town to forward this matter would never condescend to such a clause. Besides, it was to no purpose since the petitory part of the address itself was the calling of a new Parliament, whose province it was to take this affair under consideration.

Whilst two or three days were spent in endeavouring to reconcile and adjust this difference, the country gentlemen grew weary of hanging on to no purpose in Edinburgh, so many of them dropt off and went away to their country seats.[18] And the government (confounded to see such numbers in the streets) coming to understand the design, resolved to obstruct it, and for that end the Chancellor on the twenty-seventh of December acquainted the house that notice had been sent to the Commissioner that several letters had been sent and dispersed through the country inviting persons of all ranks to come to Edinburgh and demand an answer from the Parliament to their addresses; that such meetings might occasion disorders and trouble.[19] For which cause he presented a proclamation discharging any such meetings and gathering together during the sitting of Parliament, which was approven of, but protested against by George Lockhart of Carnwath in the following terms:

> I do protest for myself and all that shall adhere to this my protestation, that this proclamation now to be emitted, discharging the barons, freeholders and heretors from coming to Edinburgh in time of sitting of Parliament shall no ways prejudice the rights and privileges of the barons, freeholders and heretors of this kingdom, competent to them by the laws of this nation.[20]

And took instruments thereupon. To which the adherers were: the Dukes of Hamilton and Athol; the Earl of Errol; the Earl Marishal; the Earls of Wigton and Selkirk; the Viscounts of Stormont and Kilsyth; the Lords Oliphant, Balmerino, Blantyre, Bargeny, Belhaven, Colvil and Kinnaird; Sir James Foulis of Colintoun, Sir John Lauder of Fountainhall, Andrew Fletcher of Salton, Sir Patrick Home of Renton, John Brisbane of Bishopton, William Cochran of Kilmaronock, James Graham of Bucklivy, Robert Rollo of Powhouse, Sir Patrick Murray of Auchtertyre, John Murray of Strowan, Alexander Gordon of Pitlurg, John Forbes of Culloden, David Bethune of Balfour, Henry Balfour of Dunboig, [Thomas] Hope of Rankeiller, Patrick Lyon of Auchterhouse, James Carnegy of Phinhaven, David Graham of Fintrie, James Ogilvy of Boyn, Alexander Mackie of Palgown, James Sinclair of Stempster and George Mackenzie of Inchcoulter, barons; Alexander Watson, Francis Molison, John Lyon, Sir Robert Anstruther, John Carruthers, George Home and John Bain, burrows.

The letters to which the Chancellor in his discourse referred were writ by Hay of Craignethan, Sheriff Deputy under the Duchess of Hamilton in the shire of Clydesdale,[21] to most of the heretors in that shire (and a copy of one of them brought to the Commissioner by one Cunningham of Harperfield)[22] in the same terms as the Commissioner asserted. And truly I must acknowledge both the stile and method of giving this advertisement were very improper. Other people upon the concert took other ways privately to advertise their friends without running the hazard of thus exposing and discovering the whole design, and that too in such a strange stile.[23] But many, adding this piece of management to the Duke of Hamilton's conduct in relation to the address, concluded it was done on purpose to elude the project. But be that as it will, the foresaid bone that was thrown in the address's teeth, and this publication of these letters, rendered the whole of no effect.

A guilty conscience is a strange thing, and still discovers itself. For the government, not sufficiently secured by this proclamation, gave orders to the officers of the guards if they saw any considerable number of gentlemen approaching the Abbey of Holyrood House, to stop them and deny them access. But they might have spared their pains, for the discord that on this point arose betwixt the two Dukes of Hamilton and Athol, who were after this so jealous and out of humour with one another, disconcerted all and the measure was entirely dropt, the country gentlemen returning home highly enraged at their being thus baulked, and exclaiming as highly against those whom they believed the chief instruments thereof.

During the time that the country had been thus, though to no purpose, employed in endeavouring to obstruct the designed Union, the Parliament went fast through the articles, and being advanced to the twenty-second article (wherein the quota of Scotland's representatives in the British Parliament was adjusted) there was no more time to be lost. Whereupon the Duke of Hamilton convened a good number of the most leading men of those who had opposed the Union, pathetically[24] exhorting them not to look backwards upon what might be thought done amiss by any, but to go forwards now at the last hour to do something to save the nation just come to the brink of ruin.[25]

To which, after all present had declared their chearful concurrence, though the consequences should be never so fatal, his grace did propose that the Marquis of Annandale should renew his motion of proceeding to settle the succession of the crown of Hanover. And as it was not to be questioned but the same would be rejected, that a protestation should be entered and adhered to by all that were against the Union, who should in a body together immediately thereafter make a separation from the other members by leaving the house, not to return again. Which being done, that the national address that was concerted when the barons were to have waited on the Commissioner should be forthwith signed by as many hands as possible and dispatched to the queen. His grace told them he was perswaded that if anything would weigh with the English and prevail upon them to let the Union drop it was this measure. For they might remember the last treaty of union, which was authorized by the Rump Parliament [of] 1702, came to no effect, and one chief reason was that the English ministry thought they had no security in treating or agreeing with commissioners who derived their power from a Parliament against whose proceedings and actings so many, and such considerable, members had protested. And concluded that this separation upon the back of so bold a protestation would startle the English more than anything besides, and convince them that this Union would not be founded upon a secure and legal basis, a back door being left open to evade the same whenever a fair occasion should offer. And then his grace offered the draught of the protestation.

I know the Marquis of Annandale put it into his hands, but whether or not his lordship or some other person was the author of it is more than I can tell. Only I was informed, but I cannot affirm it is a truth, that it was drawn by Sir James Stuart the queen's Advocate, who, though he could not be persuaded to speak and declare his mind against the Union in Parliament, yet was heartily averse to it, and as soon as it came under serious consideration deserted the house and could not be prevailed upon either by the threats or [the] cajoling of the Court to return and assist them in promoting it.[26] But be the author who will, the paper well deserves to be inserted at large, and was as follows:

> Whereas the peace and safety of mankind, and the security
> of all well-established nations and their governments, civil
> and ecclesiastical, do chiefly depend upon the careful and
> religious preservation of those original, fundamental and

indissolvable constitutions by which men are joined in societies amongst themselves, these fundamental constitutions can never be sheltered from the precarious vicissitudes and insults of factions unless they are placed above the reach of the ordinary course of administration and legislature. And whereas it does evidently appear by the ancient constitution and practice of this kingdom that though our Parliaments are empowered to enact all manner of laws for the security of the constitution, yet they were never impowered, nor never did attempt, to lessen or invert the priviledge which the peers have of sitting and voting in Parliament, which priviledge is a part of their property and cannot be touched without impeachment and forefaultrie.

Neither hath the Parliament been impowered, nor have they ever attempted, to lessen the number of representatives of the barons or burrows, seeing no representative can lessen or alienate the power by which they represent without express power and warrant for that effect from the constituent.

Neither have our Parliaments ever been empowered, nor have they at any time attempted to lessen or transfer the power and authority of Parliament. And whereas it appears by the same ancient constitution and practice that whenever any extraordinary juncture did occur, or any incroachment was made upon our fundamental laws and constitution, or that any extraordinary remedy or innovation was found necessary, there was always a convention of estates called upon such an extraordinary juncture, as being a representative cloathed with a more than ordinary power and instructed with a more immediate sense of the nation. And whereas many noble and worthy members of this house, and the subjects of this nation of all ranks and qualities, have generally shown an utter aversion to any such union as is contained in the Articles of Union now lying before the house, as appears by several protests entered in this house upon the fourth, twelfth, fifteenth and eighteenth days of

November last bypast, by an address from the Commission of the General Assembly, by several unanimous Presbyterial addresses, by an address of the Royal Burrows (the third state of the nation) and by an unprecedented number of addresses subscribed by the generality of the freeholders, magistrates and burgesses, especially of all those shires which had shown themselves most early and active in the late Revolution, and all declaring their aversion to the present treaty of union. And whereas to prevent these threatning disorders and dangers, and to calm people's minds, and to show our neighbours of England that there is a more expedite, safe and certain method for establishing a good understanding betwixt these nations, there was an offer made on the [6th] day of [November] for settling the succession of the House of Hanover upon such limitations as should be thought necessary.

I do therefore for myself and in the name of all those shall adhere to this my protestation, protest against this Union in the terms of these articles now before this house, as manifestly tending to subvert that original, fundamental and indissolvable constitution by which the people of this ancient kingdom are joyned together in a society amongst themselves and tending thereby to divest our establishment, civil and ecclesiastical, of all manner of security, as tending to lessen and forfeit the right of the peers of this nation without crime or impeachment by inverting their proper rights of a constant share in the legislature to a precarious right. As tending to expose the whole rights and property of the nation to be forfeited and taken away upon pretext of bettering the condition of the nation. Which precedent might be of dangerous consequence and might at one time or other affect the whole rights of the nation, from those of the meanest subject to the soveraign rights of the crown. As tending to invert and annul the grants of Her Majesty's royal predecessors, and to dishonour and impair Her Majesty's royal prerogative in Scotland by subverting the nature of her patents and grants. As tending to debase the whole nobility of Scotland by degrading them to a spurious state of peerage, subaltern and inferiour to the peers of England. As tending to lessen the representatives of shires and burrows, where those shires and burrows themselves have given their recent and immediate instructions in private, and addresses in public to the contrary. As tending to translate, surrender and subjoin the power of our legislative and Parliaments (after they were thus dismembred and lessened) to the entire Parliament of another nation. As tending to subject the security and administration of two incompatable [sic] church establishments, and the security and administration of different municipal laws and judicatives to the vote of one and the same Parliament, to the unavoidable confusion, jealousy and danger of these nations. As tending to drain this nation of a considerable part of its small stock of money for defraying the charge of sixty-one representatives. As tending to drain this nation of the far greater part of the product of the customs and excise which formerly remained at home towards paying our own ministry and other necessary charges of the government, but must henceforward go out, seeing upon the event of this Union our government and ministry must be translated forth of this kingdom. As tending to ruin the trade and subjects of this kingdom by engaging them into insupportable customs and burdens upon foreign trade and home consumption, and by involving the trade of Scotland under the regulations of the trade of England, though the funds, export and import, and the common means of living in the south and north are of such different natures that the regulations that are necessary in the south will be ruinous to the trade and living in the north, and generally as tending to lay a foundation of perpetual grudge and animosities amongst people whose happiness in that united kingdom is pretended to consist in their being absolutely and entirely united in all manner of interests, while at the same time they are and must be kept separate in their most valuable concerns, both civil and ecclesiastick.

And I do for myself, and in my name and behalf of all those who will adhere to this my protestation, protest and declare that we will not lessen, dismember or part with our Parliament or any part of the power thereof, or with any part of the just rights and properties of the peers, barrons, or burrows of this kingdom, and that no pretended laws, acts, or resolves, to be past, or settlements to be made in all time coming in, or by, any pretended Parliament of Great Britain, can be of force or effect to bind the subjects or property of this nation. And that if any person or persons whatsoever of our fellow subjects, of whatsoever degree, rank, or estate, under any pretext whatsoever, or by any manner or means, endeavour to dismember or withdraw themselves from us and go into any other constitution of their own invention inconsistent with, or destructive to and subversive of, our present fundamental constitution, we do look upon them as breakers of our indissolvable fundamental society, against which we cannot nor ought not to transgress. And that it shall be lawful for us by all legal and lawful means in Parliaments, Conventions and Meetings of Estates, or otherways as our ancestors in the like cases have usually done, to vindicate and assert our ancient rights and liberties, and to support, redintegrate [sic] and certify our said fundamental constitution and indissolvable society in which we have been united for so many hundreds of years. And that we will in the confidence of those sacred and indissolvable rights, under the blessing and protection of the divine vindicator of all rights, maintain, support and defend the constitution and authority of our Parliaments, Her Majesty's sovereignty and government and the present settlement both of church and state in this nation according to our Claim of Right and other laws following thereupon, against all opposition whatsoever.

When the Duke of Hamilton made this proposal there were, to

the best of my remembrance, present the Duke of Athol; the Marquis of Annandale; the Earls of Errol, Marishal, Wigton,[27] Galloway and Selkirk; the Viscounts of Stormont and Kilsyth; the Lords Belhaven and Balmerino; Mr Cochran of Kilmaronock, Mr Lockhart of Carnwath, Mr Ogilvy of Boyn [and] Mr Lyon of Auchterhouse.[28] And likewise the Earl of Panmure,[29] the Lord Nairn,[30] Mr Henry Maul and Mr James Graham of Newton, Solicitor to the late King James, who, though the two first of these four had not sworn the oaths and taken their places in Parliament, and the other two were not members thereof, were all very capable to be assistant in their advice.

These, I say, having demanded a day or two to take the proposal into consideration before they came to a final resolution,[31] the Duke of Hamilton was in the interim at great pains to convince them and such others (who were not present when the proposal was first made) to whom he thought fit to communicate it, of the reasonableness of the measure. The greatest difficulty with some was the mentioning their having been willing to settle the succession on the House of Hanover, which they said was a kind of obligation upon them to make their refuge to that family to protect them in opposing the Union's taking effect, and endeavouring to restore the nation to its ancient rights and constitution. Whereas their design was, and had ever been, to preserve the nation and at the same time to restore the king to the throne, which they thought the present temper of the people would much advance. To this the Duke of Hamilton returned that it would draw no obligation upon them to adhere to the interest of the House of Hanover since they did not protest against the motion's being rejected, the narrative only bearing the true matter of fact, viz. that such a proposal had actually been made. And even supposing it were otherwise, it was not the first time they had made greater stretches with a design that good might come of it, and he hoped this would be the last. 'For', added he (to such as he was intimate with), 'this bold and clear protestation, backed by the separation, will not only confound the English, but likewise encourage our own fellow subjects and engage them to stand by and support us.' And for his part he was of opinion, that if the English did not desist from prosecuting the Union they must have recourse to arms and call over the king, and he doubted not but the nation, to save themselves from utter ruine, would concur with them, and he was willing to venture as far as any.

By these and such considerations all were brought over, and at the next meeting declared their approbation of the measure, promising to adhere to the protestation, which it was taken for granted the Duke of Hamilton would present. Only the Duke of Athol could by no reasons be prevailed upon to adhere to the protestation, because of that clause in relation to the House of Hanover.[32] But he engaged to join in the measure of leaving the house, and all that should be afterwards thought necessary and demanded of him.

All things being thus prepared and adjusted, next day was appointed for the execution, which, being communicated to a great number of those which were against the Union, it caused an universal joy, and great numbers of gentlemen and eminent citizens flocked together that morning about the Parliament house to attend the separating members and assist them in case they should be maltreated as they came from the house. But all their hopes soon vanished and came to nothing, for that morning the Duke of Hamilton, pretending[33] to be seized of the toothach, refused to go to the house. But some of his friends having freely expostulated with him upon this his conduct, telling him this double dealing and wavering would convince the world that what was said concerning his grandfather in the reign of King Charles the first was true,[34] and that he played the second part of the same tune, he was at last prevailed upon to go to the house and prosecute the measure. But when he came there he called for his friends that were upon the concert, desiring to know from them who they had pitched upon to enter the protestation. They told him there was none so proper as his grace, being the person of the first quality and most interest in the nation, begging and imploring he would lead them on at this time, and assuring him they would stand by him with their lives and fortunes. Yet nothing would do, he still persisting in this resolution not to be the presenter of it, though he swore he should be the first adherer. And so much time was spent in wrangling upon this point that the Parliament had met and advanced so far upon business that the opportunity was lost.

It is not to be expressed what a rage all those that had been upon the concert, nay, I may say, the whole nation (for it was soon spread abroad) were in, to see the Duke of Hamilton thus three times, one after another, break the designs and measures that were laid down for opposing the designed slavery of the nation. And I was told by the Earl of Seafield that if the measure had been pursued and executed the Commissioner and other ministers of state had resolved to prorogue the Parliament and give over the prosecution of the Union. I was likewise assured by one who had it from one of the ministers of state that the reason his grace changed his mind and made so short a turn in this affair was that after his friends had left him the evening before the protestation was to be entered and the separation made, either the Commissioner himself or one from him (but I have forgot which) came privately to his grace and told him he had intelligence of what was in agitation, and could assure him if it was not let fall England would lay the blame of it upon him and he would suffer for it, and that this threatning induced him to change his mind and confound the measure [he] himself had concerted, promoted and engaged people of his principles to enter into.[35] Whether this truly was or was not the reason is what I cannot assert. But this behaviour of his gave occasion for people to talk far and wide, that he had made his terms with the Court and betrayed the Country party, and did so exasperate and discourage them, and create such jealousies and dryness betwixt him and the Cavaliers, that for the future no other measures were concerted and everyone did that which was good in his own eyes. And in a few days great numbers of those that had appeared zealously against the Union deserted the house in despair. So that when the twenty-second article (which took the house up two or three days in adjusting) came to be approved, there was little or no opposition against it.[36] Only, before voting it, Mr Lockhart of Carnwath entered a protestation with relation to the privileges of the barons in these terms:

> I do protest for myself and such other barons as shall adhere to this my protestation, that neither this vote nor any other vote, conclusion or article in this treaty of Union shall prejudice the barons of this kingdom from their full representation in Parliament as now by law established, nor in any of their privileges, and particularly of their judicative and legislative capacities, of which they are deprived by the terms of this treaty of union. And I crave this my protestation may be admitted and recorded.[37]

To which most of the barons that were against the Union did adhere.

There were likewise five [other] protestations entered. The first, by the Duke of Athol, with relation to the several branches of this article, in these terms:

> Whereas by my protest given in the fourth of November last, before voting [on] the first article of the Union, I did reserve liberty to renew my protestation against any other article of the treaty. And as I protested for the reasons therein mentioned, so I do now for myself and all others who shall adhere, protest against any vote for approving the twenty-second article of this treaty of union, and against all the parts thereof, for these reasons. Because the peers of the realm who are hereditary members of Her Majesty's Great Council and Parliament do hereby become elective, and so Her Majesty is deprived of her born councellors, and the peers of their birth-right. And whereas they are at present one hundred and sixty in number, they are by this article reduced to sixteen, and are to be joined with the House of Lords in England, whose number at present consists of above one hundred and eighty. Whereby it is plain that the Scots peers share of the legislative and judicative powers in the British Parliament is very unequal with the English, though the one be the representatives of as independent a nation as the other,

and that it is a plain forfeiture of the peerage of this kingdom. And as it is the height of injustice, and against the laws and practice of this and all well-governed nations, to forfeit any person without an heinous crime, so it is against all laws to forfeit either the peers that are now present, or those that are minors and absent, without so much as being called or cited for that end. It is likewise contrary to the true honour and interest of Her Majesty and the monarchy to suppress the estate of peers, who have formerly been the greatest supporters of the monarchy. And it is dishonourable and disgraceful for this kingdom that the peers thereof shall only have rank and precedency next after the peers of the like order and degree in England, without regard to their antiquity or the dates of their patents, as is stipulated by the following articles of this treaty.

In the next place, each shire and royal burgh within this kingdom have the number of their representatives determined by Acts of Parliament, whose number, at present being one hundred fifty-five, are by this article of [the] treaty reduced to forty-five, and to be joyned to five hundred and thirteen in the House of Commons, where they can have no influence by reason of the vast disproportion of their numbers. Besides that the barons and burgesses of this nation, by this way of uniting, are deprived of their inherent right of being fully and individually represented in Parliament, both in relation to their legislative and judicative capacities. And they are not only highly prejudged in lessening their representation, but also degraded from being members of the Parliament of this kingdom, where they sit as judges in all causes civil and criminal, to be joyned to the Commons of another nation who are accustomed to supplicate for justice at the bar of the House of Lords.

The barons and burrows are further prejudged in this, that whereas now every shire and royal burgh have their own representatives, one commissioner will hereafter represent several shires and burghs, who, it cannot be supposed, will understand the several interests and concerns of the said several shires and burghs whom they may represent. And further, for the present representatives of the barons and burrows in Parliament to offer by any vote or deed of theirs to incapacitate their consitituents, or deprive them of any part of their inherent right, is that which their constituents may and do justly disallow, they only having their commissions with the ordinary power of making and amending laws and giving supplies, but no ways to alter fundamental constitutions, or to take away or diminish their representation, which is also a plain forfeiture of their constituents, of their inherent rights and undoubted privileges, and is contrary to the fundamental laws of this nation, which are the birth-right of the people thereof.

From all which it is plain and evident that this, from a soveraign independant monarchy, shall dissolve its constitution and be at the disposal of England, whose constitution is not in the least to be altered by this treaty and where it is not to be supposed the Scots shall have any weight in the making of laws, even though relative to their own kingdom, by reason of the vast disproportion and disparity of their representation aforesaid. And therefore I do also protest that no vote may hinder or prejudge the noblemen, barons and burrows as now represented in Parliament to retain, bruke, enjoy and exercise all their rights, liberties and priviledges as fully and freely as hitherto they have enjoyed them. And since it evidently appears not only from the many protests of the honourable and worthy members of this house, but also from the multitude of addresses and petitions of the several parts of this kingdom of the barons, freeholders, heretors, burrows and commons, and from the Commission of the General Assembly, that there is a general dislike and aversion to the incorporating union as contained in these articles, and that there is not one address from any part of the kingdom in favour of the Union, I do therefore protest against concluding this and the following articles of the treaty until Her Majesty shall be fully informed of the inclinations of her people, that, if Her Majesty think fit, she may call a new Parliament to have the immediate sentiments of the nation, since these articles have been made publick. Where it is to be hoped they may fall upon such methods as may allay the ferment of the nation, satisfy the minds of the people and create a good understanding betwixt the two kingdoms by an union upon honourable, just and equal terms, which may unite them in affection and interest – the surest foundation of peace and tranquility for both kingdoms. And this my protestation I desire may be received and inserted in the minutes, and recorded in the books of Parliament, as a testimony of my dissent and the dissent of such as shall adhere to me.[38]

The next protestation was made by the Earl of Buchan,[39] with relation to the rights of the peers, as follows:

Forasmuch as the changing of the rights of the peers of this realm, from a constant and hereditary right to one that is elective, and the debarring all or any of them from taking [their] place and voting in Parliament, conventions or publick councils is subversive of the birth-right and undoubted privilege of the peers, dishonourable to the whole kingdom and contrary to the fundamental laws and constitution thereof, as well as to all justice and equity. I do therefore for myself and in the name of all who shall adhere to this my protestation, protest that the aforesaid right of the peers of this kingdom to sit and vote in all Parliaments, councils and conventions do after the intended union with England, and notwithstanding thereof, continue in full force, and remain to them as their undoubted right and property, and that no vote pass in this house to prejudice all or any of them from claiming the same in time coming.[40]

The third protestation, with relation to priviledges of peers, barons and burrows, was entered by Walter Stuart of Pardovan, representative of the town of Linlithgow,[41] in these words:

I do protest for myself, and in name and behalf of all others who shall adhere to this my protestation, that the restriction of the representatives in Parliament for this kingdom, as contained in the twenty-second article of the treaty of union, is contrary to the birth-right of the peers and rights and privileges of the barons and freeholders and royal burrows, and fundamental laws and constitution of the nation. And if any vote shall pass approving of the said article in the terms that it stands, that it shall not prejudge the birth-right of the peers, the rights and privileges of the the barons and freeholders and royal burrows, competent to them by the laws and constitution of this kingdom, and I take instruments upon this protestation and desire it be inserted in the records of Parliament.[42]

The fourth protestation, by the Earl of Errol, with relation to his heretable office of High Constable, in these terms:

I do hereby protest that the office of High Constable of Scotland, with all the rights and privileges of the same, belonging to me heretably and depending upon the monarchy, sovereignty and ancient constitution of this kingdom, may not be weakened or prejudged by the conclusion of the treaty of union betwixt Scotland and England, nor any article, clause, or condition, thereof. But that the said heretable office, with all the rights and privileges thereof, may continue and remain to me and my successors entire and unhurt by any votes or act of Parliament, or other proceedings whatsoever relative to the Union. And I crave this my protestation may be admitted and recorded in the registers and rolls of Parliament.[43]

The last protestation was by the Earl Marishal, with relation to his heretable office of Mareschal of Scotland, in this manner:

I do hereby protest that whatever is contained in any article of the treaty of union betwixt Scotland and England shall in no manner of way derogate from, or be prejudicial, to me or my successors in our heretable office of Great Marishal of Scotland in all time coming, or in the full and free enjoyment and exercise of the whole rights, dignities, titles, honours, powers and privileges thereto belonging, which my ancestors and I have possessed and exercised as rights of property these seven hundred years. And I do further protest that the Parliament of Scotland, and constitution thereof, may remain and continue as formerly. And I desire this my protestation to be inserted in the minutes, and recorded in the books of Parliament, and thereupon take instruments.[44]

To the three first protestations, viz. the Duke of Athol's, the Earl of Buchan's and Mr Stuart's, most of these members that had been opposite to the Union, and had not left the house, did adhere.[45] But the Courtiers being unwilling to let the world see the good grounds that moved them to oppose the Union, refused to allow those three and Mr Lockhart's protestations, and the names of those that adhered to them to be printed (as was always usual in the minutes of Parliament. And having a majority on their side, the said protestors were obliged to compound the matter thus: that provided the said protestations were recorded in the books of Parliament, they should not be printed at length, but that mention should be made in the minutes of such protestations being entered by such persons, and of the adherers names. But the Earl of Marchmont, not satisfied with allowing this, entered his protestation against it in a most virulent stile, asserting that these protestations were presumptious, illegal and unwarrantable, and tending to raise sedition. But the Lord Balmerino entered another protestation against receiving this of Lord Marchmont's, as the same was unmannerlie and illegall. And the members, as they favoured the parties and cause, adhered to the one or the other of these two protestations.[46]

From this day forward the house was almost quite drained of the Anti-Unioners, and so the Courtiers acted how and as they listed, till they had finished and approven all the articles of the treaty and engrossed them into an act, and that they received the royal assent, without meeting with much opposition. Only when the method for chusing the representatives for Scotland to the next, British, Parliament was under consideration, the Duke of

Hamilton and Mr Cochran of Kilmaronock did each of them protest against their being chosen out of the Parliament by the members of the house as being contrary to the twenty-second article of union, wherein the method of electing the peers is regulated and determined, inconsistent with the birth-rights and privileges of the barons and burrows, and contrary to the principles of Common Law and diverse Acts of Parliament. To which the Earls of Errol, Marishal, Buchan, Eglinton and Galloway; the Viscount of Kilsyth; the Lords Semple, Balmerino, Blantyre, Bargeny, Belhaven and Colvil; Sir John Lauder of Fountainhall, Andrew Fletcher of Salton, Sir Robert Sinclair of Longformacus, John Brisbane of Bishopton, Sir Humphrey Colquhoun of Luss, John Graham of Killearn, Robert Rollo of Powhouse, Thomas Sharp of Houston, Sir Thomas Burnet of Leys, Sir David Ramsay of Balmain, John Forbes of Culloden, Thomas Hope of Rankeiller, David Graham of Fintrie, Alexander Mackie of Palgown, James Sinclair of Stemster, James Dunbar of Hemprigs, Sir Henry Innes of Innes and George Mackenzie of Inchcoulter, barons; Alexander Edgar, James Scott, Francis Molison, Robert Scott, John Hutchison, Archibald Sheilds, John Lyon, George Brody and John Carruthers, burrows, did adhere.[47]

But the Courtiers being conscious to themselves that the nation was displeased with them, that they could not expect any of their stamp would be returned from the shires or burrows,[48] were resolved not to 'swallow a cow and stick at the tail'. And as they had begun, carried on and finished their projects contrary to all the ties of justice and honour and the welfare of the country, so they continued the same well pathed road and commenced the Union with as great an invasion upon the rights of the subject by depriving them of the powers of naming their own representatives, as ever was done to a free people. For they picked out sixteen peers, thirty barons and fifteen burgesses of this present Parliament that were thorough paced and altogether at their becks.[49] Whereby it came to pass that some shires had their whole number of representatives as in the Scots Parliament, such as Argyleshire, etc, while some had two, some one, and some of the chief shires, such as Edinburgh, Fyfe, Stirling, etc, none at all.

Having brought affairs so far, I have now no more to say to the Parliament's actings. Only let me add, that, notwithstanding the Commissioner had solemnly engaged to the Duke of Hamilton that he would not hinder any person from giving him his vote to be one of the sixteen peers, yet just as they were going to elect he produced a letter from the queen which he had, as he apprehended, at that instant received, discharging any of her servants from voting for him, under the penalty of her displeasure. And thus several who had engaged to vote for the Duke of Hamilton were obliged to resile,[50] and his grace was baulked, to the great satisfaction of many who thought he had been too much imposed upon and were glad to see him cheated by the Court.[51]

It is not to be doubted but the Parliament of England would give a kind reception to the articles of union as passed in Scotland when they were laid before that house, as was evident from the quick dispatch in approving of and ratifying the same.[52] And so the Union commenced on the first of May 1707, a day never to be forgot by Scotland. A day on which the Scots were stripped of what their predecessors had gallantly maintained for many hundred years – I mean the independency and soveraignty of the kingdom. Both which the Earl of Seafield so little valued that when he, as Chancellor, signed the engrossed exemplification of the Act of Union, he returned it to the clerk, in the face of Parliament with this despising and contemning remark: 'now there's ane end of ane old song.'

Notes

1. *Seafield Letters*, p. 107: Seafield to Godolphin, Edinburgh, 16 Nov. 1706; HMC *Portland*, pp. 352, 364, 365: Defoe to Harley, Edinburgh, 16 Nov. and 7 Dec. 1706. Cf. HMC *Portland*, iv. 366: Defoe to Harley, Edinburgh, 9 Dec. 1706.
2. HMC *Portland*, iv. 349: Defoe to Harley, Edinburgh, 13 Nov. 1706.
3. The militantly presbyterian nonconformist followers of Richard Cameron, whose principal strength lay in the southwest of Scotland.

4. Scotland north of the Tay was predominantly episcopalian at this time.
5. HMC *Portland*, iv. 352: Defoe to Harley, [Edinburgh] 16 Nov. 1706.
6. Major James Cunningham of Aiket.
7. GL is either decidedly disingenuous or surprisingly ignorant in his account of Cunningham's early career (which included involvement in the Glencoe massacre and the desertion of his post at Darien), for which see: Prebble, *Darien Disaster*, pp. 59, 103, 150, 156, 161, 220.
8. GL and those who were suspicious of Cunningham were both partially correct, according to Clerk: Somerville, *History*, p. 219 note 31.
9. John Brisbane jr, of Bishopton, Commissioner for Ayrshire; *PS*, i. 68.
10. John Murray of Strowan, Commissioner for Perthshire; *PS*, ii. 533.
11. John Hepburn; HMC, *Laing MSS* ii. 101–9.
12. HMC *Portland*, iv. 374: Defoe to Harley, [Edinburgh] 27 Dec. 1706.
13. John Macmillan, formerly minister of Balmaghie.
14. *Hooke Correspondence*, ii. 353, 372–3.
15. GL may be referring to the Parliament hastily summoned after the death of James IV at the battle of Flodden in 1513.
16. Spokesman.
17. *DNB*, xxxvii. 85–6.
18. HMC *Portland*, iv. 376–7: Defoe to Harley, [Edinburgh] 2 Jan. 1707.
19. *APS*, xi. 369; HMC *Portland*, iv. 374: Defoe to Harley, [Edinburgh] 27 Dec. 1706.
20. The printed version in, *APS*, xi. 369, differs slightly from that given here by GL.
21. Andrew Hay of Craignethan jr, Sheriff-Depute of Lanarkshire for Anne, Duchess of Hamilton.
22. Alexander Cunningham of Harperfield.
23. HMC *Mar and Kellie*, pp. 363–4: Mar to Nairne, Edinburgh, 28 Dec. 1706.
24. Emotionally.
25. Cf. *Lockhart Letters*, p. 37: GL to Maule, [Edinburgh] c. 28 Dec. 1706.
26. HMC *Mar and Kellie*, p. 280: Mar to Godolphin, Edinburgh, 21 Sept. 1706.
27. John Fleming, 6th Earl of Wigton; *CP*, xii (2). 640–1.

28. Patrick Lyon, Commissioner for Forfarshire; *PS*, ii. 441–2.
29. James Maule, 4th Earl of Panmure; *DNB*, xxxvii. 86–7.
30. William Nairne (né Murray), 2nd Lord Nairne; *DNB*, xl. 26.
31. GL's account of the Jacobites' hesitation here is at odds with Mar's description of their response to Annandale's first motion along these lines in November: HMC *Mar and Kellie*, pp. 313–14: Mar to Nairne, Edinburgh, 5 Nov. 1706.
32. HMC *Portland*, iv. 378: Defoe to Harley, Edinburgh, 4 Jan. 1707.
33. In contemporary parlance this meant 'claiming', and did not necessarily carry any implication of deceit.
34. James Hamilton, 1st Duke of Hamilton, was notorious for his cunning tergiversation, by means of which he managed to stay in with both the Covenanters and Charles I until 1648.
35. Clerk offers a more direct solution: 'The duke of Hamilton ... held private correspondence with the commissioner [Queensberry], and was resolved to do nothing that might effectually mar the union' (Somerville, *History*, p. 218 note 29); HMC *Portland*, iv. 347: [D. Fearns] to Harley, Edinburgh, 12 Nov. 1706. See also: HMC *Portland*, iv. 338–9: Hamilton to Harley, Holyrood House, 22 Oct. 1706, for evidence of Hamilton's friendly relations with Harley.
36. *APS*, xi. 386–398: 7–10 Jan. 1707. Cf. HMC *Portland*, iv. 380: Defoe to Harley, [Edinburgh] 9 Jan. 1707.
37. For a slightly different version see, *APS*, xi. 387.
38. For a slightly different version see, *APS*, xi. 386–7.
39. David Erskine, 9th Earl of Buchan; *CP*, ii. 381–2.
40. For a slightly different version see, *APS*, xi. 387.
41. *PS*, ii. 670–1.
42. For a slightly different version see, *APS*, xi. 387.
43. For a slightly different version see, *APS*, xi. 387–8.
44. For a slightly different version see, *APS*, xi. 388.
45. *APS*, xi. 390: adhering to Atholl's protest, for the lords, the Earl of Caithness, Viscount Stormont, Lords Oliphant, Balmerino, Bargany and Kinnaird; for the barons, John Brisbane jr of Bishopton, Sir Humphrey Colquhoun of Luss, Sir Patrick Murray of Ochtertyre, John Murray of Strowan, James Ogilvie jr of Boyn, Alexander McKye of Palgown, James Sinclair of Stempster, Alexander Robertson, Alexander Duff, Francis Molison, Robert Scott, Archibald Sheills, John Lyon, John Carruthers, George Home, John Bayne and Robert Frazer.

Adhering to GL's protest, for the barons, Andrew Fletcher of Saltoun, Sir Robert Sinclair of Longformacus, Sir Hugh Cathcart of Carletoun, John Brisbane jr of Bishoptoun, William Cochran of

Kilmaronock, Sir Humphrey Colquhoun of Luss, Robert Rollo of Powhouse, James Carnegie of Phinhaven, David Graham jr of Fintrie and James Sinclair of Stempster.

Adhering to Buchan's protest, the Earls of Crawford and Galloway.

46. *APS*, xi. 390–1: 8 and 9 Jan. 1707. The adherers to Balmerino's remonstrance were: for the peers, the Dukes of Hamilton and Atholl, the Earls of Errol, Marischal, Buchan, Eglinton, Wigton, Galloway and Selkirk, Viscounts Stormont and Kilsyth and Lords Sempill, Oliphant, Blantyre and Bargany; for the barons, George Lockhart of Carnwath, Andrew Fletcher of Saltoun, William Cochran of Kilmaronock, Sir Humphrey Colquhoun of Luss, Robert Rollo of Powhouse, John Murray of Strowan, James Carnegie of Phinhaven, David Graham jr of Fintrie, Alexander McKie of Palgown, Alexander Edgar, Alexander Duff, Francis Molison, Archibald Scheills, John Lyon, John Carruthers, George Home and Robert Fraser.

47. *APS*, xi. 415–16, 417: 21 Jan. 1707.

48. *Baillie*, p. 181: Baillie to Johnston, [Edinburgh] 21 Jan. 1707.

49. GL's implication that all those chosen to represent Scotland 1707–8 were adherents of the Court is misleading. Following the broad alignments outlined by R. R. Walcott, *English Politics in the Early Eighteenth Century* (Cambridge, Massachusetts, 1956), pp. 233–5 (as corrected by Riley, *Union of England and Scotland*, pp. 330–4 and *PS* i and ii) and House of Lords Record Office, Memorandum 39 (1968): J. C. Sainty, 'A List of Representative Peers for Scotland 1707–1963 and for Ireland 1800–1961' (I am indebted to Clyve Jones of the Institute of Historical Research Library for this reference), they may be categorised as follows:

Court: Duke of Queensberry; Marquess of Lothian; Earls of Crawford, Glasgow, Ilay, Leven, Loudon, Mar, Rosebery, Seafield, Stair, Sutherland and Wemyss; Alexander Abercromby of Glasshaugh; Sir George Allardyce of that ilk; Daniel Campbell of Shawfield; James Campbell of Ardkinglass jr; Sir James Campbell of Auchinbreck; John Campbell of Mamore; John Clark of Penicuik; Sir David Dalrymple of Hailes; William Dalrymple of Glenmure and Drongan; Sir Alexander Douglas of Egilshay; Archibald Douglas of Cavers; Sir John Erskine of Alva; John Erskine of Carnock; Alexander Grant of Grant; Sir Peter Halkett of Pitfirrane; Sir John Johnston of Westerhall; Sir Patrick Johnston; Sir Kenneth Mackenzie of Cromarty; Alexander Maitland of

Pitrichie; Patrick Moncrieffe of Reidie; Francis Montgomerie of Giffen; Hugh Montgomery of Busbie; William Morrison of Prestongrange; John Murray of Bowhill; Patrick Ogilvie of Cairnbulg; Sir Robert Pollock of Pollock; John Pringle of Haining; Hugh Rose of Kilravock; James Scott of Logie; William Seton of Pitmedden jr; Sir James Smollett of Stainflett and Bonhill; John Stewart of Sorbie; Sir John Swinton of Swinton.

Squadrone: Marquesses of Montrose and Tweeddale; Earl of Roxburghe; George Baillie of Jerviswood; William Bennet of Grubbet; John Bruce of Kinross; Sir Thomas Burnet of Leys; John Cockburn of Ormiston; Mungo Graham of Gorthie; John Haldane of Gleneagles; James Haliburton of Pitcur; Sir Andrew Home of Kimmerghame; Sir William Ker of Greenhead; William Nisbet of Dirleton.

Anti-Union: Sir David Ramsay of Balmain.

50. Withdraw.
51. HMC *Mar and Kellie*, pp. 373–6: Mar to Nairne, Edinburgh, 13 Feb. 1707.
52. *Journals of the House of Commons*, xv. 258–326: 28 Jan. – 6 Mar. 1707. N.b. however, that some English Tories had been trying to work up sufficient opposition to block the Union since the summer of 1706 (*Marlborough-Godolphin Correspondence*, ii. 629).

[Jacobite Conspiracy, 1707–1708]

I have now brought the affairs of Scotland from Queen Anne's accession to the throne to the conclusion of the last Scots Parliament. I proceed next to give an account of what happened after the commencement of the Union, [and] particularly of the projects that were set on foot to subvert the same and restore the king. It is not to be expected I can discover all the secret transactions at the time I write this, for many of them were carried on in France, and others, though at home, were kept very secret. Yet you will perceive I have come at the knowledge of so much as will sufficiently enable you to understand the true origin and progress of the designed invasion from France in March 1708.

To begin then. No sooner was the first of May past than the ministry (now of Great Britain) took care to establish the Union of the two kingdoms. And as by the articles it was agreed there should be the same regulations, impositions, etc, of trade throughout the united kingdom (that is to say, that the laws relative to trade in England should take place in Scotland) a set of commissioners was immediately appointed, one for managing the customs, the other the excise of Scotland, consisting partly of English and partly of Scotsmen, though these latter had no pretensions to intitle them to that name, save their being born in that country.[1] They and all that were employed afterwards as commissioners for managing the Equivalent, or advanced to any of the new posts being downright renegadoes, and rewarded on no other account than the assistance they gave in selling their country. At the same time vast numbers of surveyors, collectors, waiters, and, in short, all or most of the officers of the customs and excise were sent down from England,[2] and these, generally speaking, the very scum and canalia of that country.[3]

Which remembers me of a very good story. Sometime thereafter a Scots merchant travelling in England and shewing some
apprehensions of being robbed, his landlady told him he was in
no hazard, for all the highwaymen were gone. And upon his
enquiring how that came about, 'why truly', replied she, 'they are
all gone to your country to get places.'[4]

These fellows treated the natives with all the contempt, and
executed the laws with all the rigour, imaginable. So that before
the first three months were expired there were too apparent
proofs of what had been often asserted in relation to the bad
bargain Scotland had made.[5] It is true indeed, some particular
merchants made a vast gain at this juncture, for the duties upon
wine and most other foreign commodities being much less in
Scotland than in England, great quantities were imported into the
former before the commencement of the Union, and being
afterwards carried into England returned an extraordinary profit.
But as discerning people saw, that was only the accidental
consequence of what could not be well avoided at this juncture
and that these sunshine days would be soon over-clouded (as the
merchants have since effectually experimented),[6] it did no ways
lessen the dreadful apprehensions of the consequences of the
Union. And people of all ranks and perswasions were more and
more chagrined and displeased, and resented the loss of
soveraignty, and were daily more and more perswaded that
nothing but the restoration of the royal family, and that by the
means of Scotsmen, could restore them to their rights. So that
now there was scarce one of a thousand that did not declare for
the king. Nay, the Presbyterians and Cameronians were willing to
pass over the objection of his being papist. 'For', said they
(according to their predestinating principles),[7] 'God may convert
him, or he may have Protestant children, but the Union can never
be good.'[8] And as the reader may remember, the commons
shewed a greater alacrity and readiness to join against the
promoters of the Union whilst it was in agitation, than did those
of better rank and quality, so were they at this time more uneasy
at their subjection and zealous to redeem the liberty of the

country. And thence it was that on all occasions, in all places, and by all people of all perswasions, nothing was to be heard throughout all the country save an universal declaration in favour of the king and exclamations against the Union and those that had promoted it.[9]

Nay, so great a length did their indignation lead them that the presbyterian ministers became universally hated and despised, and lost all their interest with the commons. These not sticking to tell them publickly that they were time-servers and had preached up against the Union whilst they thought their Kirk not well enough secured, but that once being done, they valued not the country nor the people's liberties. And thus were the commons come to this lucky pass that they would have entered into and prosecuted any measure without the previous advice and constant concurrence of their ministers, who formerly, on all other occasions, acted only with a view to themselves, could never be guided by the nobility and gentry and rendered the commons ungovernable by the influence they had over them.

As these were the people's inclinations, so likewise was there an universal expectation of the king's coming over to them. Whence this came I cannot tell, but people were over all parts prepossessed, and pleased themselves with an opinion it would happen very soon. So that for several months they were in constant expectation of him – and this was before any measure for the purpose was finally concluded, and in such countries where few or none were privy to the concert.[10] Besides, they acted consequentially to this, their belief and expectation, in preparing themselves to receive and assist him. For the western shires had their private delegates from each parish to meet and concert measures together, and, amongst others, they appointed several of their number to apply themselves towards getting of intelligence. They named their officers who should head them, till once the nobility and gentry took the command upon them. They had arms making in all places, and appointed people to buy horses. So that a worthy friend of mine, in the shire of Ayr, assured me that very summer twelve or fifteen hundred good horses had been brought over from Ireland, which were picked and brought up by country people and carried where nobody knew. And some of these ringleaders and delegates in Clydesdale did come to Mr Lockhart of Carnwath, telling him they were ordered by a considerable party to enquire of him against what time he thought the king would land. And upon his answering that he wondered how they could ask such a question of him and that he knew nothing of such matters, they answered he might indeed be shy in divulging his mind to them, but they doubted not but he knew, and they would be glad to know likewise, that each of them might spare one or two of their best horses from work and have them in good condition against he landed. And on another occasion one of the chief Cameronians told him they were content to join in an army with the episcopalians, for it was not now a time for Scotland to be divided amongst themselves [sic].[11]

I have instanced these two particulars to shew the inclinations of the people, the like to which happened to several other people in all parts of the kingdom. So that I may well aver that the commons were almost impatient at the king's delay in coming over, and were most sincerely ready to have made him welcome by assisting him to the utmost of their powers. And though the commons appeared with less caution and more barefacedly, yet were not the nobility and gentry less desirous to have him amongst them, so that never was a prince or deliverer more longed for by a people. And what Ovid observed long ago:

> Nescio qua natale solum dulcedine tangit
> Humanas animas...[12]

was remarkably evident on this occasion. For from hence arose that unanimity amongst the episcopals, presbyterians, Cavaliers and many of the Revolutioners, so that, according to the Scots proverb, 'they were all one man's bairns', had the same desire, and were ready to join together in the defence of their country and liberties.[13]

It is not to be doubted but these accounts would soon reach the ears of those at St Germains and Versailles, for, in the first place, during the time that the articles of the Union were under the consideration of the Scots Parliament, the English ministry allowed, or rather, encouraged, their newsmongers to ascribe the opposition they met with to a spirit of Jacobitism. And next, care was taken [by the French] to inform [themselves] how averse the people were to the Union and press the king's coming over as the luckiest opportunity for restoring of him and advancing the affairs of France, by giving a diversion to English arms. And the French king, by the bad success of his arms during the last campaign (wherein he lost the battles of Ramillies and Turin and several strong towns) being brought to a weak pass, began to relish the proposal and seemed in earnest to do something for our king. For which end he sent over Colonel Hookes to get intelligence and treat with the people of Scotland.

I have elsewhere given account of this gentleman,[14] and I have good grounds to believe he was palmed upon the Court of St Germains, being pitched upon by the French king as one that would follow his directions and be true to his interest.[15] And indeed he was not disappointed, for the Colonel showed more concern to raise a civil war at any rate (which was what the French king chiefly wanted), than so to manage and adjust measures as tended most for King James's service and to encourage his subjects to do something for him.[16]

Now it will be proper to remember that the two Dukes of Hamilton and Athol had for some time been on bad terms with one another. The first claiming merit upon the account of his past actions, his interest and qualifications (which are seldom undervalued by great men), and the other thinking that he was to be valued and would yield to none because of the interest he had of late got with the north country gentry, and the great number of men he could raise. But he never considered these would have joined the king not out of affection or obedience to his grace (though he might have a considerable stroke with them, and was therefore to be valued), but from principle of loyalty which they had manifested on all occasions.[17]

These Dukes had their several friends, and some honest men, being disgusted with the Duke of Hamilton on the account of his behaviour during the last Parliament, inclined to think the Duke of Athol would venture further for the king.[18] Which, as it picqued the one, so it elevated the other, nay, to so great a degree that the Duke of Athol and his partizans railed openly against the Duke of Hamilton, and pretended to do all themselves.

There were others again, who, remembring the Duke of Athol's conduct at, and on several occasions since, the Revolution, were afraid he was not thoroughly well founded, but acted more from a desire of revenging himself of the Courtiers who had slighted him than a true principle of loyalty. And considering that he was by no means qualified to be the head of a party, though in general a useful man in promoting so good a design, thought he was to be humoured, but not so as to disgust the Duke of Hamilton altogether. For though the last's behaviour in all points was not approved by them, yet being thoroughly convinced that he was altogether loyal, and though perhaps a little too cautious, or rather timorous, in concerting of measures, would infallibly join the king and venture as far to serve him as any man alive. And it being evident to a demonstration that he was absolutely necessary to be with the king because of his interest, courage and conduct, and particularly his dexterity in managing the different parties in the kingdom. Upon these considerations, I say, they thought he was to be valued, respected and advised with. And having notified the same to the Earl of Middleton[19] (who agreed with them in it)[20] and he again to the king, the Duke of Perth,[21] who was of quite a different interest from the Earl of Middleton,[22] soon made up with the Duke of Athol. And having more interest with the priests and Roman Catholicks than the Earl of Middleton, prevailed so far with the Court of France,[23] or at least with Hookes himself, that when Hookes arrived in Scotland he should make his chief application to his correspondent the Duke of Athol.[24]

It may seem strange that such divisions should have lasted amongst those of the Court of St Germains, but the same happened during the exile of King Charles II,[25] and is a clear proof that nothing can separate statesmen from that selfish, ambitious principle that overrules all their projects, though often to the prejudice of their master and (as on this occasion) of themselves. For sure unanimity and concord were necessary to people in their circumstances.

These being premised, I go on to acquaint you that Hookes set sail from France and landed in the northern parts of Scotland some time about the latter end of February or beginning of March 1707. And, being conducted to Slains Castle, after he received some further account of the present posture of affairs from the Countess dowager of Errol[26] (who was entirely of her brother the Duke of Perth's interest, and a very pragmatical[27] woman) and acquainted some of those with whom he was to traffick of his arrival, he set out towards the south.[28] And came into the shires of Perth and Angus, where he met with great numbers of gentlemen (who were for the most part of the Duke of Athol's party), with whose frankness and hospitality he was so much taken, and they again with his business and errand, that he openly avowed the same and was caressed as an ambassador indeed. And I have been told he took it well enough to be called His Excellency.[29]

After he had remained some time in this country, felt people's pulses and pitched upon those with whom he would treat, he fell to business. I cannot indeed say that he had a personal interview with the Duke of Athol, but certain it is they concerted measures together.[30] But [sic] there were several with whom he met and to whom he made his proposals. The first thing he produced was a letter from the king, and another from the French king, being his credentials, impowering him to treat with the people in Scotland in order to bring about the king's restoration and recover the nation's soveraignty and ancient privileges.[31] Then he produced a long paper containing several queries drawn [up] by Monsieur de Torci,[32] relating to the number of men that could be raised in Scotland, the conveniency of subsisting troops with meat, cloaths and quarters, and their carrying on the war, and the number of men, sum of money and quantity of arms, ammunition and other warlike stores necessary to be sent from France.[33] These and suchlike matters being concerted and adjusted, an answer to M.

de Torci's questions was compiled which gave a distinct resolution to each query, contained a full account of the state of affairs, particularly the inclinations and forwardness of the people to venture all for the king's service, and earnestly entreated him to come over as soon as possible.[34]

I should be glad I were master of a copy of those papers, so that I might insert them at large. However, I have often read them, and this is a short abstract of the most material heads contained in them.

This paper was signed by about fifteen or sixteen noblemen and gentlemen, viz. the Duke of Athol, Lord Drummond,[35] the Earls of Errol and Strathmore, Viscount of Stormont, Lord John Drummond,[36] Lord Nairn,[37] Fotheringhame of Powrie,[38] Lyon of Auchterhouse, Graham of Fintrie,[39] Drummond of Logie,[40] Ogilvy of Boyn and others whose names I have forgot, and was lodged in the hands of Colonel Hookes, to be by him transported to France.[41]

While all this was a-doing they kept not their affairs so secret but that great numbers at that very time, and afterwards every little body that pretended to be a Jacobite, knew of Hookes being here, and though not all the particulars, yet the main design and result of his negotiations.[42] And though I am very far from derogating from the honour and praise those gentlemen deserve upon account of the evident demonstration they gave of their loyalty upon this occasion, yet I must join with those who are of opinion that they took too much upon themselves. It being too much for a few private men in a corner of the country to negotiate and lay down schemes upon so weighty an affair without the advice and concurrence of others whom they knew to be as loyal and as capable to serve the king as they were themselves, nay, without whom they could not pretend to influence other parts of the kingdom. And I can ascribe it to nothing so much as the Duke of Athol's ambition to be thought the chief and first promoter of the king's restoration, and to the other gentlemen's great zeal and firm perswasion that, if they could have the honour of bringing the king over, the nation was so dissatisfied and disgusted at the

Union that everybody would join with them, and they be each of them valued as another Monk.[43] And indeed, afterwards, when people argued with them upon this point, alledging they had not acted prudently with regard either to the king's or their own interest thus to foment divisions at a juncture when everybody was to be pleased, and, as far as possible, honoured, some of them did not stand to answer, that they did not value that, they doubted not of success, and as they had run the hazard they expected the honour of it.

If Scotland had been only concerned they might have ventured to do what they did. And done the king's affairs with a small power, for indeed I do believe there were very few that would have opposed him. But, alas, they little considered that England was in the play and the united strength of all Scotland little enough to effectuate the great design. It is true Hookes brought over letters from the king to the Duke of Hamilton and Earl Marishal.[44] But before he transmitted these letters to them he had so closely attached himself to the other set, and made such advances in the treaty, that these noble lords could not but see how much they were despised and maltreated, and therefore did not think fit to send their answers by him, but chose another hand to communicate their opinions to the Earl of Middleton. Upon which Hookes sent them more than once or twice impertinent, haughty, threatening letters.[45] And so great was the schism upon this account, betwixt those that carried on this business with Hookes and such as enclined to correspond with the Earl of Middleton, and were thus neglected, particularly the Duke of Hamilton, the Earl Marishal, Viscount Kilsyth,[46] Cochran of Kilmaronock, Lockhart of Carnwath, Maul of Kelley and Captain Straton, that the former in all companies where they used the freedom to tell their minds (which was indeed too many), and by the accounts they gave to the Court at St Germains, made no bones of calling the other people cowards and lukewarm, and giving them all the harsh epithets imaginable. Though the Duke of Hamilton and his friends bore them no enmity, and wished them good success, and were very far from envying any man the honour, provided he brought the king home in safety and did so regulate matters as that he might become successful.[47]

And therefore in all their accounts to the king they told him they would strive with none that were doing him service, save in outdoing them in that point if it lay in their power; assuring him they were ready to venture all when he required it, and advising him, as they thought themselves in duty bound, not to hazard his royal person, unless he were so attended and in such a capacity as to be able to accomplish his design. In order to which they at least thought ten thousand regular troops absolutely necessary (the other set having demanded only six or seven thousand) to be brought over with him, and recommending to him to fall upon measures to satisfy the people as to the security of their religion and rights (which by the others was wholly neglected), without which he could not expect to succeed and in doing which there were great difficulties, because of the different parties in the kingdom.[48] These gentlemen thought it their duty to represent matters thus to the king since a faint attempt might have proved fatal to the king's person, and, if it miscarried, ruined the future prospect of his affairs and the hopes of recovering Scotland's rights, by rivetting rebellion and the Union, since it was clear, as [the] Duke of Hamilton expressed it, they must throw away their sheaths. And therefore they continually remonstrated that it was better to suspend making any attempt than not to do it to purpose. Now let God and the world judge if these gentlemen, by giving such advice did deserve to be slandered and misrepresented as they were. However, they had this satisfaction: that they could not blame themselves and were, notwithstanding, resolved to join with the king upon his landing, though he should not bring such a force as they thought necessary for him. The truth of which would have appeared had not the design miscarried.

Hookes had no sooner finished his negotiations than he took his leave of his friends, assuring them that the French king should be in Scotland by the next August, and went in a French ship which waited upon him on the north coast, to France, where he arrived in May 1707. And having given an account of his embassy and the reception he met with, triumphed no little over the Earl of Middleton, whom [he] and his friends in Scotland he [sic] accused of backwardness to serve the king.[49]

In the meantime everybody expected to have heard of the designs being put in execution. But some weeks before the month of August (the time appointed for making the attempt) notice was sent that it could not be done then. And thereafter several diets[50] were prefixed which took as little effect, and it was next to a miracle that so long delay and so many off-puts did not bring all to light, and occasion either then, or at least afterwards when the attempt was made and miscarried, the ruin of many people. For, as I said before, the design was known to so many people and discoursed of in common conversation that it was strange witnesses and proof should be wanting to have hanged many honest men. But such was the loyalty and affection of the people to the king that though the government knew there had been a correspondence with France, yet they could not procure any certain intelligence, nor afterwards the least accusation against any one of the many who they knew were deeply dipped and concerned in it.[51]

But to proceed. After several times had been appointed for making the attempt, and nevertheless no appearance of its being executed, people began to think that the French king's affairs being somewhat retrieved by the battle of Almanza,[52] which happened during the time Hookes was in Scotland, he was resolved to reserve this design in favour of the king to another occasion. And this proceeded from reflecting on Hookes's behaviour here, and a jealousy, I am afraid too well-grounded, that the French king only minded our king in so far as his own interest led him, and made use of him as a tool to promote and be subservient to his own private designs.

None was more of this opinion than the Duke of Hamilton. And, having waited (without seeing any reason to believe the French king was in earnest) till the end of January 1708, his affairs in England requiring his presence, he set about that time from Kinniel to Lancaster. I know his enemies have upbraided him highly on this account, as if he had fled or at best retired just when he saw the king a-coming. But as I have not spared him when I thought he deserved it, so I hope my reader will believe me when I vindicate him from this aspersion.

Before he was positively determined to go away he communicated his design to the Viscount of Kilsyth, Mr Cochran of Kilmaronock, Mr Lockhart of Carnwath and Captain Straton, asking their opinion and whether they believed the king would come over to Scotland, in which case he would not stir. And these gentlemen, seeing no reason to believe what they desired would happen so soon, could not obstruct his going to a place where they knew his affairs so necessarily required him. What induced them to that opinion was that, some little time before, from a letter by the Earl of Middleton's direction to Captain Straton, they understood that the king and his ministers often pressed the French king and his ministers (with whom they had frequent conferences) to enable the king to recover his crowns, and that though they had got good words and fair promises, they had come to no determination as to the time or method of accomplishing it. Besides, Mr Ogilvy of Boyn (being so straitned in his circumstances that he could not reside in Scotland, and trusted by the Duke of Athol and his friends to negotiate for them and press the execution of what had been agreed to by them and Hookes) had likewise wrote from France to the same purpose to his correspondents.

Matters being in this posture, the Duke of Hamilton resolved, and did make, his journey, as I have said, and with him his Duchess and family. But on the third morning after he set out, as he was preparing to move on from Sir David Murray of Stanhope's house, where he had been all night, an express from Captain Straton overtook him, intimating that by the post which came in the night before he had received letters with an account that at last the expedition was resolved on, and would be executed betwixt then and the middle of March. Mr Lockhart of Carnwath, having convoyed his grace so far, he shewed him Captain Straton's letter, and seemed extreamly puzzled how to behave.

But, after some consideration, resolved to proceed on his journey. 'For', said he to Mr Lockhart,

> the design cannot be long a secret, since the preparations for it will be publick to all the world. And if I, after I am come so far on my journey with my family, do all of a sudden return back, everybody will conclude it is with a design to join the king, and so I shall be exposed to the malice of my enemies and be certainly clapt up in prison and sent to England. Whereas, if I go on, perhaps they may think I am not very forward in hazarding, and have stept out of the way on purpose, and an express can be easily at me in two or three days. I shall be always ready, and am able to force my way through England to Scotland. Besides, the people of Scotland are all ready enough to join the king at the instant he lands and I do not know but I may do him better service by being in the north of England, to excite his friends there to appear for him.

Mr Lockhart having little to say against these reasons, his grace desired him to communicate the same to Captain Straton and his friends, and that they should send off an express to him as soon as they had reason to believe that the king was ready to sail, and another as soon as he was landed. And he concerted with Mr Lockhart that upon the king's landing he should instantly repair to the shire of Lanark (where both their chief interests lay) to raise and lead their friends, and such as would take arms, to meet the Duke at Dumfries, where he promised to meet him, and where he was sure to be joined with a great number of horse and foot both from that country and the western borders of England, and would instantly proclaim the king there and thus be in a condition to defend the borders of Scotland against any attempt from England until a Scots army was formed, the Parliament convened, and the king's affairs settled. Thus they two parted, and you shall see by and by his grace would have executed what he then proposed.

It is beyond my reach to determine the cause of this sudden change in the French king's councils. Some were pleased to say that it was long ere he could be prevailed upon to make the attempt.[53] Others again, that he all along designed it, but the time of its being accomplished was kept a mighty secret as long as possible from anybody but his own ministers because of the divisions that were at the court of St Germains and the intelligence that was found to have gone too often from thence to England. It would not be much out of the way to leave them for some time in France, busie in making preparations for the design, and have under consideration what probability the king had to expect success.

In the first place then, he was sure to be made welcome in Scotland, to have his right asserted by the Parliament and an army of thirty or forty thousand men (picked out of the many thousands that would have offered their service) raised, the nobility, gentry and many of the commons being prepared to receive him and having provided themselves with good horses.[54] The regular troops wanted ammunition and other warlike stores, and did not exceed two thousand five hundred men, of whom at least two thousand would have infallibly joyned with him. Nay, the very Guards done duty on his person the first night he had landed.[55] All the garrisons were unprovided and must have yielded at the first summons.[56] The Equivalent money, which came down the preceeding summer from England, was still in the country, and a good part of it in the castle of Edinburgh, and would have helped well to carry on the war. And a fleet of Dutch ships had some time before run aground on the coast of Angus, wherein was a vast quantity of powder, cannon and small-arms and a great sum of money, all which the gentlemen in that country would have secured. In short, all things concurred to render the design successful in Scotland.

In England the regular troops were scarcely five thousand men, and those for the most part newly raised. And the opposite parties and factions so numerous, and jealousies and animosities so great,[57] that it might reasonably be expected (as it actually happened) all would be in the greatest confusion imaginable, for every party suspected the other was privy to the design. So that in all appearance, everybody would have succumbed, or, if any resistance had been made, the Scots would have given such a diversion to the English arms that France had a fair opportunity of reducing Holland[58] and by that means breaking the confederacy, and then the hardest part was over.

It would appear odd that England should be thus catched napping, when, as I told you before, they knew what temper Scotland was in; and that there had been trafficking with France was no secret. For, besides that the design was too much divulged at home, the Duke of Hamilton was assured by a certain general officer that during the last campaign the Duke of Marlborough had information of the whole project from a person belonging to the Earl of Melfort.[59] Whether the English did not believe that the French king would have prosecuted the measure, or, as some think, that the Duke of Marlborough and the Earl of Godolphin were privy and had consented to it, or were content it should go on, resolving ere it ended to provide for their own security, or what other reason to assign for England's being so unprovided, is what I cannot determine. But certain it is that England was no ways in a readiness to oppose such a storm. And it is more than probable if the king had but once set his foot on the Scots shore all his subjects would have soon submitted, the fatal Union been dissolved and [he] himself restored to his crowns.

The king's part was to hasten over to Scotland, to bring money, arms and ammunition for the men he could raise, where [*sic*], upon his landing, to march strait to Edinburgh, there to proclaim himself King of Scotland, declare the Union void and null, emitt a declaration or manifesto promising to maintain and govern his subjects of both kingdoms by the established laws thereof, calling a new and free Parliament to whom should be referred the determination of all religious affairs, and further providing for the security of both civil and religious concerns. Lastly, [a declaration] requiring all his good subjects to assist him in his design of recovering his own and the nation's rights and privileges, and, as soon as the Parliament had adjusted affairs and formed an army, to march without delay into England. These then being the grounds whereupon the king was to form his design, let us return to where we left off.

No sooner did the French begin to make their preparations at Dunkirk than all the world, save Scotland, was amazed. England was confounded and Holland afraid of their own territories. But upon the king's coming to Dunkirk in person the design was clearly discovered in Scotland, and nothing was to be heard but prayers for a lucky voyage. And when the time drew near, most people of note slipped privately out of Edinburgh to the country to prepare themselves for joyning the king. In England the consternation was general, the publick credit gave way to so great a degree and there came such a demand of money upon the Bank,[60] that had the news of Sir George Byng's[61] having chased the French off the Scots coast come a day later it had broke and been shut up, and with it the credit of the government, which alone was a sufficient compensation for all the expence the French were at.

However, it being high time to provide against the storm, Major-General Cadogan[62] shipped in Holland ten British battalions to be ready to, and which actually did, sail for Tinmouth, as soon as the French fleet was sailed. Among these troops were the Earl of Orkney's regiment[63] and the Scots Fuziliers, who declared they would never draw their swords against their country. But before these troops could have come to Scotland the first brush had been over and all things in a readiness to have given them a warm reception. Neither could the forces which were ordered to march from England (most of them being in the southern part of it), and from Ireland, have come in time to prevent Scotland's being in arms and drawn together to support their king and country. And in that case it would have been no easy matter to have dissipated them.[64] For, as the quarrel was just, so were all men bent to hazard the utmost in defence of it. But that on which England depended most was the fleet, and indeed it is incredible how soon a mighty one was fitted out which proved too strong for the French and the only means to frustrate the design and undertaking. Though, had not several cross accidents happened, the French might have landed notwithstanding the English fleet. As soon as the French fleet was ready to sail, the king dispatched Mr Charles Fleming (brother to the Earl of Wigton) to acquaint his friends in Scotland thereof, and with him he sent several copies of a paper containing instructions to his subjects how they were to behave, particularly desiring them not to stir till they were sure he was landed, and that then they should secure all the money, horses, arms and provisions that were in the hands of such as were not well-affected to him, and even their persons if possible. And Mr Fleming was to cause provide pilots to meet him at the mouth of the Firth of Forth and guide his fleet up the same, being resolved to land on the south side thereof, at or about Dunbar.

Mr Fleming arriving at Slains, the Earl of Errol immediately sent him to Perthshire, where he communicated his instructions to such as he thought proper. The Earl of Errol likewise sent Mr George, a skipper in Aberdeen, to be ready to go from Fifeness with Mr Malcolm of Grange,[65] to pilot the king up the Firth, and further advised him to make a trip over the water to Edinburgh and advertise Captain Straton and Mr Lockhart of Carnwath of Mr Fleming's arrival and instructions. Which having accordingly done, instead of returning immediately to his post he was so elevated with the honour of his employment that he remained drinking and carousing with his friends in Edinburgh till it was so late he could not have liberty to repass the Firth, for by this time the publick letters were full of the French preparations to invade Scotland. Nay, the French king had solemnly taken leave of the king, and, wishing him a prosperous voyage, concluded with a wish that he might never see him again, and had ordered his Ambassadors at foreign courts to notifie his design to the princes at whose courts they resided.[66]

All things being prepared, and the French fleet ready to sail, on the twenty-eighth of February the English fleet came before Dunkirk. Whereupon the French Admiral Forbin[67] sent an express to his master, from whom he received orders that notwithstanding the English fleet he should endeavour to get out of Dunkirk. But in the interim the king became indisposed of the measles, whereupon the troops disembarked for some few days, by which time the English fleet was returned back to the Downs. So that, without opposition, the French fleet sailed out of Dunkirk on the sixth of March about four-o-clock in the afternoon. But the wind chopping about in the evening, they were detained in Newport pits till the eighth, at which time, the wind proving fair, they set sail, and on Friday the twelfth in the afternoon arrived in the Firth of Forth, where at night opposite to Crail they dropt anchors, designing next morning to have sailed further up the river and landed their men and ammunition. But early next morning, perceiving the English fleet was come upon them, they immediately cut their anchors, and, having a good breeze of wind, stood out to the ocean. And the French fleet consisting of lighter and cleaner ships than the English soon outsailed them, only the *Salisbury* (formerly taken from the English) during the chase, which lasted all day, fell into Sir George Byng's fleet and was taken, aboard of which was the Lord Griffin,[68] the Earl of Middleton's two sons,[69] Monsieur La Vie, a Major-General, Colonel Francis Wauchope, some other officers and three or four hundred soldiers.

The French fleet during the chase being separated, did not rendezvous till the fourteenth, at which time, being at a good distance from the English fleet, a council of war (as we are informed by a letter from Monsieur Gacé, now Marshal Montignon,[70] then Commander-in-Chief of the land forces aboard the fleet, to Monsieur Chamillard,[71] printed in the *History of Europe for the Year 1708*)[72] was called, wherein the Marshal proposed to the Admiral that since they had been prevented landing in the Firth they should land elsewhere, and Inverness was proposed. Which the king agreeing heartily to, pilots were sent for. But, in the meantime a storm arising, there was no getting to land to procure them, and the Admiral fearing great inconveniences might happen in case the fleet should be separated (notwithstanding the earnest and pressing desires of the king at least to set him, and such as were his own subjects, ashore) steered his course directly to Dunkirk, where he safely arrived. This is the French account. But after this we shall take occasion to examine their conduct particularly, whether they might have landed in the Firth had they managed their affairs right. One thing is certain: had not the wind chopt about and kept them bound up in Newport Pits, they might have been in Scotland before Sir George Byng knew of their sailing from Dunkirk. For, having sailed from thence in the evening, ere next day they would have been out of land's sight. But being wind bound in the Pits occasioned their being discovered from off the steeples of Ostend. Notice of which being immediately dispatched to Sir George Byng, he instantly sailed with the English fleet and arrived at the mouth of the Firth in the night time, some few hours after the French.

No sooner did the French fleet appear in the Firth than an express was sent from Dunbar to notifie the same to the Earl of Leven, Commander-in-Chief of the Scots forces, and his lordship was at a great deal of pains to make the world believe he could and would make a vigorous defence. But it was well enough known that his army, although willing, was of too small a number to prevent the king's landing, or stand before him after he was landed. And of this he himself was so conscious that he was positively determined to have retired with as many (which indeed were few) as would have followed him, to Carlisle or Berwick. It is impossible to describe the different appearances of people's sentiments. All this day, generally speaking, in every person's face was to be observed an air of jollity and satisfaction, excepting the General, those concerned in the government and such as were deeply dipt in the Revolution. These indeed were in the greatest terror and confusion. And it was no great wonder that the Earl of Leven did afterwards, in one of his letters to the Secretaries of State, complain that the Jacobites were so uppish he durst hardly look them in the face as they walked in the streets of Edinburgh. For uppish they were indeed, expecting soon to have an occasion of repaying him and his fellow rebels in the same coin he and they had treated them for these twenty years past.

But next day advice was sent from Sir George Byng that he had come up with, and was then in pursuit of, the French fleet, and then it was that everybody was in the greatest pain and anxiety imaginable, some fearing it would, and others that it would not, determine as it did. In this perplexity were people when on the next day, being Sunday, a great number of tall ships were seen sailing up the Firth. This put our general in such a terror and confusion as can scarcely be well expressed. He drew his army up in battle array on the sands of Leith, as if he would oppose a landing, and in this posture did he remain for several hours when at last his fears, which truly had almost distracted him, vanished by the landing of a boat, which acquainted him that it was the English fleet returned from chasing the French. For Sir George Byng, after a day's pursuit, finding the French outsailed him, tackt about for the Firth, which was the place he designed chiefly to guard. Besides, he had sailed so unprovided that most of his ships wanted water and provisions. Here he lay several weeks, and for the most part the wind was easterly so that he could not well have sailed down the Firth. And the French might, and everybody believed would, have landed in the north, or sailed round and landed in the west. But instead of that they went sneaking home without doing any good, but on the contrary, much harm to the king, his country and themselves.

You have heard the reasons for not landing alledged by Marshal Montignon in his letter to Monsieur Chamillard, but these will appear too frivolous. And yet consider the want of resolution and firmness that has of late appeared in the French councils, and it is not improbable that having mist of the first aim of landing in the Firth, and being afraid of the English fleet's falling upon them, they might be at a stand and despair of succeeding. But is it not strange they should have undertaken such an expedition, and not reflected on, and been provided with, orders for all accidents that might happen? And was it so extraordinary a thing that they could not forsee that the English fleet (which was then at sea) might have endeavoured to prevent the landing in the Firth, and yet on such an emergency leave all to the Admiral's own disposal? But since, as I mentioned before, the king was so pressing to have landed on the north, I am apt to believe Forbin had secret orders from his master which he did not communicate to the king.[73]

And therefore I cannot altogether condemn those who are of opinion that the French king did never design the king should land, for being fully perswaded and satisfied that the Scots were zealously bent to rise in arms, he might think that upon his fleet's arrival on the coast they would have appeared. And having once set the island by the ears together and kindled a civil war, he might spare his men and money and reserve the king in power to serve him on another occasion. 'Else', say they, 'why did he not send such a number of forces as was capitulated?' For the treaters demanded six or seven thousand, and others ten thousand, which was promised, and yet they were but betwixt four and five thousand and those none of the best. Neither was the sum of money nor quantity of arms and other warlike stores near so great as was demanded and agreed to.[74] And since he had been at so much charges in equipping this expedition, and made such a noise of it all the world over, why did they not land in the north or west, where they could meet with no opposition? It is true indeed the south side of the Firth was the place advised and most proper (though other places both in the north and west had been spoke of too), because the north country was secure against any attempts and well inclined to serve the king, and the landing on the south side of the Firth gained them Edinburgh and opened a communication betwixt the north and the south and the west of Scotland, and north of England. But sure the difference betwixt west, south and north was not so great that if anyone failed the whole design was frustrated.

But not to insist further on the French king's secret designs (which are all misteries to us), this is certain: that had the French managed their affairs right they might have landed even in the Firth. For had they sailed their course directly from Newport pits they might have reached it a day sooner than they did. But in place thereof, though they knew the English fleet was in quest of them and that England and all the world knew of their design, stood out so far to the North Seas for fear, as they since alledged, of alarming England, that the first sight they had of Scotland was near thirty miles to the north of Aberdeen. And so though they had the start by near a day of Sir George Byng, yet he arrived in the Firth in a few hours after them, and one of their ships which proved leaky and was obliged to return to Dunkirk and remained there two days after they sailed, reached the Firth several hours before them. And if it was true, as I have been informed, that the French king's orders to Forbin were that, provided he could land on any place on the south of the Firth, rather than lose the opportunity he allowed him to destroy his ships and join his seamen to the land forces, why did they drop their anchors at the mouth of the Firth and lose half a day and a whole night? For had he sailed on he might have reached the windings in the head of the Firth before the English fleet could have come up to the Firth, and lain sometime concealed from them who we saw knew not where the French were but dropped their anchors too. But supposing the English had discovered them next day? They would at least have got so many hours sailing of them that before they came up their great ships might have been unloaded and the lesser ones run into creeks and shallow places (which abound there) where the English big ships could not have come at them. Lastly, it was unaccountable in them to come from Dunkirk where there were abundance of Scots seamen who would have been glad of the occasion, and not bring a pilot who knew the coast with them, the loss of which they found when they arrived there, and were obliged to take in some fishermen for that purpose off Montrose.

I know that some have attributed their not landing to the Duke of Perth, whose heart, they say, failed him when it came to the push.[75] But, for my part, I cannot conceive how his opinion or inclination (supposing the fact was true, though at the same time it is not probable) could have had such weight in the managing a matter of such importance. Again, it has been said that the Earl Marishal omitted to answer the signal of a ship which was sent by agreement to the coast near his house, to learn intelligence from him of the state of affairs. It is true indeed his lordship failed on his part. But can it be thought that the vigorous execution of the project could stop on so slight a disappointment? Besides, Mr Malcolm of Grange did actually go aboard that ship which I told you came after the French out of Dunkirk and arrived in the Firth before the fleet, and informed them of all that was needful. But to leave these speculations with this animadversion, that the French might have landed, if they had pleased, or managed their affairs right and that time must discover the true reason of their not landing, of which (by the by) none of the court of St Germains, though often wrote to on this subject, will give any return, which makes it the more misterious.[76] I proceed to tell you, never was a people so much disappointed as the Scots, for all were ready to have shown themselves loyal subjects and good countrymen. Particularly Stirling of Keir,[77] Seaton of Touch,[78] Stirling of Carden[79] and many others, having, as they thought, received certain intelligence that the king was landed, mounted their horses and advanced in a good body towards Edinburgh from the shire of Stirling, but being quickly informed of the bad news, returned home again. However, they were imprisoned and brought to tryal as guilty of treason by being in arms for the Pretender (the title now given to the king), but the probation against them being defective, they were acquitted.

As soon as certain accounts of the French being ready to sail came to Edinburgh, Mr John Hamilton, son to Mr Hamilton of Wishaw, was dispatched to the Duke of Hamilton, and, having reached Ashton in Lancashire in three days, gave his grace an account of the joyful news. Whereupon he made all things ready, and sat up three nights expecting every moment the other express with the account of the king's being actually landed, in which case he was resolved with about forty horses to have rid night and day, and forced his way from the Messenger[80] (his grace being put in Messenger's hands upon the first account of the invasion, by orders of the Council of England) and through the country till he had reached Scotland, which no doubt he might and would have accomplished. But, alas, the first news he had was of the sad disappointment.

It is too melancholy a subject to insist upon the grief this disasterous expedition raised in the hearts of all true Scotsmen. The reader may easily conceive it was very great, since thereon depended the nation's freedom from oppression and slavery.

On the other hand, the Revolutioners were not able to bear the good fortune, but triumphed over all they thought inclined towards the king and against the union. Immediately, the castles of Stirling and Edinburgh, and all the prisons in Edinburgh, were crammed full of nobility and gentry. At first, no doubt, the government expected to have had proof enough to have brought several of them to punishment. But failing, blessed be God in that, the next use they made of them was to advance their politicks. For no sooner did any person who was not of their party pretend to stand for a candidate to be chosen a Parliament man at the elections, which were to be next summer, but he was clapped up in prison, or threatened with it, if he did not desist. And by these means they carried, generally speaking, whom they pleased. But to return to the prisoners. After they had been in custody for some weeks, orders came from London to send them up thither. Which was accordingly done, being divided into three classes, and sent up at three several times, led in triumph under a strong guard and exposed to the raillery and impertinence of the English mob. And now it appeared to what a fine market Scotland had brought her hogs, her nobility and gentry being led in chains from one end of the island to the other merely on account of suspicion and without any accusation or proof against them.

Whilst this was a-doing, the Duke of Hamilton being likewise brought up prisoner to London and taking the advantage of the discord betwixt the Treasurer and the Whigs, struck up with the latter and prevailed with them to obtain not only his, but all the other prisoners' liberation (excepting the Stirlingshire gentlemen, who were sent home again to undergo their tryal) upon their finding bail to appear again against a certain day (which was likewise soon remitted), and engaging to join with them (the

Whigs) and their friends in Scotland, viz. the Squadrone, in the election of peers for the Parliament of Great Britain.[81] Which having accordingly done, several of the Court party were thrown out.[82] This certainly was one of the nicest steps the Duke of Hamilton ever made, and had he not hit upon this favourable juncture, and managed it with great address, I am afraid some heads had paid for it. At best they had undergone a long confinement. So that to his grace alone the thanks for that deliverance were owing.

Notes
1. P. W. J. Riley, *The English Ministers and Scotland 1707–1727* (1964), pp. 38–47.
2. Cf. Ibid., p. 56.
3. HMC *Portland*, iv. 427: Defoe to Harley, Edinburgh, 19 July 1707; Riley, *English Ministers and Scotland*, p. 57.
4. Official posts.
5. HMC *Portland*, iv. 403, 408: Defoe to Harley, Edinburgh and Glasgow, 24 Apr. and 15 May 1707.
6. Experienced.
7. The belief that individual human destinies were already known to, and planned by, God before he made the universe.
8. GL's assertion that there was (at least temporarily) a pro-Jacobite tendency among the more radical Presbyterian congregations is supported by John Forbes of Culloden's account of a conversation with a 'wast country minister' in December 1706, for which see *More Culloden Papers*, ed. D. Warrand, 3 vols (Inverness, 1925), ii. 9: Forbes to Jean Forbes, Edinburgh, 15 Dec. 1706. See also, HMC *Mar and Kellie*, p. 397: Harry Maule of Kellie to Mar, Edinburgh, 3 June 1707.
9. HMC *Portland*, iv. 390, 431–2: Defoe to Harley, Edinburgh, 23 Feb. and 7 Aug. 1707.
10. HMC *Portland*, iv. 425: Defoe to Harley, 8 July 1707.
11. *Hooke Correspondence*, ii. 359, 369.
12. GL apparently quoted either from memory of from a poor edition of Ovid, since the likely origin of the lines is *Epistolae ex Ponto*, I, 3, lines 35–6:
    Nescio qua natale solum dulcedine conctos,
    Ducit, et immemores non sinit esse sui

(All men are drawn somehow by the sweet attraction of their native soil, which will not let them forget.)

13. HMC *Portland*, iv. 433: Defoe to Harley, [Edinburgh] 9 Aug. 1707.

14. See above, pp. 124–5.

15. Hooke's mission was regarded as unnecessary by both St Germain and himself, on the grounds that his previous scouting of the Scottish Jacobites' capabilities had told the French government all they needed to know, but GL's implication that Hooke himself was foisted on the Jacobite court is not supported by their attitude towards him. *Hooke Correspondence*, ii. 121–2: Middleton to Hooke, St Germain, 13 Feb. 1707 ns.

16. *Hooke Correspondence*, ii. 88–92, 157, 348.

17. GL's assertion receives some support from the behaviour of the clan in 1715, when it followed Atholl's heir, the Marquess of Tullibardine, into rebellion in defiance of Atholl (A. and H. Tayler, *1715: The Story of the Rising* (1936), p. 47: the Earl of Mar to Lord Forbes of Pitsligo, Kirkmichael, 16 Sept. 1715).

18. *Hooke Correspondence*, ii. 349, 351–3, 360.

19. Charles Middleton, 2nd Earl of Middleton, the Jacobite Court's senior Secretary of State; G. H. Jones, *Charles Middleton. The Life and Times of a Restoration Politician* (Chicago, 1967).

20. In fact, when Hooke arrived in Scotland he found Middleton and Queen Mary of Modena were positively trying to obstruct his mission and urging all Scotland's Jacobites to follow Hamilton's lead; *Hooke Correspondence*, ii. 353–4.

21. James Drummond, 4th Earl and 1st (titular) Duke of Perth, Queen Mary of Modena's Chamberlain at St Germain; *DNB*, xvi. 29–31.

22. By this time both Middleton and Perth had converted to catholicism. Middleton, however, favoured an accommodationist policy towards Protestant Jacobite demands for religious securities whereas Perth espoused a more inflexible, 'Catholic', line. See: D. Szechi, 'The Jacobite Revolution Settlement, 1689–1696', *English Historical Review*, 108 (1993) 610–28.

23. The French court was by this time a very pious institution, Louis XIV having repented his formerly licentious ways in the 1680s; F. Bluche, *Louis XIV*, transl. M. Greengrass (Oxford, 1990).

24. Puzzlingly, the Old Pretender's instructions for Hooke omit any reference to visiting or otherwise negotiating with Hamilton (*Hooke Correspondence*, ii. 141), but Hooke was nonetheless given a letter to deliver to him from the Old Pretender: ii. 149–50.

25. There the rivalry was between three factions: the Protestants, headed by Sir Edward Hyde, the Catholics, led by the Earl of Bristol and

Queen Henrietta Maria, and the Adventurers led by Prince Rupert of the Rhine. See: R. Hutton, *Charles II. King of England, Scotland, and Ireland* (Oxford, 1989), pp. 71–132 *passim*.

26. Anna Drummond, widow of the 12th Earl of Erroll.
27. Shrewd.
28. *Hooke Correspondence*, ii. 348–61.
29. The care Hooke took not to commit either himself or Louis XIV to any formal agreement with the Scottish Jacobites at this stage suggests these allegations of vanity on his part may have owed more to GL's hostility to him than anything Hooke said or did. Cf. *Hooke Correspondence*, ii. 375–83.
30. Atholl and Hooke in fact never met (*Hooke Correspondence*, ii. 375–89), but they did engage in serious negotiations.
31. *Hooke Correspondence*, ii. 152–4.
32. Jean-Baptiste Colbert de Croissy, Marquis de Torcy, Louis XIV's Secretary of State for foreign affairs.
33. GL is incorrect here: Hooke's list of questions came from Michel Chamillart, the French Secretary of State for War (*Hooke Correspondence*, ii. 118–210).
34. HMC *Portland*, iv. 460, 464–7: Ogilvie to Harley, Edinburgh, 17 Nov. and 25 Dec. 1707; *Hooke Correspondence*, ii. 256–62.
35. James Drummond, subsequently 5th Earl and 2nd (titular) Duke of Perth; *DNB*, xvi. 31.
36. John Drummond, subsequently 2nd Earl and 2nd (titular) Duke of Melfort.
37. William Murray, 2nd Baron Nairne; *CP*, ix. 445–6.
38. Thomas Fotheringham of Powrie.
39. David Graham of Fintry, Commissioner for Forfarshire; *PS*, i. 292.
40. Thomas Drummond of Logiealmond.
41. The signatories were in fact the Earl of Errol, Viscount Stormont, the Marquess of Drummond, Lord Kinnaird, George Moray, James Ogilvie, William Keith, Patrick Lyon, Thomas Drummond, Thomas Fotheringham and Alexander Innes, but each claimed to be signing on behalf of many others: *Hooke Correspondence*, ii. 238–9, 262.
42. HMC *Portland*, iv. 424: John Forster to Harley, Stonegarthside, 30 June 1707, indicates that one at least of Anne's English ministers was being alerted to the danger by his spies.
43. George Monk, 1st Duke of Albemarle, the Cromwellian general primarily responsible for the restoration of Charles II in 1660.
44. *Hooke Correspondence*, ii. 149–50, 151.
45. *Hooke Correspondence*, ii. 363–5, 384–6, 393–4, 396–9, 400–1.

46. William Livingston, 3rd Viscount Kilsyth; *CP*, vii. 266.

47. In making this claim GL may not have been aware of Hamilton's efforts to undermine Hooke's negotiations with the Atholl faction of Jacobites: *Hooke Correspondence*, ii. 351–2, 367–8.

48. *Hooke Correspondence*, ii. 394: Memo by Hooke for the Marquis de Torcy, [Paris] 9 July 1707 ns; ii. 475–6: Fr James Carnegy to Hooke, 2 Aug. 1707. GL traduces the Errol-Atholl network of conspirators when he alleges they neglected to secure a commitment regarding Scotland's religious liberty in the event of a Jacobite victory: cf. i. 294–5; ii. 333–4, 335, 335–6.

49. *Hooke Correspondence*, ii. 347–409 *passim*.

50. Dates.

51. HMC *Portland*, iv. 450–80 *passim*, esp. letters by John Ogilvie, John Forster and Defoe. The Scottish ministers, however, seem to have been blithely unaware of what was going on: HMC *Mar and Kellie*, p. 409: Seafield to Mar, Edinburgh, 31 July 1707.

52. Fought on 14 Apr. 1706 between Bourbon forces commanded by the Duke of Berwick and Allied forces under the Earl of Galway. Berwick's victory checked the Allied advance in Spain.

53. He was only finally persuaded to commit himself to the expedition by his 2nd wife, Madame de Maintenon, in December 1707 (Gibson, *Scottish Card*, pp. 103–4).

54. HMC *Portland*, iv. 450: Forster to Harley, Newgarthside, 18 Sept. 1707.

55. HMC *Portland*, iv. 466: Ogilvie to Harley, 25 Dec. 1707; HMC *Mar and Kellie*, p. 429: Grange to Mar, Edinburgh, 2 Mar. 1708.

56. I.e. the garrisons had no supplies stockpiled and could not have withstood a formal siege.

57. Possibly a reference to the maneuvering and intriguing which followed the fall of Secretary Harley in February 1708: HMC *Mar and Kellie*, pp. 426–8: Mar to Lord Grange, Whitehall, 5, 10 and 19 Feb. 1708.

58. Forcing the surrender of the Dutch Republic.

59. John Drummond, 1st Earl and (titular) 1st Duke of Melfort, an embittered Jacobite ex-Secretary of State; *DNB*, xvi. 35–7.

60. The Bank of England.

61. Subsequently 1st Viscount Torrington; *DNB*, viii. 115–18.

62. William Cadogan, subsequently 1st Earl Cadogan; *DNB*, viii. 182–6.

63. George Hamilton, 1st Earl of Orkney. He was Hamilton's brother.

64. Mar indicates his concurrence with GL's opinion in a letter to his steward detailing the preparations necessary to minimise damage

to his home and estates in the forthcoming conflict: HMC *Mar and Kellie*, pp. 431–2: Mar to George Erskine, Whitehall, 12 Mar. 1708.

65. James Malcolm of Grange.
66. Louis XIV's parting advice to James 'III and VIII' can be found in: *Jacobite Threat*, pp. 101–2.
67. Claude Forbin, Comte de Forbin.
68. Edward Griffin, 1st Lord Griffin, a Jacobite exile in France since 1693.
69. John Middleton, Lord Clermont, and Charles Middleton; *CP*, viii. 697.
70. Charles Auguste de Matignon, Comte de Gacé, Maréchal de Matignon.
71. Michel de Chamillart.
72. I have been unable to trace this publication.
73. The French navy was certainly very unhappy about the whole project, as may be seen in their grudging support for Hooke's second expedition to Scotland: *Hooke Correspondence*, ii. 155n.
74. In fact Hooke had brought the Atholl faction of Jacobites to agree to the number of troops, money, etc, assigned to the expedition being left to the discretion of the French government: *Hooke Correspondence*, ii. 259–61.
75. Cf. Gibson, *Scottish Card*, pp. 128–9.
76. The Old Pretender at least purported to blame the failure of the expedition on bad weather and bad luck, going by the instructions issued under his own hand to the Jacobite emissary Charles Farquharson in April 1708: *Original Papers*, ii. 101.
77. James Stirling of Keir.
78. Archibald Seaton.
79. Archibald Stirling.
80. These were the official agents of Parliament, who were often used to arrest or supervise suspects.
81. *Baillie*, pp. 192–3: Roxburgh to Baillie, London, 27 Apr. 1708; *Lockhart Papers*, i. 293–5.
82. The final results of the peers' election (after the House of Lords voted the Marquess of Annandale duly elected over the Marquess of Lothian – a Courtier) were as follows:

Court: Earls of Crawford, Glasgow, Ilay, Leven, Loudoun, Mar, Northesk, Rosebery, Seafield, Wemyss.

Squadrone: Dukes of Montrose and Roxburghe; Earl of Rothes.

Independent/Tory: Duke of Hamilton; Marquess of Annandale; Earl of Orkney.

[Reflections on the State of Scotland]

Having thus finished the account I designed to give of the Scots affairs [*sic*], I may appositely conclude with the words of Aeneas when he began his melancholy story:

> ...Quis talia fando,
> Myrmidonum, Dolopumve, aut duri miles Ulyssei,
> Temperet a lacrymis[1]

And surely the consideration of Scotland's present circumstances must be grievous to any true Scotsman that will but take a short view of the state from which that kingdom is fallen, and what it was before England usurped such a dominion over it.

And first then, notwithstanding the false assertions of the English historians of old,[2] and late attempts of the learned Usher[3] and Stillingfleet,[4] the great Mackenzie[5] and others have made it clear that the Scots nation is for its antiquity, and upon the account of its being governed by a race of kings of one and the same lineal succession, altogether independent, and, notwithstanding the many attempts, yet never conquered nor under the dominion of any other prince or state whatsoever, preferable to all the nations of Europe. Old England will indeed tell you that Scotland was not worth the pains of conquering. But I must beg leave to say that such reflection is not to be regarded. For it is well known the English vanity and self-conceitedness reaches so far as to despise all kingdoms but their own, and all people but themselves. On which account the world hates them. But besides, there is no ground for this assertion, for it is plain the Romans were not of this mind else they would not have been at so much pains to reduce the Scots. The Danes, Normans and Saxons (that is to say, all the different nations that prevailed as soon as they attempted the conquest of England) did not remain satisfied with

England, but spent much blood to reduce Scotland likewise. But to close up all, has England spared her blood? No. The many bloody battles fought in all ages, with various success, manifests the contrary. Did she spare her treasury? No. The vast sums expended by her kings and, to say no more, the late Equivalent, testify otherwise. Did she neglect any means, fair or foul, to reduce Scotland? No. King Henry VII: his preferring the Scotch to the French king, when both demanded his daughter in marriage; King Henry VIII: his earnest desire to marry his son to Queen Mary, and the great terms offered afterwards by that prince to obtain her; the treacherous dealings of their beloved Edward I in the case of Bruce and Baliol; the inciting the subjects of Scotland to rebel against, and the ungenerous murder of Queen Mary, by their pious Queen Elizabeth; and the constant bribes bestowed by the ministers of England since the accession of the Scots race to that crown, are all, besides many more here omitted, evident proofs, that England covets nothing so much as a reduction of Scotland.

That this should be so is no strange thing, for though Scotland is not the best, yet neither is it the worst, country in Europe, and God has blessed it with all things fit for human use, either produced in the country itself, or imported from foreign countries, by barter with its product. So that the necessaries, and even comforts and superfluities of life, are as plentiful there as any where else.[6]

As for the inhabitants, none, I think, will deny them to have been a brave, generous, hardy people. If any do, there's no nation in Europe but can furnish instances of heroic actions performed by Scotchmen, who have been honoured and employed in the greatest trusts in later and former ages. And that this has not been confined to some single persons starting up now and then (which happens in the most dastardly countries), but that they have constantly behaved themselves well, the French and the English may be allowed competent judges to determine. The former, in old times, owed much to the Scots' valour in assisting them against the latter. And these have, in many pitched battles, besides a thousand skirmishes and incursions, found the sad effects of it. And even in this present age have not been a little obliged to the Scotch valour in the wars with France, though when they conquered for England they did but drive the English chains so much the harder and faster upon Scotland. But I need not insist upon what all histories agree in, especially since a full account of the atchievments of the Scots' heroes is shortly expected from Dr Abercrombie.[7]

As the Scots were a brave, so likewise [they were] a polite people. Every country has its own peculiar customs, and so had Scotland, but, in the main, they lived and were [as] refined as other countries. And this will not seem strange, for the English themselves allow the Scots to be a wise and ingenious people, for, say they to a proverb: 'They never knew a Scotsman a fool.' And if so, what should hinder them from being as well bred and civilized as any other people? Those of rank (as they still do) travelled abroad into foreign countries for their improvement. And vast numbers, when their country at home did not require their service, went into that of forreign princes, from whence, after they had gained immortal glory and honour, they returned home. And as it is obvious that at this very time (which must chiefly proceed from this humour of travelling) the Scotch gentry do far exceed those of England, so that in the one you shall find all the accomplishments of well-bred gentlemen and in your country English esquires all the barbarity imaginable, so doubtless the odds were the same, nay greater, in former ages, for the Scots took as great care to improve themselves then as now. Whereas it is well known that it is but of late that any inclination to travel has seized the English (though not near to such a degree as in Scotland), and that the improvement of their gentry is much owing to their being employed of late in armies abroad.

At home the Scots king kept a court to which resorted ambassadors from foreign princes, and to whom again ambassadors were sent from Scotland. And that the Scotch court was sufficiently splendid may be easily guessed at were it from no more but the stately fabricks of King James the Fifth's palaces (viz.

Stirling, Linlithgow, Faulkland and Holyrood House), he being the best-lodged prince of any in Europe at that time, [going] from the Acts of Parliament regulating the apparel and attendants of people of all ranks, and mentioning the numerous offices belonging to the king's family, and from the high and honourable offices of state.

As Scotland was a brave and polite nation, so likewise from thence arose great numbers famous in all ages for all kinds of learning. Here the Christian religion soon took footing, and was preserved in purity, when most other nations were corrupted. And though in process of time the church of Scotland became, as did the rest of Europe, subject to the Papal hierarchy, yet she was among the first that shaked it off. The happy constitution of government, well-digested laws and regular courts and forms of justice, established in Scotland are a plain proof that the Scots were a wise and learned people. Besides, the numerous colonies of learned men (as all histories, and particularly Dr Mackenzie's late treatise, do give an account of) furnished by Scotland to foreign countries is an undeniable testimony of it.[8] Some may hence infer that there was no encouragement for learning at home, but that is a great mistake. For it is well known that the churches and universities of Scotland were not only adorned with noble fabricks,[9] but likewise endowed with considerable revenues in the time of popery. And even since the Reformation there was a more orderly and equal distribution of the clergy's revenues in Scotland than in England. It is true indeed in the former none were so largely, or rather profusely, provided as some in the other, but there was none but had a sufficient competency there-upon to live easily and conveniently (which cannot be said of England).[10] And before the abolition of episcopacy the bishop-ricks and deanries were a sufficient encouragement for study, and had the desired effect.

I proceed next to consider her power. And here we shall find Scotland courted by all the neighbouring states, and the kings matching themselves and [their] daughters with the greatest potentates. It is true indeed, her situation led her to have most to do with England, and hence it was that she always joined [coalitions] to prevent England's growing power. And this was the origine of the famous league entered into by Charlemagne and Achaius;[11] a league which their posterity for many ages kept so inviolably, and proved so advantageous for both the kingdoms of France and Scotland, that no history relates the parallel of it. The Scots king was without doubt a powerful prince. It is foreign to my purpose to debate whether he had an absolute or limited power. So far is certain: he was endowed with a revenue consisting of duties upon trade, the reddendo's[12] of his subjects' estates (which all held of him as their supream lord and superior, and did pay a yearly rent, or feu) and the crown lands, which sufficiently enabled him to keep a splendid court and maintain the dignity of his royal character. It is but a late practice to impose taxes through the country, and formerly there was no occasion for them. For when the nation's service required the subjects were obliged, and did attend, the royal standard, where they maintained themselves and gave as signal proofs of fidelity and courage as the mercenary troops nowadays. In those happy days the king fought for the people and they for the king, against the common enemy, looking upon their interests and prosperity to be reciprocal. And by these means they did, for many hundreds of years, defend themselves against the powerful attempts of the Romans, Picts, Normans, Danes, Saxons and kingdom of England, bringing into the field armies consisting of ten, twenty, thirty, forty or fifty thousand men. Nay, not only defended their own limits, but had men to spare for the assistance of their allies abroad, it being universally known that not only private persons flocked over to the assistance of France, but even royal armies were sent, as during the captivity of King James I, and afterwards led in person by King James V when he understood the French king was hardly put to it. And I'm told there are still to be seen in France authentick records of that prince's having lent the French king eleven ships of war, one whereof was the biggest then in Europe. Which leads me to mention that not many years ago the Scots were able to keep their own with, nay, fight and defeat, the English fleet at sea.[13]

Neither were those wanting who did prosecute trade and brought home riches to themselves and the country. Which is sufficiently conspicuous from the many considerable towns situated over all the kingdom where the merchants lived and followed their trades and employments, and from the stipulated regulations and priviledges of trade with France, Holland, Dantzick[14] and other places.

To conclude. The Scots were a people loyal to their king, and zealous asserters of their liberties. There needs no greater proof of the first, than the lineal succession of so many kings of one and the same race and descent. And where is the nation can boast of the like? And the other is as evident from the gallant opposition they made to all invaders. How manfully did they recover their country and liberties under the auspicious command of King Fergus II,[15] when their enemies flattered themselves that the name of Scot was wholly extirpated out of the island! How highly did they resent Baliol's base surrender of the independency of the kingdom! (It is more [than] probable these our progenitors would never have entered into an union with England.) And how courageously did they stand it out under the happy conduct of King Robert Bruce against the reiterated efforts of England and, at last, after the effusion of much blood, drive those invaders out of the country and fill their souls with such an apprehension of the Scotch valour that even their own historians own fifty English would have fled before a dozen of the Scots! And now show me any country but Scotland that can boast of having defended their liberties so long and so valiantly against a more powerful and numerous people bent upon their ruin, and that frequently without the assistance of allies and having nothing to confide in save their own heroick valour and God's blessing, by means of which they always made good their king's motto: 'Nemo me impune lacesset'.[16]

In these happy circumstances and under this glorious character was the Scots nation of old. But that kind providence which had supported her so many hundreds of years at last grew weary and entirely deserted her after King James VI's accession to the throne of England. For the union of the two crowns may be reckoned the fatal era from whence we are to commence Scotland's ruin. And whoever will consider the history of the two preceding reigns, and the minority of this, may perceive the face of affairs mightily altered and paving, as it were, the way to accomplish the ruin of the kingdom. Formerly the animosities and feuds proceeded from the quarrels of one family with another, or the ambition of some aspiring great man. But then the authority of the king did dissipate and quash them, and they never, or at least seldom, failed to be suspended when the honour and defence of their king or country required it. And if there was any who on such occasions did continue obstreperous, or side with the enemy, they were esteemed by all their fellow subjects, and declared and treated by the states, as rebels. So that the English seldom or never reaped much advantage of intestine divisions. And to this unanimous and hearty concurrence of all the subjects towards the defence of the country is chiefly to be ascribed the so long continuance and duration of the Scots kingdom and monarchy. But in these latter days differences of religion came in the play, which stirred up the consciences of some, and were a fair pretence to cover and carry on the ambitious and selfish designs of others. Of which Queen Elizabeth taking advantage, so fomented and encouraged these divisions (by supporting the weaker party and keeping the contenders in as equal power as possible that they might destroy one another) that the nation was totally divided and at odds.[17] And such grudges and heartburnings arose as have never been abated, far less extinguished, to this very day, and did at last bring the kingdom to ruin.

When King James succeeded to the crown of England people were weary of these disorders, and flattered themselves with the hopes that now he would be in a capacity of establishing peace and order. But it is amazing that though the people were weary of these wars, civil and foreign, which had raged in the country for so many preceeding years, they did not foresee that to be freed thereof by the union of the two crowns was such a change as to

leap out of the frying pan into the fire. For who is it that would
not prefer the greatest hardships attended with liberty, to a state
that deprived him of all means to defend himself against the
oppressions that must inevitably follow? And who is it that could
not forsee that such consequences would follow the union of the
two crowns? We are told that when King James was preparing to
go and take possession of his crown of England his subjects of
Scotland came to take their leave of him and attend him part of
his way thither with all the state and magnificence imaginable.
But amongst these numerous attendants, decked up in their finest
apparel and mounted on their best horses, there appeared an old
reverend gentleman of Fyfe, cloathed all over in the deepest
mourning. And being asked why, whilst all were contending to
appear most gay on such an occasion, he should be so singular?
'Why truly', replied he,

> there is none of you congratulates His Majesty's good
> fortune more than I do, and here I am to perform my duty to
> him. I have often marched this road and entered England in
> an hostile manner, and then I was as well accoutered in
> clothes, horses and arms as my neighbours, and suitable to
> the occasion. But since I look upon this procession as
> Scotland's funeral solemnity, I am come to perform my last
> duty to my deceased and beloved country with a heart full
> of grief and in a dress correspondent thereto.

This gentleman, it seems, foresaw that by the removal of the
king's residence from Scotland the subject wanted an occasion of
making so immediate an application to the fountain of justice,
and the state of the nation could not be so well understood by the
king. So that the interest and concerns of every particular person,
and likewise of the nation in general, would be committed to the
care of ministers of state, who, acting with a view to themselves,
could not fail to oppress the people.

He foresaw that England being a greater kingdom, made (as
said Henry VII when he gave his daughter to the King of
Scotland rather than the King of France) an acquisition of
Scotland, and that the king would lie under a necessity of siding

with and pleasing the most powerful of his two kingdoms, which were jealous of, and rivals to, one another, and that therefore ever after the union of the crowns the king would not mind, at least dare, encourage the trade of Scotland, and that all state affairs would be managed, laws made and observed, ministers of state put in and turned out, as best suited with the interest and designs of England. By which means trade would decay, the people be oppressed and the nobility and great men become altogether corrupted. Besides these inconveniencies which would arise from the management of public affairs, he likewise foresaw that the very want of the royal presence necessarily would occasion other losses. It deprived the kingdom of a court where were spent the revenues of the crown, and which drew foreigners to the country and was an encouragement to trade, artificers and the manufactures of the country. So that the product of the country would prove a drug, the species of money be drawn from thence and vast numbers be obliged to desert the kingdom for want of employment and others flock to London to make interest at court to obtain redress of their grievances, or places, or preferments. Which besides would not be so numerous as when the court remained in Scotland.

As these and many more suchlike were the obvious and plain consequences of the union of the two crowns, it is strange the Parliament of Scotland took no care to provide at least that after the decease of His Majesty the two crowns should disunite and be enjoyed by different stems of the royal line. This is what other nations, nay private families, usually have done. But the truth on't is, the preceeding gloomy, and the hopes of better, times, drew people in to neglect this measure, and King James proved so kind to his countrymen (many of them he advanced to great posts in England) that others, without thinking, drove on till they had run themselves and country over head and ears into the gulf, though they might have forseen that as a Pharoah arose who proved unmindful of, and unkind to, the Jews, so their beloved king (who, being born and bred amongst them, knew and loved them) could not always live, and would be succeeded by kings strangers to them, who would rule them as seemed most for the advantage of their other designs. Lastly, in process of time the nobility and gentry turned, generally speaking, so corrupted by the constant and long tract of discouragement to all that endeavoured to rectify the abuses, and advance the interest, of the country, that the same was entirely neglected and religion, justice and trade made tools of to advance the private and sinister designs of selfish men. And thus the nation being for a hundred years in a manner without a head, and ravaged and gutted by a parcel of renegados, became, from a flourishing happy people, hewers of wood and drawers of water. For at the union of the two crowns[18] the odds betwixt Scotland and England was computed but as one to six, whereas at the union of the two kingdoms as about one to fifty.[19] The plain reason of which was that ever since the Scots king's accession to the English crown Scotland has been on the decaying hand, and England (and all the states of Europe) advancing through the encouragement and protection they met with in advancing and carrying on their trade. But no sooner did Scotsmen appear inclined to set matters upon a better footing than the union of the two kingdoms was projected as an effectual measure to perpetuate their chains and misery.

It is beyond the reach of man to assign reasons for the good or bad fate that attends kingdoms, families, or single persons, for the ways of God are past finding out. Yet, there are two consider-ations that I have often reflected on, and which seem to have had a great share in bringing down those judgements which have of late fallen upon the kings and kingdom of Scotland. For, since the union of the two crowns, many and heavy have been the misfortunes of both. The first is, the mean-spirited behaviour of King James VI in not revenging his mother's murder. Ought he, with a view of not irritating Queen Elizabeth, been guilty of such an unnatural submission [sic]? Was it not a servile acknowl-edgement of England's dominion, to suffer the sacred person of the Queen of Scotland to be tried, condemned, and executed, without so much as daring to say it was ill done? And was it not a connivance at the greatest violation and encroachment that was ever offered to the divine rights of crowned heads, thus silently to see her treated after such a manner, who was accountable to none but God? How much was he degenerated from the illustrious stock from whence he sprung! And which of his royal progenitors would not have resented it with fire and sword? For my part, I'm afraid the indignation of God was stirred up upon this account against his posterity, and that particularly in the case of his son, Charles I. God visited the iniquity his father committed by shewing so little duty and natural affection to his mother, and regard and value for the sacred rights of crowned heads. For though we often read of conquerers having dispatched conquered kings, and subjects murdering their soveraigns, yet she was the first instance of a royal pannel,[20] and the only precedent to the hard fate of her grandson.

The other consideration is the share the Scots had in the rebellions against King Charles I and King James II. For sure it was both their duty and interest to have assisted and supported them against their rebellious subjects of England, but to act the part they did was, besides the folly, such a crime as I am afraid is not wholly as yet avenged, and has no small share in bringing us to the miserable state to which we are reduced. The Jews were God's chosen people, and he assumed a more particular and immediate share in the administration of affairs in Jewry than in other nations, but upon their rebelling against him and his anointed, he gave them up to the power and laws of a forreign people, and at last subverted their monarchy, defaced their government, destroyed their country, and, as the greatest temporal curse, cut them off from having the name of a people on the face of the earth. How near a relation there is betwixt the gross and crying sins of the Jews, and those of Scotland, and what a resemblance there is in their punishment, let such who have been the instruments of the first, or executing the last, seriously consider. For the Almighty God, the wise and supreme governour of the world, hath permitted such things to come to pass, yet I doubt much if the authors and abettors of them can produce any authority to justify their proceedings in the sight of

God or man. It is true that God hath in all ages and countries raised up wicked and tyrannicall princes and rulers, and also rebellious and treacherous subjects, both of clergy and laity, as a scourge to sinfull nations, but their wickedness, tyrannies, rebellions and treacheries were never to be esteemed the less criminal. And if so in preceeding times, those of the present age, when they reflect upon the part they have acted with respect to Scotland, have no reason to expect to be justifyed in this world or that which is to come.

FINIS

Notes

1. 'Who would attempt to speak of such things, of the Myrmidons or of Dolopus or the soldiers of harsh Ulysses, without tears' (*Aeneid*, book 2, lines 6b–8a).
2. GL is referring here to attempts by English historians to prove that Scotland had been an English dependency time out of mind, for an account of which see: R. A. Mason, 'Scotching the Brut: Politics, History and National Myth in Sixteenth-Century Britain', in *Scotland and England 1286–1815*, ed. R. A. Mason (Edinburgh, 1987), pp. 60–84.
3. James Ussher, Archbishop of Armagh, the famous Biblical scholar; *DNB*, lviii. 64–72.
4. Edward Stillingfleet, Bishop of Worcester; *DNB*, liv. 375–8.
5. Sir George Mackenzie of Rosehaugh; *DNB*, xxxv. 142–5.
6. Many, if not most, of GL's contemporaries would have felt he was letting his patriotism gets the better of his judgement here, as he is clearly overlooking Scotland's recent, and terrible, experience of famine in the mid-1690s; T. C. Smout, *A History of the Scottish People 1560–1830* (6th impression, 1985), p. 225.
7. Dr Patrick Abercromby, subsequently author of *The Martial Achievements of the Scottish Nation*, 2 vols (vol 1, 1711, vol 2, 1716).
8. Dr George Mackenzie, author of *Lives and Characters of the Most Eminent Writers of the Scots Nation*, 3 vols (Edinburgh, 1708, 1711, 1722).
9. Architecture.

10. The poverty of many of the lower clergy (and even some of the higher clergy) of the Church of England was a chronic problem in the early eighteenth century.
11. Probably this Scottish king, and certainly his alliance with Charlemagne, are mythical.
12. The duties or services paid by Scots tenants to their feudal superiors.
13. It is not clear to what battle or encounter GL is referring here.
14. Danzig (modern Gdansk).
15. Fergus son of Earc, one of the first rulers of the Irish kingdom of Dalriada in western Scotland; *DNB*, xviii. 336.
16. None provokes me with impunity ('Wha daur meddle wi' me').
17. Elizabeth I was in fact very reluctant to get involved in Scottish politics; K. M. Brown, 'The Price of Friendship: the "Well Affected" and English Economic Clientage in Scotland Before 1603', in *Scotland and England*, pp. 139–62.
18. 1603.
19. These ratios refer to the relative wealth of the two countries.
20. Defendant in a court case.

[Appendix A]
The Appendix to the Memoirs

In the preceding *Memoirs* I have given a particular account of what appeared to me the origine of the treaty of union, and of the several views and designs of the Scots and English Whigs and Courtiers in carrying on and concluding the same, and have given notice of the many cross accidents and disappointments which happened to those who opposed it, and of the various illegal and arbitrary methods that were made use of to make the Scots members swallow it down. But since the compiling these *Memoirs* a further discovery hath been made, which evidently verifying what was with too much reason suspected, viz. that money was remitted to Scotland from England and employed in bribing members of Parliament, I shall give a very distinct and clear account of the matter, as it was discovered and reported to the British Parliament by the Commissioners appointed in the year 1711 for taking, stating and examining the publick accounts of the kingdom.[1]

These gentlemen, having got the scent, so closely pursued the game that they discovered from Sir David Nairn, late Secretary-Depute of Scotland, that the sum of twenty thousand pounds sterling was remitted by the Treasury of England to the Earl of Glasgow in the year 1706, the occasion of which was [as follows]. After the treaty of union was concluded at London the Ministers of State in Scotland, being sensible that they would meet with great opposition in the carrying on their designs in Parliament, and chiefly in the affair of the Union, did conclude it was absolutely necessary to make payment of part of the arrears of salaries and pensions lest some of the persons to whom these arrears were due might prove humorous[2] and ungovernable.[3] And, the Scots funds being all anticipated, they applied to the queen, laid a state of her Scots revenue and debts before her and prevailed upon her to lend her Scots Treasury the sum of twenty thousand pounds, to be employed for payment of part of these arrears and salaries. That this was the origin and pretence of that loan and remittance of money is evident from the queen's letter to the Lords of the Treasury, a copy whereof the said Sir David Nairn did upon oath exhibit to the Commissioners of Accounts, which was by them delivered into the Parliament and is as follows:

Right trusty and right well beloved cousin and Chancellor, right trusty and entirely beloved cousin and Councellor, right trusty and well beloved cousins and Councellors,
We greet you well,
Whereas there has many representations been made to us by our servants and by those who have been employed in our service, desiring payment of what is justly owing to them by us. We did thereupon order you to lay before us the state of these funds. And it appearing that they are entirely exhausted and pre-engaged for some time to come, so that there remains nothing at present for defraying the charges of our government, which is so indispensably necessary for our service, and to enable you in some measure to pay such part of the debts of the Civil List as we shall by particular warrants direct, we have therefore remitted unto you the sum of twenty thousand pounds sterling, to be disposed of by you for the ends and uses abovementioned, in such manner as you shall find most fit for our service. And for which sum you are to hold account to us. And you are to pass an Act of Treasury, acknowledging that you have received the said sum in borrowing, to be refunded to us out of the funds of the Civil List, or for paying the debts thereof, and that at such time as we shall demand the same. For doing of which this shall be your warrant. And so we bid you heartily farewel.

Given at our court of Windsor-Castle the twelfth day of
August 1706, and of our reign the fifth year.

By Her Majesty's Command,

Loudoun

After the Scots Ministers of State had prevailed with the queen
to write this letter and advance this sum, they went to Scotland.
And finding the country extremely bent against, and averse to, the
Union, they conceived it improper to deliver and read the queen's
letter to the Treasury, and own the receiving of this money from
England lest it had afforded a handle to strengthen and increase
the opposition to the Union. For at that time of the day everybody
would have believed that this money was remitted to bribe
members of Parliament. To prevent which, they proposed to
change the course in which the queen had placed this loan, and
for that purpose wrote the two following letters to the Earl of
Godolphin, then Lord High Treasurer of England, copies of
which Sir David Nairn likewise delivered on oath to the
Commissioners of Accounts.

My Lord,

We are convinced that what Her Majesty by her royal letter
to her Treasury here has promised to advance for defraying
the necessary charge of the government, and paying some
part of the debts of the Civil List, is so needful that the
government could not subsist without it, all the funds of the
Civil List being so far pre-engaged, as did plainly appear to
Her Majesty before granting of that letter. Neither can we
think there can be any reasonable objection to the doing it.
But because opposers will do everything in their power to
obstruct the Union and might probably make some noise if
the letter were read in the Treasury before the meeting of
the Parliament and before the treaty is well received, we
think it therefore necessary for Her Majesty's service for
some time to delay making use of the letter, and have
thought fit to represent this to your lordship. And to desire
that in the meantime ten thousand pounds may be paid to
Sir David Nairn upon his receipt to your lordship. Whereof

the said David Nairn is to retain four thousand five hundred on my Lord Commissioner's account. Which sum his grace my Lord Commissioner is to allow for his equipage and daily allowance. And for the remaining five thousand five hundred pounds the said Sir David Nairn is to give an obligation to your lordship to remit the same to the Earl of Glasgow, who has given us obligation to disburse the said sum by Her Majesty's order, or Acts of the Treasury in Scotland, so soon as the same comes to his hands. And the said Sir David's receipt and obligation in the terms above-mentioned shall oblige us to procure to your lordship from the Treasury of Scotland a receipt in the terms of Her Majesty's letter for the said ten thousand pounds in a short time, when it may be more seasonable and convenient for Her Majesty's service to present it. We earnestly intreat your lordship to grant this our desire, being so necessary for Her Majesty's service.

We are, my lord,

Your lordship's most obedient and most humble servants,

Queensberry. Seafield. Mar. Loudoun. Glasgow.

My Lord,

Your lordship having complied with what was in our former letter ha[ving] been of great use for Her Majesty's service, we now again find ourselves obliged to desire that the rest of that sum agreed to be lent to the Treasury of Scotland, being ten thousand pounds, be likewise remitted as soon as possible. We have been obliged to give promises to several persons for a considerable part of [their] arrears, and without this sum they will be disappointed, which may prove of bad consequence. We all agree in this, that it is unfit as yet to make use of Her Majesty's letter to her Treasury here, or to have it known that Her Majesty lends any money to her Treasury. But afterwards we shall, in the safest and best method, advise in what manner what Her Majesty proposes in her letter may be most effectually done. And in the meantime no money to be remitted shall be employed but for the Commissioner's daily allowance, the payment of the salaries of the other servants and for payment of a part of the debts upon the Civil List since Her Majesty's accession to the crown. We desire your lordship may pay in the money to Sir David Nairn and take his receipt for the same, together with his obligation to remit the money to the Earl of Glasgow, Lord Treasurer Depute. And we hereby declare that his receipt and obligation, together with this letter shall be effectual for the ends proposed in Her Majesty's letter to the Treasury here. We are with great respect,

My Lord,

Your lordship's most obedient and most humble servants,

Queensberry. Seafield. Mar. Loudoun. Glasgow.

The Earl of Godolphin having nothing so much at heart as the preventing everything which might obstruct the Union, was pleased to grant the desire of these noble lords. And though the queen had expressly required that the Scots Lords of the Treasury should give her Treasury in England a publick security for the repayment of that money, did accept of these lords' missive letters as a sufficient security for the same and ordered the money to be paid to Sir David Nairn, who carefully, about the time that the Scots Parliament met, remitted it to the Earl of Glasgow, to be employed by his lordship for promoting his country's ruine and misery.

This money being remitted after this manner, was attended with another advantage besides the concealing it was from England. For had the loan been as the queen designed it -publickly owned and received – all the several persons who had arrears due to them would certainly have expected, and could not well have been refused, a share thereof. But now the Ministers of State were absolute masters of it, to whom, after what manner and to what purposes they pleased. And fatal experience teaches us that they did it to the best advantage by distributing it after the manner, and to the persons, contained in the following account exhibited on oath by the Earl of Glasgow to the Commissioners of Accounts:

	£.	s.	d.
To the Earl of Marchmont	1104	15	7
To the Earl of Cromarty	300	0	0
To the Lord Prestonhall	200	0	0
To the Lord Ormiston, Lord Justice Clerk	200	0	0
To the Duke of Montrose	200	0	0
To the Duke of Athol	1000	0	0
To the Earl of Balcarras	500	0	0
To the Earl of Dunmoor	200	0	0
To the Lord Anstruther	300	0	0
To Mr Stuart of Castlestuart[4]	300	0	0
To the Earl of Eglinton	200	0	0
To the Lord Frazer[5]	100	0	0
To the Lord Cesnock, now Polwarth[6]	50	0	0
To Mr John Campbell[7]	200	0	0
To the Earl of Forfar[8]	100	0	0
To Sir Keneth [sic] Mackenzie[9]	100	0	0
To the Earl of Glencairn[10]	100	0	0
To the Earl of Kintore[11]	200	0	0
To the Earl of Findlater	100	0	0
To John Muir, Provost of Ayr[12]	100	0	0
To the Lord Forbes[13]	50	0	0
To the Earl of Seafield, Lord Chancellor	490	0	0
To the Marquis of Tweedale	1000	0	0
To the Duke of Roxburgh	500	0	0
To the Lord Elibank[14]	50	0	0
To the Lord Bamf[15]	11	2	0
To Major Cunningham of Eckatt	100	0	0
To the Messenger that brought down the treaty of union.	60	0	0
To Sir William Sharp	300	0	0
To Patrick Coultrain, Provost of Wigton[16]	25	0	0
To Mr Alexander Wedderburn	75	0	0
To the Commissioner for equipage and daily allowance.	12325	0	0
	20540	17	7

Which balance of five hundred and forty pounds seventeen shillings and sevenpence was, as the Earl of Glasgow did acknowledge, paid him by the Earl of Godolphin when he accounted to his lordship for the twenty thousand pounds he had received as aforesaid, and expended as by the particulars mentioned in the abovesaid account.

The Commissioners of Accounts in their report of this affair to the Parliament do observe that they are at a loss to explain some expressions in these letters (meaning [the] two letters from the Scots Lords to the Earl of Godolphin), such as that opposers of the Union would make some noise if Her Majesty's letter were read in the Treasury, that they had been obliged to give promises to several and without the sum desired they would be disappointed, which might prove of bad consequence. And that they would not have it known that Her Majesty lends any money to her Treasury. And then these Commissioners add that they will not presume to guess at the reasons of these insinuations, but humbly conceive that if the money had been fairly applied to the pretended purpose there could have been no such occasion for so much caution and jealousy.

Such as endeavoured to justify the conduct of the Ministers of State in this matter seem to wonder how the paying of just debts can be reckoned a fault, and especially a bribing of Parliament. To which I answer, that it may with far more reason be alledged that the bestowing of employments would not admit of such a construction, since there must under all governments and in all countries be employments and persons appointed to officiate in them. And yet, who is it that does not know that often, nay, for the most part, all pensions and employments have been bestowed, or continued, in order to procure friends to assist the designs of such as have the disposal of them? But supposing that this matter, when taken in a general view, might be fair and could be justified, yet if the tables are turned and you consider the particular case and circumstances of it, the reverse will evidently appear. For though the Ministers of State in Scotland were very lavish in obtaining pensions to stop the mouths of hungry gapers, yet they

THE APPENDIX TO THE MEMOIRS

seldom or never paid them but as a particular favour, and upon particular views. And whoever will impartially reflect upon the grand affair under agitation when this pretended payment of arrears was made, the place from whence the money came, the clandestine manner of obtaining and disposing of it, and, lastly, that all the persons (excepting the Duke of Athol) on whom it was bestowed did vote for and promote the Union. Whoever, I say, will impartially reflect upon these particulars must conclude that the money was designed and bestowed for bribing members of Parliament.

I mentioned that the Duke of Athol, notwithstanding he got part of this, did oppose the Union. And this some would urge as an argument to prove that the same was not applied as has been alledged. But, alas, one swallow does not make a summer, and though his grace did nevertheless stand his ground, yet who knows what the managers did expect, and with what intention they gave it?

But what follows puts this matter beyond all manner of controversy. For the Commissioners of Accounts having required from the Auditors of the Exchequer in Scotland an account of all pensions and salaries due at any time from the queen's accession to the throne to the commencement of the Union to the persons contained in the aforesaid account exhibited by the Earl of Glasgow, and a particular account of payments and the time when [they were] made, to such persons on account of such pensions and salaries, it did appear from the return that several of these persons, such as the Dukes of Montrose and Roxburgh, Sir Keneth Mackenzie, the Earl of Balcarras, Patrick Coultrain, John Muir, the Lords Frazer, Bamf and Elibank, had no manner of claim, all that they on such pretence could have demanded being paid to and discharged by them a considerable time before the distribution of this money. And others, such as the Dukes of Queensberry and Athol, Lords Englinton and Anstruther, Mr Stuart of Castlestuart, Lord Prestonhall and the Marquis of Tweedale, gave no acquittance for, nor is there any notice taken in the records of the Treasury, of the money thus received from the Earl of Glasgow. So that in a few months thereafter, when they obtained certificates from the Lords of the Treasury of what was due to them on account of arrears of pensions and salaries, some of them had no regard at all, and others only in part, to what they had received from the Earl of Glasgow. And being thus entituled to the full of their arrears out of the Equivalent, many were consequently twice paid in whole or in part. These facts being undoubtedly true, it evidently appears that what was given in either of these cases must have been with some other view, and on some other pretence, than arrears of pensions and salaries.

The Duke of Queensberry having after the Union received the sum of twenty-two thousand nine hundred and eighty-six pounds twelve shillings and twopence sterling out of the Equivalent, being the full [amount] of his equipage money and daily allowance as High Commissioner to the Parliament, did afterwards repay what he had received from the Earl of Glasgow on the same account. But was it paid back again to the Treasurer, as the queen first designed it? No. But, as the Commissioners of Accounts discovered (after a great many oaths and examinations of the Earls of Godolphin and Glasgow and Sir David Nairn, altogether repugnant and contradictory to one another) to the queen herself in a private, clandestine manner. And since the said Commissioners do affirm in their report that it was not applied to the use of the public people generally believe that Her Majesty was pleased to return it to the Duke of Queensberry and the said two Earls as a reward for their good services in carrying on the Union.[17]

Murder will out, and what is thus discovered is sufficient to satisfie any man of the true motives that induced the ministry of England to lend this money, and directed the ministry of Scotland in the distribution of it. It is abundantly disgraceful to be any manner of way a contributor to the misery and ruine of one's native country. But for persons of quality and distinction to sell, and even at so mean a price, themselves and their posterity, is so scandalous and infamous that such persons must be contemptible in the sight of those who bought them, and their memories odious to all future generations.

Notes

1. This was a backbench Tory commission, of which GL was elected a member, designed to find sufficient evidence of corruption to impeach prominent members of the Whig administration ousted in 1710; D. Szechi, *Jacobitism and Tory Politics 1710–14* (Edinburgh, 1984), pp. 76, 80–1, 107–8.
2. Wilful.
3. *Seafield Letters*, p. 182: Earl of Glasgow to Godolphin, Edinburgh, 4 Oct. 1706.
4. William Stewart, Commissioner for Wigtownshire; *PS*, ii. 664.
5. Charles Fraser, 4th Baron Fraser; *CP*, v. 568–9.
6. Sir Alexander Home Campbell of Cessnock (a.k.a. Home of Castlemains), heir to the Earl of Marchmont and Commissioner for Berwickshire; *PS*, i. 349–50.
7. Of Mamore, Commissioner for Argyll; *PS*, i. 100.
8. Archibald Douglas, 1st Earl of Forfar; *CP*, v. 555.
9. Probably Sir Kenneth Mackenzie of Cromarty, son of the Earl of Cromartie and Commissioner for Cromartyshire, but possibly Sir Kenneth Mackenzie of Scatwell, Commissioner for Ross-shire; *PS*, ii. 455–6, 459.
10. William Cunningham, 12th Earl of Glencairn; *CP*, v. 675.
11. Sir John Keith of Inverurie, 1st Earl of Kintore; *CP*, vii. 327–8.
12. Commissioner for Ayr; *PS*, ii. 514.
13. William Forbes, 13th Baron Forbes; *CP*, v. 548.
14. Alexander Murray, 4th Baron Elibank; *CP*, v. 47.
15. George Ogilvy, 3rd Baron Banff; *CP*, i. 410–11.
16. Son of William Coltrane of Drummorall, Commissioner for Wigtown; *PS*, i. 139.
17. All analyses of the passage of the Act of Union have to deal at some point with this enigmatic payment. For two contrasting modern interpretations see: W. Ferguson, *Scotland's Relations With England: a Survey to 1707* (Edinburgh, 1977), pp. 246–51, and Riley, *Union of England and Scotland*, pp. 256–9.

[Appendix B]
The Introduction to the 1714 Edition
By Sir David Dalrymple

The surprize upon the imagination would be too great, and the light too strong upon the eye of the reader, from the naked view of the following memoirs, without conveying the important matters contained therein to the senses, by a proper medium, and preparing them to dwell upon such prodigious wickedness for some time, with a restraint of temper.

The strokes in many places indeed are so bold, and lye so open to the senses of every man, as will raise the blood of the most phlegmatick. And it's happy for some deluded people, who have hitherto doubted of a plot being carryed on against their country, that the author of these memoirs has so freely discovered the flagitious attempt of his party.

The many impious schemes the reader will meet with through the course of these sheets, laid down for the entire subversion of liberty and the Protestant interest in Scotland, will often oblige him to carry his reflections higher, and wonder how a government so emabarrassed with faction, and attacked in her vitals by such a number of parricides, has subsisted to the date of this happy minute.

The imagination will be always kept warm with great variety of incidents, and no person can propose to read some passages coolly, whilst he is encountered with such a vicissitude of passions, horror and pleasure rising alternatively in his breast, from the projected wickedness on one hand, and the successful defeat of it on the other.

The noble struggles which have been made for keeping out popery and slavery, and rescuing the constitution out of the hands of its oppressors, must give inexpressible delight to the asserters of liberty and men of true Revolution complections. Whilst the parricides, and those who had sworn her destruction, must be covered with shame at the thought of so unnatural an attempt.

Though the following transactions are chiefly confined to Scotland, yet they will serve to clear up many speculations relating to the English affairs. And by this clue we may be able to come at the paralell wickedness of a set of men in both kingdoms, who had the same villainous intentions towards their country, even those who have been a constant dead weight upon the Revolution, perplexed King William's affairs, and gave no small disturbance to the reign of Queen Anne.

The barbarous designs of these men you will find, through the whole strain of the memoirs, artfully disguised with the plausible name of publick spirit, and a tenacious love of their country. But they who observe upon what foundations all their measures were built, and that compassing them must inevitably have been the destruction of all civil and religious rights, will never be very forward in approving the means, when the end was so pernicious.

The following sheets, one may readily discern, were designed for the triumph of another day, a day which would have extinguished the very name of liberty, and even the form of religion amongst us, and which all true Britons deprecate and never desire to see fill up a space in their kalendar. And what perhaps might have been designed to make a merit upon the arrival of the Pretender is now sacrificed to a more glorious occasion, and published to dispossess some unhappy people of their prejudices, and give all King George's subjects an abhorrence of those wicked practices which were levelled at the happy Revolution, and, consequently, at the title of our present king.

The test of assurance at the Revolution, which was of the same nature as a qualifying act, we find loudly stormed at. Not so much upon the account of its irregularity, but because the Parliament consisted of a majority of Williamites, who, being apprehensive of the Jacobites crowding in to distress the government, under the formal acknowledgement of King William's title as a nominal, or *de facto*, king, were resolved to make the oath as explicit and binding as they could think of, and therefore required all persons in publick stations to take it to him as rightful and lawful sovereign.

This was an effectual check upon several, and disabled them from doing any legal mischief. Thus, being disappointed of their aim, we must expect to find their passions disburdened in bitter invectives against those worthy patriots who took all the necessary precautions for the support of so glorious a cause.

The reasons given for some gentlemen not appearing as candidates for the Convention, viz. their confidence of a speedy breach in so young and uncompacted a settlement, and their unwillingness to be present at any councils which might seem to countenance King William's pretentions, or favour his right, are lucid proofs of their disposition to return back to their former chains, and their ardent zeal for popery. Their rancour against the Revolution made them refine too much in their politicks, and so infatuated them till the opportunity was past of obstructing so great a felicity, that perhaps it was never known that such prepense[1] malice ever contributed so much to the promotion of a cause which was intended to be disserved by it.

It is plain to a demonstration the unexpected present of the crown to King William first waked all the dormant passions of their souls, and the establishment of the presbyterian church of Scotland fired them to a degree of frenzy. No man would make himself such a novice in Scotch affairs, as not to be sensible that an episcopalian in Scotland is a professed Jacobite. The Revolution men therefore, knowing that no limitations would bind them, or concessions engage them to become entirely in the interest of King William, thought fit to lodge an incapacity over their heads, whereby their measures were broken, both as to their authority and legal assistance to any contrivance against the Revolution and Protestant interest. The source of all the bitter invectives against the promoters of them, under the invidious names of rebel and fanatick.

It will in a great measure alleviate the complex scandal thrown upon the least distinguished worthies who contributed so bravely to the support of the Revolution, when they find themselves ranged with the most illustrious blood of Scotland, for having acted so strange a part (in the dialect of the popish faction) of serving [sic] their country.

The great Duke of Queensberry's unbounded zeal for the publick good, his easy addresses to the froward and obstinate, only to soften their rugged spirits and bend them to humanity and a love of their proper interest, which seldom stands in need of strong arguments, merits no better title with this memoir-author than profound dissimulation. His falling-in with the staunch Protestant Revolution interest after a promise to the opposite party of joining them only in just and honourable measures, has no better graces assigned it than revolt and apostacy. And the accumulation of honours heaped on his family under the reign of Charles and James the seconds [sic] is displayed to enlarge the view of his ingratitude to those patrons of his family, in the generous assistance he gave to King William, and the bleeding state of his country, which was dearer to him than all the presents in the gift of a crown, for which the author is pleased to give him the civil appellation of the first rebel.[2]

The personal failings of the great Duke of Argyle, which are always to be weighed down by superior virtues, are introduced in the character of that brave man to sully his early appearance for King William, and to insinuate that as the Revolution was a work begun by profligate and flagitious men, so consequently it had nothing to recommend it but successful wickedness. The unwilling concessions made to his penetration, judgment, addresses and elocution are put in that light only to raise an indignation in persons that they were not more usefully employed. His want of application one would think should atone in some measure for the mischief he did, with this memoir-writer, but the least vigilance in a good cause, we find, is not to be forgiven by those who are ever watching for the destruction of their country. Still, amidst these pointless assertions, he lives warm in the hearts of all honest Revolutioners, and will triumph in history when the invidious memoirs of a disappointed faction will moulder with their own envy. We are well assured that glosses would not have been wanting to varnish the worst of his infirmities, could he have been prevailed upon to go over to the interest of a party which makes even damnable sins venial in transgressors of the greatest magnitude of their own perswasion. That part of the character which charges him with ingratitude for abandoning the interest of King James when he had so fair a prospect of being restored to his forfeited estate would have fixed a greater blemish upon him, even that of an unwarrantable credulity, if he had trusted to a promise which would never have been made good without forfeiting his honour and conscience in lieu of his fortune.[3]

The probity of these memoirs is further illustrated in the attack upon the character of the unblemished Earl of Stair, inaccessible, one would think, even to envy itself. What quarter must persons expect in the lower orbs of life from the rage of a faction when such sublime virtues are so prophanely insulted? One who commanded assemblies by a masculine, unforced eloquence and gave conviction to the most prejudicate minds. His early and ardent zeal for the Revolution and incessant toils for establishing it upon a lasting basis are services never to be forgiven by one set of men, or forgotten by another. But the plan he laid for consolidating the two kingdoms, and thereby giving a sanction to the title of the illustrious house of Hanover to these realms, will always put the blood of a faction into the highest ferment, and make them gnash their teeth, though [sic] they are grinded down by this happy conjunction. We see to what miserable shifts they are reduced, when, in opposition to the brightness of his merit they are forced to glance at the freshness of this great man's family, whilst they must be content to enjoy the solitary title conveyed to them by a fortuitous generation, unaccompanyed with those honours which flow from an exemplary desert and a superior genius. But what will entail their malice upon this noble family is to find the hereditary vertues of the father shine out so conspicuously in all the actions of a most accomplished son.[4]

The consummate merit of the Duke of Roxburgh cannot be passed over without having its share of the tainted breath and virulency of this author. The elegance of his manners, his fine parts, greatness of soul and all the endearing qualities which go into the composition of a great man, were misapplyed, according to the memoirs, for being a strong Revolutioner, and his strenuous support of the Hanover interest.[5]

The Duke of Montrose's vigilance and zeal for so good a cause could not escape unmarked by this author. His generous warmth for carrying the resolve about the succession for the house of Hanover is basely traduced as heat and passion. And his earnestness for ratifying the Revolution sets him at the head of the Hanoverian whiggish faction. Whatever ignominy our author and party thought to fix upon this great man by these two epithets, yet they will always appear among the shining lights of his character. And the noble pushes he made for securing the Protestant interest and establishing this glorious succession will yield a solid satisfaction to him whilst the popish, Jacobite, Tory faction must suffer all the agonies of mind, and contempt from the world, for having gone all extremities towards accomplishing the ruin of their country.[6]

It is no wonder to find the passions of this virulent writer boil higher when he falls in with the present Duke of Argyle's character. The hereditary spirit of a family that always detested even the most distant approaches of popery,[7] and knew not how to bend to arbitrary rule, could not fail of receiving many impotent lashes from the pen of an abject author, who was never easy in the possession of liberty, and enjoyed it at the hands of a government which owed him no protection.[8] The firmness of my lord Duke to the true interest of his country has given a fresh accession of glory to his family, in having abandoned all his honours and leaving himself at large and unincumbred to serve his country and maintain the succession of our present glorious King George, if any struggles had been made to the contrary.[9]

The Earl of Cromarty's character is treated in a contemptible manner for favouring the episcopal party at first, and then deserting them when their violent actions rendered them incapable of protection from the civil government. The names of

Marchmont, Loudoun, Leven, Glasgow, could not hope to escape the rage of this memoir-writer, their zeal against popery and slavery being registred in such lively characters. As little favour could those worthy patriots [the] Dalrymples, and Mr Baily of Jerviswood, expect at the hands of a faction after having confirmed the Revolution in the very teeth of rage and tumults, and so vigorously succoured the title of our present king.[10]

These, with many other illustrious names, we find drawn at full length by this memoir-writer, but wretchedly mangled. A few virtues here and there have been artfully interspersed, and so coolly represented, that the warm colourings of their vices should strike more forcibly upon the eye. This seems to admit of some mitigation when we consider his usage to those of his own faction and the reproaches he has heaped upon them in that light he has placed them, under pretence of making their characters appear brighter to the world.

Had he studied a satyr upon his friend the Duke of Athol, he could not have exposed him more to the common censure of mankind. His excess of love to King William, so as to form all his gestures upon the model of that great prince, and then flying off from his interest because his recommendation was not so powerful as another's, and from a jealousy of a noble lord's being a greater favourite, are such low and contemptible characters as will just suit with our ideas of a person not come to years of discretion. He is owned a trimmer, by this good friend, between Court and Cavalier. After that he becomes a violent Jacobite, at the same time a diligent hearer of the presbyterians, willing to go into any desperate measures against the Hanover succession. And to confirm the world in this opinion, he had, by the memoir-writer's account, six thousand Cavaliers upon a loyal bottom to sacrifice for the king's service.[11]

In what a fine situation does this scribe put this noble lord! Upon what slender bottom are his disgusts founded! How lively his inconstancy and inconsistencies are painted! And how nakedly he exposes his zeal for the service of the king, as the faction stiles the Pretender, which, for the safety of his noble friend, might, one would think, have been softened by dashes or ambiguities!

The Duke of Hamilton's character is rendered almost as conspicuously bad by this author in his trimming capacity, and desertion, when the Cavaliers thought they had him sure. Joyning sometimes with one party, then another; consenting to the Queen's nomination of commissioners to treat; and his resolution questioned because he could not be induced to go all the desperate lengths of the faction.[12]

The loyalty of the Earl of Errol to the royal family is very much illustrated by the Earl Marishal's fidelity to his prince and country. And Lord Balmerino is complimented in a most horrible manner for not taking the oaths to the government till 1704, with a view to obstructing the Hanoverian succession. I will pass over the large pourtraiture of Mr Fletcher, the author having blended so many contrarieties in his character, that it is impossible to reconcile them to any man's apprehension.[13]

When the reader finds the terms Cavalier, royal family, prince, king, episcopal, dispersed through these memoirs, he cannot be at a loss for the meaning of them, they being terms of great significance amongst the faction, but in Revolution dialect go for no more than Jacobite, a spurious issue, Pretender, mock-monarch, and popish persuasion. These terms will be fully explained, and the desperate attempts of the faction appear in lively colours, when the barefaced treason against the late Queen Anne shall glare in your eyes and astonish you.

I shall pass by the Union without any remarks upon the author's relation, only beg leave to say that though some rights and privileges in Scotland may have been weakened by this conjunction, yet they have their religion and liberty secured to them by it. For it had been impossible to have defeated the attempts of the Jacobites, or extinguished their sanguine hopes, without declaring the succession to the crown of Scotland to be in the illustrious house of Hanover. This is evident from the alarum it gave the whole party. For no sooner was the Union settled, but projects were concerted for restoring their king, as they called him. But this conspiracy against the queen and the Protestant religion was of a quite different management from all the plots recorded in history. Besides the general expectation and ardent wishes for his arrival, the Jacobites had their delegates to treat about the manner of his restoration, and set meetings in the western shires. But we shall cease wondering at the insolence of these open attempts, under the eye of government, when we read of a black list of sixteen nobles and gentlemen who subscribed to a solemn invitation, with a Duke's name in front.

This passage, methinks, should have made the author of the memoirs a little more temperate in his foregoing reflections upon the Duke of Queensberry and some other nobles, who are represented as trumping up a sham plot upon the abovementioned Duke. If people should once make use of their reason, and compare the former account laid before the Lords of England with what is set forth here in so many capitals, it would be no great strain upon the imagination to conclude him embarked in the same designs before, as this author, upon his knowledge, assures the world he was of later date.[14]

There was no manner of caution observed in keeping this conspiracy a secret. As the general opinion of the kingdom had decreed a great share in the restoration of their king to the Duke of Hamilton, so our author scruples not to let the world know that letters were sent from the Pretender to that duke and the Earl Marishal, by the mediation of one Hookes, an agent from the court of St Germains, but that from some jealousies and disgusts they chose to convey their sentiments to the Earl of Middleton by another hand.[15]

Happy was it for the tranquillity of Scotland, that two great men, equally engaged in the conspiracy, should through emulation and jealousy of each other's power keep upon the reserve, and, each affecting the prime direction of that great affair, propose to make a superior merit of it. By which means the communication between them was cut off, and the mutual confidence weakened which was absolutely requisite to a design of that extent.

None, I presume, hereafter will arraign the ministry in England at that time of severity for laying the Duke of Hamilton under a modest restraint, after this memoir-writer has affirmed that the said Lord was so bent upon the restoration, as they termed it, that he had determined even to break through the Messenger's hands to his king, with a guard of horse which were to be sent to his relief. Such discoveries from the author of these memoirs, who was upon the main secret, entrusted with the conduct of the most important affairs relating to it, and who cannot be imagined so flagrant in his malice as to relate each circumstance and punctuality in so solemn a manner against his friends and confederates in treason, must be credited by bigots of the rankest credulity.

After so frank a declaration we defy the faction, with the most studied sophistry, to reconcile their allegiance and duty they so much boasted of to Queen Anne, to the active obedience they showed to the Pretender, under the title of their king, or satisfy any Revolution Protestant, why any toleration should be granted to a Scotch episcopalian after such notorious perjuries, collusions, mockeries of God and abuses of the Queen's clemency. And if a rebellion of that black dye was carried on against a queen of the greatest indulgence to their follies, and who was wickedly represented by them as having concealed inclinations to serve their interest and keep the crown in trust for their king, what rancour, what hellish malice may not King George expect from a faction who put their country in a flame to oppose his succession, and were reducing it to an heap of ruins, to prevent his being sovereign of the soil?

Notes

1. Premeditated.
2. Cf. above, pp. 11–12.
3. Cf. above, p. 32.
4. Cf. above, pp. 58–9.
5. Cf. above, p. 104.
6. Cf. above, pp. 92–3.

7. In fact two of the five Earls, Marquesses and Dukes of the family of Argyll 1584–1743 converted to catholicism at some point in their lives.

8. Cf. above, pp. viii–xiv.

9. Argyll was dismissed from all his offices in March 1714 as a punishment for having opposed the (Tory) Harley ministry, of which he was originally a supporter, at the polls in 1713 and in Parliament 1713–14.

10. Cf. above, pp. 42–3.

11. Above, pp. 40–2.

12. Above, pp. 22–3 and *passim*.

13. Cf. above, pp. 43–5, 111.

14. Cf. chapter 3.

15. Above, pp. 213–4.

[Lockhart's Reply]
Additional Preface to the Copy Corrected and Left for Publication by the Author

When the following memoirs were published at London some time after the Elector of Hannover's[1] accession to the crown, they appeared under all the disadvantages imaginable. For the copy, from which that printed edition was taken, was noways prepared and designed for the press, and many errors appeared in it. Several words, nay sentences, being, some omitted, and some inserted instead of others, by which in many places the sense of the whole was confounded.

But the greatest misfortune arose from the then state of affairs, which was by no means fit for propaling several facts therein contained. However, this book was printed without the consent or privity of the author. For he having lent it to a particular friend[2] under the strictest tyes of secrecy, he was so faithless and imprudent as to give it out to be transcrived by a common mercenary scrivener at London, who in turn deceived his employer and gave copies thereof to those who soon after published it.

It is impossible to express what a noise and bustle was made about this book over all Britain. Some apprehended danger from the discovery of those measures they had been concerned in for King James's restoration, and that it would clear the way towards frustrating all future attempts of that nature. Others again rejoiced at the accounts contained in it. Some, because they served as a handle to represent their enemys as disaffected to the then settlement of the crown and government, and some, that the methods by which the kingdom of Scotland was betrayed were so clearly set forth, that the persons guilty thereof must needs appear odious, and lose their interest with all true Scotsmen. But this consideration on the other hand did highly provoke another set of men, who could not endure that their actions, and the motives inducing them thereto, should be set in a true light and made publick. And their resentement ran high against the person whom they supposed the author, and the book itself. But as they could not get proofs whereby to fix it on any particular person as the author of it, the book stood its ground with respect to the facts contained in it, and obtained universal credit. And though those who were most irritated at it gave it no other appelation than a villainous book, they did not care to enter into particulars, and some of them were so ingenious as to own it contained much truth.

That they had nothing to alledge against the veracity of it is evidently apparent from the introduction published with it. Seeing nothing of that kind is so much as insinuated. This introduction, whereof Sir David Dalrymple was the author, is also published with this edition, that posterity may know what objections were then made against the book. And I refer to an impartial reader, if ever he perused any thing more insipid, fulsome and unmannerly, than this introduction. But such indeed are most of the performances of the author of it.[3]

The chief or only purport of it is to tell the world that the Scots Jacobites, and the author of the *Scots Memoirs*, were rather for King James than King George. A notable discovery indeed of that which nobody denyed, nor was ignorant of! But it is strange that any man should have the impudence, after so many years fatal experience, to justify the Union and those who advanced it. With what confidence can this introductor accuse the Cavaliers for endeavouring to restore that prince, who they believed had an undoubted and only right to the crown, even though the same should be attended with the calamities he asserts, when he at the same time freely confesseth that to secure the succession of another prince, who had no manner of title but what this introductor and such as he gave him, the party for which he contends gave up the soveraignty, independence, constitution, libertys, freedom, rights, laws, religion, riches and trade of their native country? For such, wofull experience hath taught us, are the natural effects of the Union with respect to Scotland. And yet the same was contrived and carried on to establish and secure the Hannoverian succession, if this introductor may be credited. And now taking it as he would have it, that is, that the Union was undertaken on no other view than what I have mentioned, and yielding that the Cavaliers, in opposition thereto, designed the restoration of King James, who would certainly oppress and harrass his own faithfull subjects, and impoverish and ruin his own flourishing dominions – I say, let us suppose matters stood thus, the question naturally arising from it is, which of the two schemes was most detrimental to Scotland? Why, for my own part I truly think the former, because King James might change his mind, and be persuaded by reason and interest to act otherwise. If not, he might be controlled by the Parliament, resisted by the people, and sent a-packing, as was his father. And for certain he would sooner or later die, and a better prince perhaps succeed him. But the Union is of its own nature inconsistent with the prosperity of Scotland, and instead of growing better proves daily more heavy and untolerable, and withall more durable and lasting. So that of two evils, the least was to be chosen, and the Cavaliers' scheme was preferable to that of the Unioners, because it was not attended with such certain and permanent inconveniencies as the other, even though all that these Unioners did alledge had actually come to pass. Though after all, I must beg leave to think, that though indeed these gentlemen were very fond of the Hannoverian succession, yet as an incorporating Union did more effectually screen them from the punishments they richly deserved for conniving, nay contributing, to the oppressing of their country, this was what they chiefly aimed at, and more desired, than the succession of any race whatsoever to the crown, though now to conceal and cover their real designs and magnify their merit, they make the Hannoverian succession the only pretence for what they did.

But why does the introductor reckon those who were against the Union and those against the Revolution in one and the same class? Does he not know that a great many Revolutioners opposed the Union? Hath he forgot that Sir David Dalrymple, when the British Parliament passed the act concerning treason in Scotland,[4] frequently and publickly declared how much he was grieved, and repented his having been so instrumentall in promoting the Union? And did he not post from Edinburgh to London how soon he heard there was a design to propose a dissolution of it, and did any man appear more frank for the measure than he? Did not the Earl of Ilay in all companies make it his publick and constant toast, and write inscriptions on the glasses in the taverns in Edinburgh, 'To the dissolving of the Union'? And did not all of his stamp and kidney declare that the Union was untollerable, and that there was an absolute necessity of hazarding all rather than it was not dissolved? Did not all the Scots members, Whigs as well as Tories, agree unanimously to the motion which was made in the House of Lords for dissolving it?[5] Were these pretences and this behaviour in those people only grimace, and the effects of being deprived of a share in the administration of publick affairs at that time, and a desire of creating disturbance and uneasiness to the then ministry of Great Britain? If these were their motives, their insincerity and selfishness are conspicuously apparent, and we are naturally led to judge of the motives that induced them to be for the Union at first. But if they were sincere in their declarations against the Union, why this sudden change, and whence this new light, when the tables are turned and they once more at the helm of publick affairs? I will make no reflections, but leave THEM to answer, and the impartial world to judge.

But, as I said before, I can see no reason for putting the Revolution and the Union on the same bottom, especially if the latter was only designed as the means of securing the Hannoverian succession. For it is consistent enough to have been either for or against the Revolution, and an open enemy to the Union and the Hannoverian succession. As, for example, supposing I believed King James and his posterity were enemies to this country, and for that for this reason I might lawfully rise in arms against him, and seclude him and his offspring from the crown in all time coming – is it not reasonable to imagine I would also oppose the succession of Hannover, if it could not be attained without the Union which appeared to me destruction to the nation? King James had a right before and untill he was actually deprived of the crown legally, but the Elector of Hannover had none before and untill it was given him. And if for my country's service I may turn him out that actually is, I may much more keep him out that only aims at being my king. On the other hand, if I was a Cavalier believing that King James and his issue were unjustly secluded from the throne, might I not very consistently with my principles be against the Union, even though he or one of his posterity whose title I owned was on the throne and advanced the measure? Because though I own his right to rule over me, I deny that he or any power under God can dissolve the constitution of the kingdom. And therefore I might fairly oppose it in a lawfull manner, nay think my aledgiance loosed as to him my soveraign, if he was accessary to the subversion of the monarchy, as happened in the case of Baliol, who without doubt had the best claim to the crown.[6] Now if the Cavaliers did act upon and from such principles, their opposing the Union did not merely proceed from a design to advance King James's interest, which only by accident was concerned in it. It is true indeed [that] when the Union took place they did what they could to improve it to his advantage – and who can blame them for endeavouring the restoration of that prince who they believed had the only title to govern, especially when the relief of their country from poverty and oppression went hand in hand and was a natural consequence of it?

To conclude: I make a great distinction betwixt the Revolution and the Union. The one was only an alteration of one, though indeed a material, part of the constitution, the other a total subversion of it. And any person might very well declare for or against the first and be at the same time, as were a great many Revolutioners and all the Cavaliers, averse to the other. So that introductor places the opposition to the Union on too narrow a foundation when he ascribes it only to a spirit of Jacobitism, it being evident and certain that it could and did proceed from no other motives than concern and zeal for the interest and prosperity of their country. And it is no wonder that all Scotsmen who are not seduced by selfish interest and sordid gain (to use one of this introductor's phrases), 'have their blood put into the highest ferment, and gnash their teeth, being grinded by this unhappy conjunction.'[7]

The introductor snarls and is very peevish at the characters given of some of his friends. How far they are well and truly drawn both he and the author must appeal and submit to the judgement of the age in which these persons lived, and to the account of their lives and actions ingenuously handed down to posterity. And by comparing the same with the characters given them by the author people may judge how far he hath done them justice or injured them. What the introductor says in their behalf is not material, being nothing more than a rhapsody of words and repititions of 'Revolution', 'King George', 'popery', 'slavery', and such-like cant, brought in over head and ears without rhyme or reason. But when he proceeds to attack the author's probity, it had been his interest to have pitched on some other character than that of the late Earl of Stair whereby to have illustrated and made good his assertion, or obliged the world so much as to publish a few of those particulars from whence in the main he is pleased to think he deserves the title of the 'unblemished Earl of Stair'. Sure I am when this introduction came out most people ridiculed this paragraph, and from thence were confirmed in the opinion of Sir David's being the penman, seeing none but he or one of that family would have the assurance to talk or write after that manner.

What the introductor calls 'the personal failings of the late Duke of Argyle', were mentioned by the author to show that though the presbyterians affected a greater degree of sanctity and purity than they allow could be possessed by those of another persuasion, they could tolerate and connive at the vices of those who could do God as much service another way. But the introductor passes over his grace abandoning the Protestant religion to please and curry favour with King James. This, it seems, in his sight was no more than a personal failing, but had been branded as appostacy in any other than a good presbyterian. And no doubt the introductor would have affirmed that such a person deserting again from the Romish church was only because he saw the Revolution was like to succeed, whereas in the case of the Duke of Argyle, in his opinion, it proceeded certainly from a principle of conscience and conviction of his error. If any man's character is lessened, it is the present Duke of Argyle's, whose many valueable qualities and amiable perfections are ever to be esteemed and valued by all men of honour and honesty, let his principles as to government be what they will.

The author said nothing of the late Duke of Hamilton but what is true, and proves him a great man, though according to the old proverb *nemo sine crimine vivit*,[8] and his grace's memory will be fragrant to latest posterity, whilst that of this introductor and his accomplices will stink throughout all future generations. The abominable, horrid, barefaced murder of this noble patriot, and the kind reception and protection which the detestable wretch who performed it did meet with from a certain set of men, doth evidently show that his grace was odious to, and hated by, the Whigs, and consequently that he was a good man and deserved well of his king and country.[9] What the introductor means by his observations on the characters of the Earl of Errol and Earl Marishal I cannot comprehend, no more than wherein doth consist the horror of the Lord Balmerino's swearing [allegiance] to Queen Anne with a design to oppose and obstruct the succession of Hannover before that Elector had any legall pretence to the crown of Scotland – unless this introductor thinks the settlement of the crown of England was a tye on Scotland.

The character of Mr Fletcher of Salton is consistent, as were all his actions (in the main), with that of a true Scotsman who preferred his country's interest to all considerations whatsoever. And it is not enough for this introductor to contradict in general terms what is said on this or any other head. He should be a little more particular, for his veracity is not so well established that his bare affirmation will obtain universal credit.

He thinks he has gained a mighty point by inferring that as the Duke of Athol was concerned in the designed invasion [of] 1708, it was reasonable to believe he was not unjustly accused in the year 1703. But with his leave, whatever weight this discovery may now have, it is ridiculous to say that what happened in 1708 could occasion a jealousy in 1703. And as this introductor knows that that plot was merely a contrivance of the Duke of Queensberry, and that no evidence was produced against the Duke of Athol, he must have a mean opinion of his readers if he imagines they will credit his account of the story grounded only from such an irregular inference, or that the charge against the Duke of Queensberry, of having forged the story, will be taken off by it. And I would willingly put the question to this introductor, if there was truly reason to accuse the Duke of Athol, why was it not exposed and judged in the Scots Parliament, as it was often and publickly demanded? Was the English House of Lords a fitter place, and they properer judges to try and determine Scots affairs? And can it be imagined that this affair would have been dropped if the contrivers had not known that their design was discovered and care taken to prevent it? I humbly, with submission, conceive the introductor had better have omitted this remark altogether, or shuffled it over as he does the paragraph concerning the Union, by saying this affair, though contrary to all the rules of honour, equity, and society, was necessary, being designed and calculated to support religion and liberty, disappoint the projects of the Jacobites, and secure the succession of the illustrious house of Hannover. In this manner does he pretend to excuse the measure of the Union. But might not this succession, if so very necessary and precious a thing, have been established and secured without the Union? Yes, it was offered,[10] and refused, because nothing but one incorporating Union suited the designs and views of England, and (as the introductor styles them) of those patriots the Dalrymples, their friends and copartners.

Having thus made a few remarks on this introductor, and having seen two books which take these memoirs into task, the one intitled, *A Letter to Lord Ilay*,[11] and the other, *The Memoirs of North Britain*,[12] both printed in 1715, I beg leave to take some notice of them. The first does little more than carp and snarl at the style, method and subject of the *Scots Memoirs*, and seems highly displeased that Mr Carstairs is called a rebellious presbyterian preacher (for which the history of the Rye-House plot[13] is a sufficient voucher), but does not pretend to contradict any of the facts mentioned and contained in these memoirs. So I proceed to consider the other book, the author whereof hath been so stupidly ignorant, that nothing he advances can lay claim to any credit. But that posterity may have something more than my assertion for this undoubted truth, I will pick out a few of the many instances of his ignorance and falsehood, and therein confine myself to such particulars as relate to the *Scots Memoirs*.

Without taking any notice of his preface, and the particular reflections he throws on the person whom he supposes the author of the *Scots Memoirs*, I begin with observing that the author of these North British memoirs (whom for the sake of distinction I will call the slanderer) manifests his ignorance by asserting that the author of the *Scots Memoirs* was obliged, as being [a] member of the four last Scots Parliaments, to take the oaths of aledgiance and abjuration, and sign the tests of assurance and association. For it is certainly true that the association was not required during all Queen Anne's reign, and the abjuration not till the commencement of the Union.

He condemns the reasons assigned in the *Scots Memoirs* why the Revolution went so easily through in Scotland. And to make good the same, he sets down a list of members of the Convention, and the names of such members as being displeased with the proceedings left the house, and he concludes that these were all who were against the Revolution.[14] But he does not take notice that the Marquis [*sic*] of Athol did not stand his ground with the resolution that became him, that there were great numbers of armed men from the western shires to overawe and intimidate the members and that a great many who would have opposed the Revolution, when they could not prevent it, submitted, and kept their places in the Convention. If this party was inconsiderable, as is by this slanderer represented, why so great a cry ever since of the danger arising from it? Is the testimony he brings from Dr Welwood a sufficient proof of what he affirms?[15] Can it be expected that one of his low descent and sullied character (having been expelled the College of Justice for a gross piece of knavery detected in him) and a stranger to the country (having left it and retired to England after his disgrace) can know much of affairs of state? And is his account of matters sufficient to overturn what is known to all the world? As for the speech of the learned gentleman which the slanderer gives at full length, as he is pleased to conceal his name, I suppose it is not considerable otherwise we should have had it.[16] And all that can be inferred from it is, that such a rebellious impudent speech was perhaps made, and no doubt there were many such besides it in that Convention. This slanderer's pretending to justify the barbarous treatment of the Scots at Darien, the murder of Glencoe and the persecutions of the episcopal clergy, are sufficient proofs of his impudence, and need no reply.[17]

His account of the act for securing the Presbyterian government does no way contradict what is asserted in the *Scots Memoirs*, viz. that if the queen had gone into the measure of establishing episcopacy, her interest would have brought over more than sixteen votes in favour of it, which being added to those who voted against that act and those who were *non liquets* (who were undoubtedly all inclined to episcopacy) would have made a majority.[18] And from thence it was apparent that the presbyterian party was not so formidable as had been represented.

The story of Sir George Lockhart's murder is grossly false and maliciously impudent.[19] To this day it was and is believed by his relations and all the nation, that he was murdered by Cheesly[20] for having been instrumentall in obtaining an aliment[21] of Cheesly for the support of his wife and children, whom the wretch had abandoned. If it was a political murder, as this slanderer affirms, it is most probable that it arose from the Whigs, for Cheesly himself was a thorough presbyterian, and the son of Sir John Cheesly, the famous stickler in the late rebellion against King Charles First and Second.[22] And the Cavaliers had no reason to desire or contribute towards Sir George's death, for it was known he was a gentleman of loyall principles, had declined being member of that Convention, as he believed it illegally conveened, and that some of the king's friends designed to have moved in the Convention to have called for him to give his opinion how far the forfaulture of King James was agreeable to the law of the land. What he affirms to prove that it was a Jacobite murder, viz. that David Lindsay was thought accessary to it, and on that account imprisoned by the Convention, is utterly false, for no such thing was ever laid to Mr Lindsay's charge, nor was he ever sent to prison on that account, nor did he appear as a witness. And alike false is what he says concerning torture, for, as the magistrates of Edinburgh, by whom the wretch was tryed, convicted and condemned, had no power to impose torture on any pretence whatsoever, there was no such thing proposed or threatned, as indeed there was no occasion for it, seeing Cheesly committed the fact at noonday in the streets of Edinburgh, before many witnesses, and gloryed, instead of denying, excusing, or repenting, of the murder.[23] To conclude: all and every part and circumstance of what this slanderer relates concerning the way and manner of Sir George's death, and the person and party he would bring in as accessary to it, are notoriously false, and were never heard of till mentioned in this infamous libell.

The turn he gives to the plot is ridiculous, and will not bear up against common sense. And the justification of the Squadrone's deserting their friends and listing with the Court, is frivolous. His account of the great Duke of Hamilton's murder is of a piece with the rest, and contrary to the conviction of all but such as averr anything to serve a party interest. His assertion that the Earl of Errol was one of the sixteen peers in the British Parliament is a gross mistake.[24]

What he says in defence of the Union with respect to the advantages arising from thence to Scotland, is contrary to reason and wofull experience. But I cannot comprehend what he means by saying that, besides the sum of £400000 given as an equivalent, England was at half as much charge in other expences.[25] Pray what expences? Was it in bribing, or what else? This is a new discovery, which we did not know of before.

Does his account of the Kirkmen's behaviour contradict what is said of them in the *Scots Memoirs*? Or does not he even acknowledge that they had no concern for the country, provided their Kirk and stipends were safe, and that the ruling elders, who were likewise Parliament men, did the same in Parliament, having so fair a copy set before them by the clergy in the Assembly?[26]

In the list he gives of those who voted against what he calls the Protestant succession, he fairly owns what he hitherto denyed, viz. that the Jacobite party was not despicable in number or power. And it might easily be accounted for, how it came to pass, that there was a majority for the Union, had he told us that above eighty of his Protestant list enjoyed places and pensions, besides those who got a share of the money sent from England. So that very few or none voted for the Union who were not influenced by downright bribery and a desire to continue the enjoyment of their places and pensions.[27] He owns in one place that the Unioners exceeded the other party in Parliament by no more than thirty-two – a majority easily to be accounted for, as I observed lately, especially when it is considered that the Squadrone made part of that number. But in another place he affirms that the Unioners were two to one.[28] It would appear this slanderer did not revise his calculations.

He reflects on the author of the memoirs because he said there was no opposition made to the twenty-second article of the Union, and yet, says he, there were no less than six protests taken against it.[29] To which it is answered, that though the Anti-Unioners (for the reasons assigned in these memoirs) did not oppose that, as they had done the other articles, with discourses containing undenyable arguments against it (though these, I imagine, will not appear an opposition in this slanderer's judgment), yet several of the members without any concert (otherwise one generall protestation as formerly on other occasions would have answered their design as well) resolved to leave their testimony and reasons against this article on record by entering their severall protestations against it. So that the account as given by the *Scots Memoirs* is agreeable to the matter of fact, and no way inconsistent, seeing a protestation cannot be reckoned a formall opposition.

In no part of these memoirs is there the least insinuation (as the slanderer pretends) that those who carried on the Union were a set of worthless beggarly people.[30] At least nothing of the last is laid to their charge. For the author does frequently in severall different places regrate and admire, that men of such estates and quality should be led into measures so dishonourable and destructive to the nation in general, and their familys in particular. And when the author advances that there was a great majority against the Union, by the context it will appear he meant of the whole body of Scotsmen, it being too great and too lamentable a truth, that the bribed, mercenary majority of the members of Parliament were quite otherwise disposed.[31]

This slanderer might have spared his observations (page 204) on the remarks he there criticises on. For it is plain, from the *Scots Memoirs*, that the author laid little or no stress on them, by his saying that he mentioned these remarks because some people were pleased and diverted themselves with them, and as he does not pretend to justify the truth or wit of them, he seems very indifferent about them. However, I cannot but take notice of the fulsome flattery contained in the slanderer's observation on the second remark. It was impudent enough in the author of the letter there cited to say that the Earl of Stair was universally lamented, but for this slanderer to add that he was the best and noblest of his country is too gross to need any reply.[32]

If any thing could be too absurd for this slanderer to assert he would not have justified the method taken by the ministry of

Great Britain in setling the Scots Customs and Excise after the Union. For though, perhaps, as he asserts, it was necessary to instruct the Scots in the way and manner of managing these according to the English rules and forms, yet there was no need of filling up most or all the best places with Englishmen, and those too of such vile characters and base morals that the ministry themselves often repented the choice they had made when they found that they were cheated and abused in the collection of these revenues, particularly in the customs. And it had been the slanderer's interest to have concealed the names of some of those, his worthy gentlemen, that were intrusted with the management of the Scots customs, seeing Sir Alexander Rigly, the most abandoned, worthless creature alive, appears in the front of his lists.[33] The aversion which almost every Scot manifested towards the Union after its first commencement is too flagrant a truth to be discredited by this slanderer's assertions of the contrary, or the letters he trumps up, from hands perhaps as disingenuous and contemptible as his own.[34]

He upbraids the author of the *Scots Memoirs* with ignorance in chronology. But if he had considered the strain of the discourse, it would have appeared the author was giving an account of the inclinations of the French court after the commencement of the Union in May 1707, and committed no mistake in saying the battle of Turin was fought the campaign preceeding this summer of 1707.[35] And the mistake of placing the battle of Oudenarde instead of Ramillies is owing to the publisher and not the author of the *Scots Memoirs*, who may retort ignorance on this slanderer from his asserting that the battle of Turin happened in the year preceeding the Pretender's attempt, seeing this was in the year 1708 and the other in 1706, which to any but this judicious critick will appear two years.

How he comes to suppose in one page that the regular troops in Scotland were 7000 men, I cannot comprehend, when in the next page the list which he sets down containing the numbers of the severall corps makes no more than 3350.[36] And if this number was the establishment, it was very fair if they realie amounted to

2500, as they are represented in the *Scots Memoirs*, and the number which the author makes the army to consist of, for the most part in England will not be found far short of the truth, if a reasonable allowance be made for non-effectives allowed by the establishment, and the great number of faggots.[37] Had this slanderer given such allowance for the errors of the press as I do to him, he would not have mentioned his observation on the state and inclination of the Scots army, but understood that sentence in the *Scots Memoirs* as it stands corrected in this edition.

I am not inclined to follow the slanderer through the remaining part of his legend, seeing the *Scots Memoirs* have no concern with what is contained in it. Allow me, however, to take notice that he is as ignorant of Scots affairs after, as before, the Union. For in the list of those Scots members of Parliament who, he says, voted with the Torys, or, as he calls them, the Malcontents, severall are mentioned who were of quite opposite principles, and voted on all occasions directly contrary to what he affirms. Such as Robert Urquhart,[38] William Johnston,[39] Sir James Abercrombie[40], Mr Roger (representative of Glasgow),[41] Sir John Shaw[42], Mr Joseph Austin,[43] and Lieutenant-General Ross.[44] And he thinks fit to mention Mr Dougall Stewart[45] as one of those members who voted for Dr Sacheverell,[46] though he was not a member of that session, having before its commencement been made a judge. On the other hand he bestows the encomium of being good Protestants on severall because they voted on the Protestant and liberty side, and as such they are mentioned in his list. Whereas in that list severall are contained who, according to his notion, were rank papists and mere tools, by adhering constantly in all votes to the Tories, viz. Sir Alexander Cuming,[47] Sir David Ramsay,[48] Sir Alexander Douglas,[49] William Grier of Lag,[50] Alexander Duff of Drummuir[51] and William Cochran of Killmaronock.[52] And in this list he adds two, viz. John Montgomery[53] and Robert Douglas,[54] Esquires, though they were not members of that Parliament, and [an]other two, viz. John Sinclair and James Abercrombie, though they were not members of that or any preeceding or succeeding Parliament.[55]

He styles his Scots peers in the list, 'Noble Patriots',[56] but sure I am it is not long since he would have given another character of some of their Lordships, such as the Earls of Orkney, Roseberry, Loudoun, Seafield (now Findlater) and Ilay, as also of his brother, the Duke of Argyle, for these, his now noble patriots joined once in a day with the Harleys, St Johns, Harcourts, etc.[57] But perhaps they have repented, and satisfyed this slanderer of their contrition since King George came to the crown.

I beg the reader would compare his account of the money sent from England during the last session of the Scots Parliament, with the attested account thereof in the *Scots Memoirs*, and observe what a poor face he puts upon that affair.[58] I will only add one further instance of his prodigious ignorance, and that is the account he gives of the prayer by the Bishop of Dundee in the Scots Convention. Whereas there never was such a bishop or bishoprick in Scotland, and this does not appear an error of the press, seeing he is again mentioned in the index.[59]

I have thus taken notice of some few of the very many gross lyes, groundless misrepresentations and false insinuations with which this scurrilous libell doth abound, being more than enough to convince any man that nothing in it contain hath any the least pretence to be credited. I could never yet learn who was so much as suspected to be the author of it. He himself pretends to be an Englishman. And indeed he writes in a style so contemptible of Scotland, and his ignorance of Scots affairs is so conspicuous that it is not improbable he was no Scotsman. And yet I can scarce think there's any stranger apprized of so many poor little out-of-the-way storys concerning Scotsmen[60] as are mentioned in this book, unless indeed he is or was one of the worthy publick officers of the revenue sent down from England, and the truth of it is, his style, learning, manners and knowledge seem more suitable and corresponding to a gauger or tidewaiter than any other.[61] But after all, whatever country he belongs [to], no great honour will be got by him. And, for my own part, I would not have been at the smallest pains or concern about what he did, or could, say, but that those of his party make a terrible noise in behalf of any story, though never so false and ridiculous, if it is not answered in due time – and so I take my leave of this slanderer.

I have nothing more to add, but that truth will be venerable and stand its ground in spite of the devil and men's malice, and that the author of the *Scots Memoirs* hath no reason to be ashamed or repent that he has discerned and propaled the designs and wickedness of those who were the chief instruments of his and their own country's ruin, and may safely remitt himself to the judgement and censure of all the unbiassed, impartiall part of mankind.

Notes

1. George I.
2. John Houston of Houston jr; M.P. for Linlithgow.
3. The Hon. Sir David Dalrymple of Hailes, M.P. for Haddington Burghs; cf. R. Sedgwick, *The House of Commons 1715–1754*, 2 vols (1970), i. 600–1.
4. In 1709. The act aligned Scottish treason legislation (which was relatively humane) with that of England (which was draconian); *Lockhart Papers*, i. 300–1.
5. In the summer of 1713, for which see, Szechi, *Jacobitism and Tory Politics*, ch. 6.
6. A reference to Robert the Bruce's repudiation of his allegiance to King John Balliol on the grounds of Balliol's surrender of the kingdom of Scotland to Edward I of England.
7. Above, p. 266.
8. None lives without sin.
9. The Duke of Hamilton was killed in a duel with the English Lord Mohun in 1712, allegedly by his opponent's second, Major-General George Mackartney. See H. T. Dickinson, 'The Mohun-Hamilton Duel: Personal Feud or Whig Plot?', *Durham University Journal*, 57 (1965), 159–65, for a careful analysis of the affray.
10. Above, pp. 161–3 and see also pp. 188–95.
11. I have been unable to trace this work.
12. [J. Oldmixon] *Memoirs of North Britain; Taken from Authentic Writings, as well Manuscript as Printed* (1715), ii – iii, v.
13. A Whig/Republican plot to murder Charles II and the future James II (then Duke of York) in 1683.
14. *Memoirs of North Britain*, pp. 59–60, 62.
15. *Memoirs of North Britain*, p. 61.

16. *Memoirs of North Britain*, pp. 62–5.
17. *Memoirs of North Britain*, pp. 78, 86, 95–9, 104–116.
18. *Memoirs of North Britain*, p. 131. N.b. GL's logic is strained at this point, because there are no grounds for assuming that all the *non-liquets* were opposed to a presbyterian church settlement.
19. *Memoirs of North Britain*, pp. 135–6, 141, 148–9.
20. John Chiesley of Dalry.
21. Food for the body.
22. Sir John Chiesly of Cresswell, Commissioner for Lanarkshire; *PS*, i. 120.
23. GL's memory (or knowledge) is faulty at this point, for the Convention did in fact order Chiesley to be tortured into revealing his accomplices: *An Account of the Proceedings of the Estates in Scotland, 1689–1690*, ed. E. W. M. Balfour-Melville, 2 vols, *Scottish History Society* (Edinburgh, 1954), i. 23: Edin, 1 Apr. 1689.
24. *Memoirs of North Britain*, pp. 152–4, 155, 156, 168.
25. *Memoirs of North Britain*, pp. 177–8.
26. *Memoirs of North Britain*, p. 178.
27. *Memoirs of North Britain*, pp. 180–1, 187–9. GL's assertion that 80 M.P.s and peers were on the government payroll should be taken more as an expression of his Country politics with regard to the executive than a statement of fact.
28. *Memoirs of North Britain*, pp. 192, 197.
29. *Memoirs of North Britain*, p. 200.
30. *Memoirs of North Britain*, p. 203.
31. Above, pp. 177–88.
32. *Memoirs of North Britain*, pp. 204–5.
33. *Memoirs of North Britain*, pp. 208–10.
34. *Memoirs of North Britain*, pp. 203, 210–11, 215.
35. *Memoirs of North Britain*, p. 216.
36. *Memoirs of North Britain*, pp. 224–6.
37. Non-existent soldiers kept on a regiment's official muster strength, usually so the officers could embezzle their pay.
38. M.P. for Elginshire.
39. William Johnston of Sciennes, M.P. for Dumfries Burghs (former Commissioner for Annan) and subsequently Sir William Johnston of Westerhall; *PS*, i. 381.
40. M.P. for Dysart Burghs.
41. Robert Roger, M.P. for Glasgow Burghs.
42. M.P. for Renfrewshire.
43. Joseph Austin of Kilspindie, M.P. for Perth Burghs.

44. The Hon. Lieutenant-General Charles Ross of Balnagowan, M.P. for Ross-shire; *House of Commons*, ii. 392–3.

45. Of Blairhall, elected M.P. for both Bute and Perthshire (former Commissioner for Rothesay), but instead took a seat on the Court of Session as Lord Blairhall; *PS*, ii. 662.

46. A High Church clergyman who was impeached 1709–10 by the Marlborough-Godolphin government for an incendiary sermon preached at St Paul's, for an account of which see G. Holmes, *The Trial of Dr Sacheverell* (1973).

47. Of Culter, M.P. for Aberdeenshire; cf. *House of Commons*, i. 597.

48. Of Balmain, M.P. for Kincardineshire (formerly Commissioner for Kincardineshire); *PS*, ii. 578.

49. Of Egilshay, M.P. (formerly Commissioner) for Orkney and Shetland; *PS*, i. 194.

50. M.P. for Dumfries-shire.

51. M.P. (formerly Commissioner) for Inverness; *PS*, i. 207.

52. M.P. for Wigtown (formerly Commissioner for Renfrew and Dunbartonshire); *PS*, i. 127.

53. Of Wrae, former Commissioner for Linlithgowshire; *PS*, ii. 509.

54. Commissioner for Kirkwall and subsequently 11th Earl of Morton; *PS*, i. 202.

55. *Memoirs of North Britain*, pp. 245, 247. Modern scholarship on the political alignment of Scotland's M.P.s during this period supports GL's categorisation of these M.P.s over Oldmixon's.

56. *Memoirs of North Britain*, p. 248.

57. The leaders of the Tory ministry 1710–14.

58. *Memoirs of North Britain*, p. 265.

59. *Memoirs of North Britain*, p. 54.

60. See for example Oldmixon's account of the furore over the Duchess of Gordon's presentation of a rare Jacobite medallion to the Faculty of Advocates in 1711, *Memoirs of North Britain*, pp. 252–63.

61. Oldmixon, as far as is known, never did visit Scotland and certainly had no visible Scottish connection; *DNB*, xlii. 115–18.

Index

Abercrombie, Alexander, of Tillibody, 115–116

Abercrombie, Sir James, 287

Abercromby, Alexander, of Glasshaugh, 207

Abercromby, Dr Patrick, 241, 250

Aberdeen, 36, 149, 225, 230

Aberdeen, Sir George Gordon, Earl of, 103, 114

Aberdeenshire, 46, 136, 291

Achaius, 243

Advocates, Faculty of, 14, 25, 291

Airth, 150

Alith, 150

Allardyce, Sir George, 207

Alloa, 140

Almanza, 219

Alves, William, 32

Andover, 137

Angus, 41, 215, 222

Annan, 150, 290

Annandale, 149

Annandale, William Johnston, Marquess of, 17–18, 26, 30–31, 53, 77, 84, 110, 134, 143, 146, 161–162, 168, 188–189, 194, 237–238

Anne, Princess of Denmark, 7, 23

Anne, Queen, 4, 7, 9, 17, 23, 25–26, 37, 41–42, 45–46, 49, 51–53, 55–57, 62, 64, 66, 69, 81, 104, 117, 126, 174, 209, 235, 263, 269, 271, 279, 281

Anstruther, 71

Anstruther, Lord, 257, 259

Anstruther, Sir John, 67, 71

Anstruther, Sir Robert, 115–116, 187

Anstruther, Sir William, 67, 71

Argyleshire, 148, 204

Argyll, Archibald Campbell, 1st Duke of, 28, 30–33, 35, 45, 49–51, 265, 278

Argyll, John Campbell, 2nd Duke of, xii–xiii, xxix, 80–81, 84–85, 87, 89, 91, 109, 125, 138, 150, 174, 267, 272, 279, 288

Ashton, 231

Assembly, General, 68, 151, 153–155, 186, 191, 199

Atholl, John Murray, Duke of, 26, 40, 51, 53–54, 67, 78, 98–99, 135, 143, 146, 165, 169, 181, 187–188, 194, 207, 213, 281

Aufrere, Anthony, xvii–xix, xxi– xxii, xxxi–xxxv,

Austin, Joseph, of Kilspindie, 287, 290

Aylesbury, 86

Ayr, 61, 148, 177, 150, 211, 261

Ayrshire, 136, 205

Bacon, Francis, 83, 88

Baillie, George, of Jerviswood, iii, 25, 54, 62, 64, 67, 69, 76, 79, 83, 99, 115–116, 208, 268

Baillie, William, of Lamington, 67, 71

Baily, David, 53–54

Bain, John, 146, 162, 166, 169, 187

Balcarres, Colin Lindsay, Earl of, 34, 46, 54–55, 257, 259

Balfour, Major Henry, of Dunboug, 115–116, 169, 187

Balfour-Melville, E. W. M., 290

Ballantyne, John, 155

Balmaghie, 205

Balmerino, John Elphinstone, Lord, 62, 70, 110–111, 115–116, 143, 161, 165, 169, 202–203, 206–207, 269, 279

Banff, 136

THE ASSOCIATION FOR SCOTTISH LITERARY STUDIES

ANNUAL VOLUMES

Volumes marked * are still available from the address given opposite the title page of this book.